China example?
Look @ WWI —
7 "Stalled aspirants" to war w/ are countries whose _____
↳ Countries we went in ___ whose be
- Conclusion was wrong on
Ukraine + Russia
. Primary governing us whats be

Afghanistan 1

Book:
"Nimitz at War"

. China/Ti dependent on Japan/Korea
getting along —

"B adminshould not have been so publicly + clearly
fearful of escalation" —

"Putin would rather lose a ~~NATO~~ war to NATO than to crummy Ukrainians"
- closer to ukrain winning, more likely for escalation
- All the stuff you hear from Russia about NATO is them
preparing to lose to NATO
- R nuke Kiev on way out in order to claim that w/ regime
change, they can now leave
- "NATO has not been this strong in the history of the
alliance, so we need to not psych ourselves out to be
as scared as they are"
- "Biggest differentiator is Russia's inability to adapt"

- Alliance dynamic: went to South Africa in 2003 to manage the
alliance + ask for help — they said no, they just had an AIDS crisis
and we did not do anything. Other countries would love to trade
their problems for our problems — they wont be there for our
crisis if we are not there for theirs.

- "We have passed the high H2O mark of authoritarian power"
- if I was an American adversary, I would want to move
quickly, because the US isnt good at having it right, we are
good at getting it right"

2 American Strengths:
1) Natural resources — minerals, water, land
2) Governing over diversity — immigrants come here so their kids can
rise to govern (they dont go to Bejing)
↳ also 3) consumer driven economy

SAFE PASSAGE

SAFE PASSAGE

THE TRANSITION FROM BRITISH TO AMERICAN HEGEMONY

Kori Schake

Harvard University Press

Cambridge, Massachusetts
London, England
2017

LIBRARY OF CONGRESS CATALOGING-IN-PUBLICATION DATA

Names: Schake, Kori N., author.
Title: Safe passage : the transition from British to American hegemony /
Kori Schake.
Description: Cambridge, Massachusetts : Harvard University Press, 2017. |
Includes bibliographical references and index.
Identifiers: LCCN 2017013637 | ISBN 9780674975071 (alk. paper)
Subjects: LCSH: Peaceful change (International relations) | Great powers. |
United States—Foreign relations—Great Britain. | Great Britain—Foreign
relations—United States.
Classification: LCC D31 .S348 2017 | DDC 327.1/140973—dc23
LC record available at https://lccn.loc.gov/2017013637

In memory of a wonderful teacher,

Tom Schelling

One held one's breath at the nearness
of what one had never expected to see,
the crossing of courses,
and the lead of American energies.

—Henry Adams, 1892

Contents

SAFE PASSAGE

1

Opening Salvo

Hegemony is the ability to set the rules of international involvement, and to create order among states by enforcing those rules.[1] Most replacements of hegemonic powers in the international order occur by violence—nearly all, in fact. Dominant states hold their position by force for as long as possible, and are eventually defeated by challengers in the form of a fresh rising power or a collection of lesser powers working together. The exception to that pattern—and there is only one—is the transition that occurred from the mid-nineteenth century to the early twentieth as dominance in the international order shifted from Great Britain to the United States.[2]

What was it about Great Britain and the United States, or the way the international order itself was changing, that made the passage of hegemonic power between the two nations peaceful? What might that illuminate about future hegemonic transitions? To answer those questions, this book focuses on nine moments in time: the establishment of the Monroe Doctrine; the Oregon Boundary Dispute; the recognition of the Confederacy; America's westward expansion; the Venezuelan debt crises; the Spanish-American War; World War I; the 1922 Washington Naval Treaties; and World War II. They are each inflection points, events that demonstrate a changing understanding by one or the other government of the power and intentions of the other. As the only peaceful transition between global hegemons since the nation-state came into being, the peculiar nature of the transition from British to American hegemony may illuminate specific characteristics that make for pacific passage among rising and declining powers or may suggest ways the international order itself changed.

The transition from Britain to America was peaceful because at that crucial time, America became an empire and Britain became a democracy. As a result, both states came to view themselves as akin to each other and different from others. As challenges arose in the form of diminished fluidity of continental balancing by European powers, emergence of reliable land transportation eroding the value of sea control, Germany becoming unified and economically dynamic, and the British public inwardly focused on the social and political consequences of industrialization, Britain made a fundamental choice that its interests were so closely aligned with America's that it could encourage an activist American foreign policy—that, in effect, American power could be harnessed to British interests. Their power relative to each other became less important than their cumulative power relative to other states.

Britain's gamble on a rising America succeeded spectacularly in the short term for solving Britain's strategic dilemma in underwriting its commitments—most importantly in providing the margin for victory in World War I. Yet once America became the hegemon, it was no longer willing to accept the rules of order that Great Britain had established. A dominant America envisioned an international order that would be a macrocosm of its domestic ideology and arrangements.[3] In the American order, Great Britain would not retain the unique status it held in transition, because empires would end and Britain would no longer be the only democratic American ally. America would establish new rules and impose them on Great Britain.

America now faces challengers to the international order of its making—in particular, the rise of China. The experience of the passage from British to American hegemony suggests that a peaceful transition from American to Chinese hegemony is highly unlikely. The passage was testy and contingent even between two countries with many more commonalities. If this earlier transition is illustrative, hegemony with Chinese characteristics will not hew to the rules of order established by the United States. Instead, should it become the hegemon, China will project onto the international order its own domestic ideology, just as America has.

At the inception of the hegemonic transition, Britain viewed itself as a liberal government and the United States as reckless usurper, an irritant and danger to the rules-based order Britain had established. It neither sought nor would welcome a strong America activist in the international arena. And the United States viewed Britain with an especial hostility, having fought it twice and defined its sense of itself as a nation in contravention to Britain.[4]

Over the course of a century—almost exactly a century—both nations and their perceptions of each other changed. The debate within Britain about political liberalization revolved around the American experience, both as hope and as cautionary tale.[5] The industrial revolution was changing the country profoundly, increasing pressure for political inclusion and requiring the British government to take public attitudes into account in foreign policy.[6] That

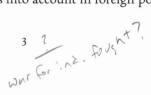

3 ?

war for int. fought?

accounting dramatically favored the United States because of its political creed and because immigration positioned America uniquely to affect its domestic political debate. Britain also began to feel the weight of its international commitments, and Henry John Temple, Third Viscount Palmerston's summation of Britain as having no permanent friends, only permanent interests, while ideally suited to a maritime power, was called into question as continental European powers began aligning. Recognition of its isolation led Britain to actively seek sharing its burden through American involvement in the western hemisphere, the Pacific region, and eventually Europe itself.[7]

Britain's search for partners occurred just as the United States began uncharacteristically behaving as a traditional great power.[8] America had always loudly championed its republican principles and insisted that this made the nation exceptionally virtuous, even as it fought wars to acquire land in every direction there was contiguous territory to that inhabited by immigrant Americans. But the United States had refrained from international involvement, considering itself unlike other nations and principally consumed with consolidating its domestic empire. With the advance of industrialization and closing of the American west, the United States began looking abroad.[9] America was in some cases a reluctant colonizer (Cuba), and in others an enthusiastic one (Hawaii), but it had given cause enough for the British government to believe America's desire for influence and need for open markets could dovetail with Britain's interests.

And those interests did dovetail for the crucial years of passage from Britain leading the international order to America replacing Britain in that role. A more democratic Britain and a more internationally engaged America felt similar to each other and different from other states. More than an alignment of interests, there also grew an affectionate regard between the governments and between the publics of Britain and America, a giving of the benefit of the doubt to each other that was not granted other states. Charles Campbell notes that "if a more democratic Britain had greater appeal for the ordinary American, the United States no longer seemed a subversive rabble-rousing republic to upper-class Britons."[10] Their national identities, if not collective, overlapped to a much greater extent than either perceived they did with other countries. Britain materially assisted America's defeat of Spain in 1898 and supported American expansion across the Pacific. America became the enforcer of Britain's interests in the Caribbean and reinforcer of Britain's side in World War I. Ostensibly neutral, Britain and the United States were considered by their adversaries to be allied.

The international order also changed, but only after the transition in hegemony. While the affectionate relationship between Britain and the United States has survived, the belief of being uniquely alike diluted once the United States became the dominant power. America proved itself not to be a traditional great power after all, episodically advocating and assisting self-determination across the international order—changing the rules in consonance with its domestic political values. The spread of American domestic political ideals internationally presaged the breakup of Britain's empire and resulted in Britain being only one among many democracies for America to have common cause with.[11] America turned out not to behave as Britain had when dominating the international order, and Britain turned out not to be the only country sharing American domestic political values. The changes in the international order toward increased acceptance of the political values Americans proclaim to be universal diminished Britain's unique claim on American cooperation.

A peaceful outcome of the transition in hegemony from Britain to the United States was by no means inevitable. In fact, it was exceedingly unlikely for a hegemon and a rising power to recognize commonality in each other and work to common purpose internationally. Peaceful transition was a highly contingent outcome, even between two countries with significant commonalities in history, philosophy, and language. It depended on the convergence of their foreign and domestic practices, the timing of domestic change, the alliance of continental European countries, technological innovation disrupting military advantage, the occurrence of international crises, and a lack of democratization in other countries. None of these variables could be controlled for, and they strongly suggest the unlikelihood of future hegemonic transitions remaining peaceful.

The complexity of this case suggests that for future hegemonic transitions to be peaceful, the hegemon being displaced would need to have a strong belief that the rising power shared both its interests and its values. Such similarity might allow the rising power's effort to be considered additive to the hegemon's rather than a challenge. Only if the relative power of both states becomes less important in this way, as did happen between Britain and the United States, would the hegemon permit the rising power to replace it uncontested.

It also merits noting that even with the two nations' wide cultural similarities and overlapping interests, Britain was disappointed in the end. A hegemonic America did not prove a faithful guardian of the order Britain bequeathed; rather, it proved to be a revolutionary power that would change the rules so that its domestic order became the basis for the international order. Perhaps that is the most worrisome lesson for America as it contemplates other rising powers: future hegemons, no matter how much commonality they exhibit through the passage of power from one state to another, will eventually seek to remake the international order in their own image, just as the United States has.

Inflection Points

The transition from British to American hegemony was a relatively slow process, encompassing nearly a century. Mostly it occurred unnoticed, as small tremors along the fault lines redistributing pressure rather than a major earthquake. But patterns accrue and are revealed as government choices. In between the rise of America as a major force in the international order and its regnancy as the hegemon of that order, several of those events form the core of this book. It is in these nine moments of decision that the supplanting of Britain by the United States is most visible, the agency of both governments most active, and the consequences of their choices determinative of their future trajectories.

The particular snapshots selected for this case study in hegemonic transition demand some explanation. A conventional telling of the relationship might begin at several alternative points: the inception, American's identification of its differences from England during the process of independence; that last of the cousin's wars, the War of 1812, in which Britain sought to contest America's rise; or the immediacy of America surpassing Britain, which might be clocked either in the late 1870s, when America's economy surpassed that of Britain, the First World War, when Britain became America's debtor, or the Second World War, when American geopolitical dominance became undeniably evident. For the purposes of this story, the American Revolution is too early, and even the 1870s is too late.

In attempting to pin down the explanation of why the hegemonic transition between Britain and the United States was peaceful, the important moments are when the rising power attempted to change the established rules. The American Revolution began not with usurpation of the established rules but with colonial Americans seeking their full participation in the established order as British citizens. The inability of continental Britons to secure the equal application of British law, political practice, and economic practice set in motion what would become a different political order in America.

Likewise, in its main allegations justifying the War of 1812, Americans were not contesting rules of the international order Britain had set; Americans were demanding that Britain heed the very rules it had established and enforced through control of the seas. As with the revolution, Americans were laying claim to rights Britain had fostered a belief they were entitled to. The War of 1812 was about preserving an international order Britain had established, not overthrowing that order.[12]

The War of 1812 also posed no real challenge to Britain's existing order. The objections Americans made to trade restrictions and impressment of sailors were, for Britain, economies and war measures necessitated by the exigencies of fighting against a genuine peer and threat to Britain's empire—namely, Napoleon's France. The trade restrictions were also cancelled before America declared war. It is truer to the experience of Britain to conclude that an upstart America took advantage of the Napoleonic Wars to become an irritant; having burned the nation's capital and prevented attempts to annex Canada, Great Britain returned its focus to the main event.

The year 1823 is relevant precisely because the United States challenged the existing order, claiming the nature of a government's relationship to its subjects as relevant in international relations, and that did pose a threat to Britain's dominance. The Monroe Doctrine propounded a different set of rules, one that uniquely advantaged American interests. That is the reason to begin tracking the story of hegemonic transition in 1823.

The Monroe Doctrine. In 1823, long in advance of Britain seeing its power wane and America's wax, the British government proposed to the United States joint action to prevent the western hemisphere—then in the throes of independence movements—from further colonization by European countries.[13] The administration of President James Monroe was strongly inclined to make common cause with Britain, provided the British would recognize the independence of Spain's American colonies.[14] Foreign Minister George Canning instead forestalled Holy Alliance intervention through agreement with France; knowing only that Britain had pulled back, the United States proceeded unilaterally on the principles that had been proposed by Britain. The American motive was not ideological; it was only in the declaration of Monroe's policy that strident republicanism was coupled to the effort of preventing further European colonies in the Americas.[15] And, for most of the nineteenth century, America was too weak to enforce the doctrine. The result was an irritating free rider problem: Britain was left carrying out America's brazen claims because it could not otherwise ensure its interests in free trade and navigation.

The Oregon Boundary Dispute. James Polk campaigned for the presidency in 1844 on extending American territory: admitting Texas to the Union, and taking the Southwest from Mexico and the Northwest from Britain. Polk's claims to Oregon were dangerously revisionist, intended to establish international precedent unique to America: a nullification of the rights of nondemocratic governments. British superiority in arms and diplomatic finesse resulted in a border along the forty-ninth parallel, but the Oregon crisis reaffirmed for Britain the unsoundness of democratic governance and the alarming precedent of America willing to become a law unto itself, tempered only by force. Within Britain, America posed a new kind of threat: the ability for a revolutionary power to mobilize British subjects against their own government. British reformists questioned the legitimacy of their nation's international claims and the nature of governance within Britain itself, causing the government to curtail its Oregon claims. America was becoming a foreign policy threat, and also a domestic one.

Recognizing the Confederacy. Before 1863, when the North embraced the abolition of slavery as a war aim, strategic arguments aligned in favor of Britain recognizing the Confederacy: it would devastate America as a rising power, better preserve the British dominion Canada, and advantage British industry. But the British government worried that supporting the South would make more difficult control of Ireland and Scotland due to familial links with the North, and also that a Southern tilt would increase pressure for expanding voting participation within Britain, since public attitudes were running in favor of the North in Britain's burgeoning industrial cities, which had little political representation. So Britain chose instead to reinforce rules of international order that might constrain a rising United States as it grew stronger, declaring its neutrality and upholding the Union blockade. Both the immigrant constituency and (for its time) broad voting participation that were fundamental to America proved unexpected capital advantages in foreign policy: they restrained a stronger power from acting on the logic of its interests out of concern for the domestic repercussions the United States was uniquely in a position to engender.

Defining Themselves. The conquest of the West became the mythic narrative symbolizing America. Politics and culture in Britain were consumed with the acts and consequences of electoral reform. The parallel seeking for identities were independent, but in a similar time frame they consolidated both countries' modern sense of themselves. For America that storytelling was politically emboldening and economically expansionist. For Britain, it emphasized stability and restraint, setting the context for a shedding, or at least sharing, of global responsibilities. As Britain became democratic and America pushed out into the world, they began to look similar to each other.

The Venezuelan Debt Crises. Venezuela's relations with European states twice brought the United States near war at the turn of the twentieth century. It is during the 1895 Venezuelan crisis that Britain took the measure of American power and chose to no longer contest it as it had previously. Confronted with the serious prospect of war, Britain conciliated. That was the moment of *anagnorisis,* Aristotle's term for the change from ignorance to knowledge of true identity.[16] The second crisis over Venezuela precipitated American enforcement of debt payments by Venezuela to Europeans.

In both Venezuelan crises, the United States took on much greater responsibility, dramatically expanding the writ of the Monroe Doctrine to a sweeping carte blanche for American actions—not just against European interlopers but, by 1903, to enforce those European claims against countries of the western hemisphere.[17] America had become a traditional power, more concerned with the balance of great power influence than with its republican creed—just as Great Britain had gambled it would.

The War with Spain. In popular history, the Spanish-American War is represented as a debutante's ball of America rising, with Theodore Roosevelt and William Randolph Hearst stampeding the country to war and empire.[18] That caricature is inaccurate; Spanish atrocities in Cuba drove an American initiative for arbitration that eventually pulled the United States into the ongoing conflict.[19] The American claim was again revolutionary: that governments that violate the fundamental rights of their subjects lose their legitimacy to govern, and the United States would intervene to protect individuals from oppressive governments. Britain might have been expected to support a government's sovereign rights, especially where colonial uprisings were at issue. Instead, Britain risked war with both Spain and Germany cementing its isolation from Europe by supporting the United States. The British expected that an America taking on greater international responsibility would become a "normal" power, by which they meant taking on colonies and shedding its revolutionary creed; in this Britain proved right, at least for a while. America's alignment as a traditional great power was, however, fleeting.

World War I. Prior to the Great War, Britain could treat the United States as a regional partner but exclude it from calculations about relations among the major (that is, European) powers. But the magnitude of resources—credit, supplies, and soldiers—the United States would add to the Allied ledger crucially influenced the Central Powers' strategy for winning the war and ultimately determined the outcome of a grinding war of attrition in which both sides were nearing exhaustion. America became a European power with World War I, when its strength proved essential for Britain to turn the tide of the war.

America reinforced Britain during the Great War, making special dispensation for its interests. In essence, Great Britain had special drawing rights on American power. But Britain's dependence was so great and the policies of the two nations at such variance that in December 1916 the British conducted a government-wide assessment of whether President Woodrow Wilson could force British compliance with the American approach. Their conclusion: "if he desired to put a stop to the war, and was prepared to pay the price for doing so, such an achievement is in his power."[20]

coalition politics (look @ 3 factors)

Both in establishing the terms for American involvement and in the war's aftermath, Wilson attempted to introduce a different kind of peace, a revolutionary kind of international order. As Adam Tooze argues, "the new order had three major facets—moral authority backed by military power and economic supremacy."[21] What Britain had imagined exclusive to the Anglo-American relationship, the United States was ambitious to establish for the entire international order.

Wilson proved unable to persuade his fellow Americans that the world merited their continued involvement, but he had found the key that would eventually become the basis for American hegemony: remaking the international order into a values-drenched simulacrum of the United States. Only when the political principles by which Americans purported to live could be universalized would American power be harnessed toward establishing order.

The Washington Naval Treaties. The damaging idealism (to British eyes) of Wilson at Versailles was more effectually practiced by his successor, Warren Harding, who became ambitious to limit military power among "all states with an interest in the Pacific." The Washington Naval Treaties promulgated restrictions on the tonnage, armaments, ship types, and shore fortifications for the navies of Britain, France, Italy, Japan, and the United States. As the dominant maritime power, Britain was disproportionately affected. Attentiveness to Britain's strategic and political concerns that had characterized compromise at Versailles was no longer operative; in fact, Britain was the country least able to affect change in the accord proposals. France and Japan both managed to exclude from the treaties elements central to their military plans. The British government achieved a more favorable balance of power than it could have achieved by building ships; but the Washington Naval Treaties represented an America grown so strong that Britain's interests were an afterthought in its greater concerns, and thus the United States made no special allowances for Britain.

At Washington in 1921–1922, the United States dominated the proceedings: it conceived the prospect of reducing the risk of war by limiting armaments among the great powers, conceptualized a series of interlocked treaties to contain great power competition in East Asia, convened the negotiations, produced policy proposals to set their terms, and used its power to broker the deals.[22] It became the moment when Britain could no longer deliver American power to British interests.

World War II. If the signs of an American-dominated international order were coming into focus at the Washington Naval Conference, they were writ large in the Second World War. A reluctant America had to be courted for years before becoming willing to commit its power to restoration of a European order, and in the Pacific it was willing to threaten Britain with stoking colonial insurrection in order to prevent "play with Japan."[23] That America could fight a two-front war in theaters half the world apart was itself an incredible statement of the breadth of its power. The resources America enjoyed, even coming off a decade of economic depression, also contrast starkly with British penury. Repayment of World War I debt, America taking over British bases in the western hemisphere in deals to provide war material to Britain, American insistence that the 1941 Atlantic Charter speak to the right of all peoples for self-determination, and military commands were all sources of friction, requiring British accommodation to the demands of a now much stronger power.

Indeed, the greatest threat to Britain after 1941 was the very real possibility that the United States would put the bulk of its effort toward the war in the Pacific. As late as July 1942, General George Marshall informed President Franklin Delano Roosevelt that "my object, is again to force the British into acceptance of a concentrated effort against Germany, and if this proves impossible, to turn immediately to the Pacific with strong forces for a decision against Japan."[24]

Both during and after the war, the "special association" of Britain to America became diplomatic strategy to deliver American power.[25] Prime Minister Winston Churchill would claim "there never has been anything like it between two allies," while many on the American side opposed any Anglo-American alliance as inhibiting wider international cooperation.[26] Churchill best summarized the change in dimensions of power, saying of Britain at the Yalta Conference, "a small lion was talking between a huge Russian bear and a great American elephant."[27] By the time of the Tehran Conference in November 1943, President Roosevelt was privately discussing with

Soviet premier Joseph Stalin ideas for Indian independence from Britain.[28] And in the war's aftermath, the intensive interweaving of Britain and America proved impossible because of ideological differences over colonialism.

Sic Transit Gloria Mundi

American foreign policy had always been grounded in the belief that the behavior of traditional great powers was both morally and practically insufficient for American interests. What began to change as American power grew relative to other states in the international order was confidence that the order itself could be transformed and the behavior of states brought into alignment with American interests by changing the domestic composition of those states.[29] The drivers of American domestic policy also became drivers of its foreign policy.[30] America at the zenith of its power attempted to recreate the international order in its image, to project as universal its domestic political values.

Rapprochement with Britain was the experience that generated American confidence that the international order could be transformed. The caution in George Washington's farewell address against alliances needs to be read in the context of its time; when he worried about America mistaking its permanent interests in the form of permanent allies, there were no other countries like the United States, politically, culturally, and economically. Democratic Britain suggested states similarly constituted could have enduring similarity of interests. Great Britain and the United States were uniquely aligned before others shared their domestic political values. It became possible to treat Britain just like other states only because other states were becoming like America and Britain.[31]

16

The expansion of representative government throughout the world has facilitated American power and given justification to Americans for caring about far-flung events. Moreover, democracies have proven slow to organize but durable in their commitments. The nature of the state has become a major factor in judgments about committing to treaties and making alliances: democratic states treat each other differently from how they treat states constituted without the consent of the governed.[32] Shared values have become the basis for enduring alliance, expanding now even beyond governance to social values.

The United States went from demanding equal treatment (in the American Revolution and the War of 1812), to exultantly propounding its domestic rights as universally applicable (in the Oregon Boundary Dispute and the Spanish-American War), to allowing Britain into the rules Americans arrogated to themselves (in the Venezuela debt crises, and in preserving Britain's colonial holdings at Versailles), to treating Britain as any other country (in the Washington Naval Treaties) and, finally, to condemning Britain's imperial policies (in World War II). The arc was ultimately descending for Britain, but its shrewd bet on American ascendency preserved British policies and influence long beyond when Britain's own strength could have.

Just how long the special relationship extends Britain's reach is debatable, but if one were to affix the zenith of British power at the defeat of Napoleon, the fillip of defanging American hostility and cajoling an international partner to share the burdens of preserving and extending Britain's international order would clock in at well over a century, making it one of history's most cost-efficient strategies.

Lessons as Others Rise

What does all this mean for America as other powers rise in the twenty-first century? Foremost, it reinforces skepticism that future transitions will be peaceful. Britain and America had so much in common, yet the peaceful transition depended on the timing of their mutual recognition of those commonalities, belief that their relative power mattered less than their cumulative power for achieving each nation's objectives, and the paucity of other countries with significant commonalities.

That the mutual belief in Anglo-American power as cumulative and its affectionate connection unique was so fleeting suggests that if American power had been attained earlier, before the government of Robert Arthur Talbot Gascoyne-Cecil, Third Marquess of Salisbury came to power, Britain might have worked to prevent America rising instead of adopting a cooperative approach. If other options had supplied the necessary heft, Britain might not have ever cultivated a special relationship with the United States. For all the genuine sympathy between the two countries, Britain did seek alliances elsewhere: with Japan, with Russia, and even with Germany. The first resulted in a limited mutual defense treaty. The second proved intractable. And the third foundered during the second Venezuela crisis.

The peaceful transition was a highly contingent outcome, unlikely to be replicable. The probability is very small of stars aligning such that both the rising and relatively declining power each possesses and recognizes in the other similarities, considers them distinguishing from all others, and fosters unique trust that enables a shifting of power without violence.

The British to American transition also cautions against optimism that a rising power will become a "responsible stakeholder." Washington's hopefulness that it can find a formula for a powerful and prosperous China probably underestimates just how much at variance with America's notions of responsibility China's notions of responsibility are, or to whom the Chinese government considers itself responsible. Great Britain was the society most like America in the nineteenth and early twentieth centuries, sharing related populations, common history, similar language, political philosophies that emerged from the European enlightenment, and cultures easily accessible to the broad population. America is likely to be far more different from potential hegemonic challengers than it was different from Britain, and even with these commonalities, America became a different kind of great power than was Great Britain.

Once in power, America changed the rules, and should expect that other rising powers will do the same in the time of their hegemony. States may be cautious while negotiating the transition, probing carefully for responses without risking too much. Established hegemons are likelier to assert their prerogatives, which will almost certainly differ from America's own because of cultural proclivities, historical experience, and myriad other specific factors.

In the American case, domestic politics was destiny: the United States reshaped the international order to advantage states adopting its form of political organization. It rewarded those states with market access, institutional creation and participation, and political and military allegiance that broke with its history of nonalignment. The truths Americans hold to be self-evident they also claim to be universal, and they worked to make them so. Rather than savor the specialness of Anglo-American commonality, a hegemonic America took those commonalities as the basis for reshaping the international order. In very many senses, the cooperation between Britain and the United States taught America how to be a hegemon.

Perhaps Americans underestimate the extent to which other states have acknowledged American power by adopting the pretense of its values; many are the states that hold sham elections or put "Democratic" in their names. If a hegemon arises with different set of domestic values to spread through the international order, it may likewise consider its values universal, giving priority in foreign relations to states that share its domestic arrangements and precipitating imitators. If the transition from British to American hegemony is illustrative, the domestic character of a state looks to be the most reliable guide to how a state will behave unrestrained in the international order.

Strongman/ junta, etc.

2

In Theory and in Practice

THIS IS NOT a book of international relations theory. It does not seek to redefine or even refine the conceptualization of hegemony. It does not seek to establish a comprehensive data set of hegemonic transitions or join the debate about which interstate engagements ought to be coded as hegemonic. This book seeks to explore in detail one case study of hegemonic transition because that one transition is distinctive in its peacefulness.

This is a book about state choices during hegemonic transition—specifically, that from British to American dominance of the international order. What made that transition, unique among hegemonic transitions, peaceful? This book seeks to answer the question by examining in detail the case of potential conflict between Great Britain and the United States from 1823 to 1923. It commences with the declaration of the Monroe Doctrine and concludes with World War II. It is a history told not continuously but focusing on potential conflicts as they emerged between the two states. The cases illustrate inflection points as Britain and the United States gauged each other's powers and sparred over their competing interests.

limited time →
false assumption
(compare w/ Germany)

The snapshots on display in this book all deal in one way or another with warfare. The practice of writing history has trended away from wars in recent decades, partly from the deeply admirable motive of filling in all the white space of people's life experiences that had been rushed past in the traditional focus on the warfare and statecraft that defined the international order; partly in another deeply admirable motive of not allowing only history's powerful to control the narrative but instead democratizing it to show many different perspectives on a common experience; and partly from the understandable motive of historians seeking fresh subjects and stories to tell.

Yet the question of how the international order reacted to a country growing in strength and activism that challenged the prevailing rules of the established order cannot be answered without relying heavily on the force of arms and its related foreign policy choices. As Geoffrey Blainey argues in *The Causes of War*, warfare is how states determine their relative strength.[1] It is how "order" is established in the international order. So this book is heavily weighted toward analysis of military determinants of state power and the choices governments make about that power.

But the argument hinges on analysis of the cultural determinants of state power. The nature of the state is central to understanding why America was different from the established order at the time of its ascendency, the new type of threat it posed to states constituted less democratically, why Britain and America found the basis for cooperation, and ultimately why America did not hew to the special relationship it had with Britain but sought to transform international relations by urging adoption more generally of its form of domestic governance.

Hegemony. The international order connotes the patterns of behavior and relations among states.[2] The international order, in a state of nature, isn't orderly. Thucydides summed up the nature of the international order as "the strong do as they will, and the weak suffer what they must." Relations among states have three modes: anarchy, in which no order exists; balance, in which states form either transient or enduring alliances to prevent one becoming dominant; and hegemony, where one state is powerful enough to establish order. In *Man, the State, and War,* Kenneth Waltz characterizes the international system as fundamentally anarchic, having no order without enforcement by a strong state compelling adherence to rules of that state's determination.[3]

Joseph Nye colloquially describes hegemony as "holding the high cards in the international poker game."[4] Hegemony is not determinant of any given outcome but provides an array of advantages. This is conceptually wrong, because a hegemon gets to determine what game card players are engaged in.

At its most basic, hegemony is the ability to set the rules of international order. It occurs when a state has a predominance of power and can impose its will on other states to create and enforce behavior. An asymmetry of power combines with the ambition to impose terms on weaker societies.[5] Powerful states contest for the ability to establish rules that advantage them, enforcing the rules while they are able through military might and incentives for cooperation.[6] When that state's power abates, challengers arise.[7]

Military strength is a necessary condition for hegemony. A hegemon must have the ability to enforce the rules of order, and in international relations, military force is the final arbiter of terms. Whether that military strength needs to be superior to the strength of every other state, or combinations of potential adversaries, depends on the degree to which military force alone is the means by which the hegemon exercises control.

A superiority of material conditions is insufficient to defining hegemony.[8] The supplementary tools of economic strength—trade, capital movement, currency, and a managed international monetary system—are valuable to a hegemon, diversifying the means by which it can coerce or incentivize behavior.[9] But they are inadequate to produce hegemony.

Culture, too, can be a means of setting and enforcing the rules of international order. Patrick O'Brien and G. A. Pigman argue that during its primacy, Britain shaped other states' attitudes in favor of the free trade that provided Britain's prosperity.[10] Shared ideology, like other incentives for cooperation, drive down the cost of establishing and sustaining hegemony. Robert Cox argues that ideas, material capabilities, and institutions are necessary for hegemony.[11]

But control alone is adequate to define hegemony. The amount of force hegemony requires is a useful measure of sustainment, but not definitional.[12] It may be despotism, and an inferior model to Rome's more efficient imperium of making subjects out of the conquered, or a Pax Americana of consensual association, but control is sufficient for establishing and enforcing the rules of international order.[13]

Some of the most interesting international relations theorists have attempted to go beyond this minimalist definition of hegemony, to festoon it with more liberal trappings. Richard Ned Lebow and Robert Kelly make a distinction between legitimated leadership and control—and even steal realists' favorite historian,

Thucydides, in support of the argument that justice as perceived by weaker states is an essential component of a hegemon's authority.[14]

Ian Clark goes even further into consensual definitional territory, arguing that hegemony is "an institutionalized practice of special rights and responsibilities conferred on a state with the resources to lead."[15] That very European approach would shift hegemony from something wrested by the strongest to something given approvingly by lesser powers with a shared normative framework.

Arthur Stein goes further still, arguing that voluntary association defines hegemony.[16] This conflates existence with cost-efficient practice of the form. Yet an "empire by invitation" would be less expensive than tyranny to enforce, and could benefit from network effects, growing and self-propagating with time.[17]

Daniel Deudney and G. John Ikenberry argue that American hegemony has unique attributes that perpetuate it through consensual practices and make it less onerous to countries than have been previous hegemonic orders. They argue that the United States has established a liberal international order characterized by "co-binding security institutions, penetrated American hegemony, semi-sovereign great powers, economic openness, and civic identity."[18] The practices of American hegemony, then, made the United States a different kind of dominant power.

Martha Finnemore also explores how rules and institutions give participants in the order overlapping interests. She argues that those practices lead to fundamental shifts in state identity in which the distribution of power is replaced by a structure of common values that create a collective identity.[19] American hegemony could thus become self-sustaining, as the idea of collective identity becomes internalized by states.

Various definitions of hegemony

The durability of hegemony is, however, different from its existence. All that is necessary for hegemony is that a state exists that is willing and able to set and enforce rules of order among nations.

Hegemony is also not potential. Prerequisites for hegemony are the willingness and ability to impose and enforce order, and no amount of wealth or power can serve as a substitute. Transition cannot be said to occur until a state demonstrates the ability to change the rules of existing order—by war or other means.

International Order? States seek to set the rules of international order to advance their interests. Why else would a government divert resources from its domestic occupations? Paramount among interests for any state is the preservation of national sovereignty: control over territory it claims, governance over populations that constitute the nation, preservation and practice of national traditions. Producing domestic prosperity is typically also high on the agenda of states engaging in international relations: attaining natural resources and creating access to new markets. In order to attain those interests, states interact. And that's where the trouble begins.

States tend not to acquire greater power and remain satisfied with their previous influence and prosperity. They begin to define their goals beyond the physical security of their territory, seeking wider latitude of activity and challenging constraints imposed on them by existing patterns of interstate relations and economic interaction.[20] These changing power relationships are typically associated with wars as states determine their respective strengths relative to each other.

Establishing international order is purposeful for a hegemonic state. Foremost among its purposes is sustaining its own security. With warfare being destructive of the wealth of nations, a hegemon typically seeks to establish rules of order that prevent it constantly having to enforce that order. Its dominant power provides the means to forestall challengers, keeping potential adversaries weak and strengthening potential allied states. Advantages can be offered to allies and exclusion to adversaries in ways that change the power dynamic between them over time.

Hegemony also allows the state to set the rules to its advantage; these rules typically include domestic prosperity and international freedom of action. So Britain and, later, the United States advocated free trade not as an abstract principle but because they, as early industrializers and major maritime powers, had advantages in low-cost production and transport. The freedom of action to impose "open-door" trading policies brought economic benefits.

As hegemons cease to be dominant powers, other states acquire the means to chip away at order and impose greater costs, either economic or political, that are advantageous to the rising powers and detrimental to the hegemon. Setting the rules matters to a hegemon's security and its prosperity.

The Mechanism. What information do we need to predict and explain state choices in the international order? Realists and neorealists posit that the distribution of power is sufficient. States have interests, and they use their power in service of those interests. Knowing a state's military strength determines its ability to preserve its sovereignty and expand its influence. Yet the richest countries do not always dominate, the strongest militaries do not always derive from the most prosperous economies, armed forces prove more brittle than anticipated in combat (and adversaries more determined), and wars won do not always translate into increased power or autonomy. As Geoffrey Blainey succinctly puts it, "history is chancy."[21] Perhaps most important for conceptualizing the international order is that the distribution of power alone does not explain why states do *not* fight. Why do strong powers permit the rise of rivals, and what triggers decisions to fight? If interests are immutable, why are states not perpetually in conflict?

Alexander Wendt posits the distribution of power approach as "undersocialized"—that is, it treats the social science of international relations theory as though it were a natural science of immutable laws.[22] It presumes state behavior is dictated according to enduring interests and the material conditions needed to advance them. Realism thus becomes "a self-fulfilling prophecy."[23] Wendt relaxes realism's iron fist of determinism, instead positing national identity as socially constructed and therefore malleable.[24] Social structures and arrangements can be formed on the basis of identities and those affect both the definition of national interests and the identification and creation of means to secure those interests.[25] So what might have caused war between, say, Britain and Germany in one epoch would not in another because how those states view their interests and each other's behavior would have changed.

Wendt outlines a "constructivist" theory of international relations in which the zero-sum power politics of realist theory is an institution of one kind of international order, not an essential feature of all kinds of international order.[26] He argues that "the structures of human association are determined primarily by shared ideas rather than material forces, and that the identities and interests of purposive actors are constructed by these shared ideas rather than given by nature,"[27] and notes that states "act differently toward enemies than they do toward friends because enemies are threatening and friends are not. Anarchy and the distribution of power are insufficient to tell us which is which."[28] Changes in interaction between states can produce more or less stability in the international system and security for states.[29]

The trajectory of relations between Great Britain and the United States from 1923 through the transition of hegemony and into the post–World War II era illustrate how profoundly constructivism's description has contributed to understanding state behavior in the international order. In the British-U.S. transition, material conditions mattered; America would not have been of interest had it not thundered to prosperity and sought an international role. But ideas also mattered.

Shifting national perceptions really did occur in both Great Britain and the United States between 1823 and 1923. Britain in 1823 considered itself a fundamentally liberal state, economically and politically, contrasting that good governance with the often illiberal democracy of America. The United States considered itself virtuously superior while practicing slavery and belligerently confiscating territory. As voting reforms democratized Britain in the mid-nineteenth century, conquest of the West gave America an imperial cast of mind, and exigencies of early industrialization pushed both economies out into the world, the two countries began looking alike to each other.

The sense of sameness was not just racial, although it certainly had some racial characteristics.[30] But, crucially, the sense of sameness precedes its congealment into a racialized Anglo-Saxonism. The sameness owes as much to the end of slavery in America; the hard realities of administering control over foreign territories (in the U.S. case, Cuba and the Philippines, and in the British case, its empire); the peaceful expansion of franchise in Britain and settling into lawfulness in the United States; patterns of transoceanic investment and capital intensive infrastructure; and trading advantages to early industrializing economies (which both Britain and the United States were). What began as wariness in mutual perception became a celebration of characteristics the two countries considered themselves to uniquely share.

The exclusive nature of the convergence between Britain and the United States evaporated relatively quickly, by 1920 or so, precipitated by American involvement in World War I. President Woodrow Wilson's "peace to end all war" looked ridiculously naive to British statesmen, but it accurately illustrated the only terms on which Americans could be persuaded to commit their country's dominant power to international involvement. Americans quickly became disaffected by European squabbling to preserve an international order (either in its endoskeleton of European wars or exoskeleton of colonial subjugation) that they didn't consider deserving of preservation. With immigrants to America having in many cases fled the wars of their native countries and benefiting from placable neighbors and oceans as buffers against much of what states fight over, convincing the American people to enforce order proved impossible, even before economic collapse gave an urgent domestic focus to government effort.

The asymmetry in British-American relations was made manifest in the 1923 Washington Naval Treaties, a set of interlocking treaties to limit naval armaments among states with interests in the Pacific region. As Adam Tooze has argued, "the train of crises that reached their nadir in 1923 ended Lloyd George's tenure as Prime Minister and exposed for all to see the limits of Britain's hegemonic capacity. There was only one power, if any, that could fill this role—a new role, one that no nation had ever seriously attempted before—the United States."[31]

It was only after the cataclysm of the Second World War that America committed to establishing and enforcing order in the international system. When in 1945 the United States did become the hegemon of the international order, it consciously constructed an order of cooperative security among states that shared its domestic political principles. Britain sought to, and to some extent did, sustain a privileged partnership with the United States.

More important from a systemic perspective is that the Anglo-American relationship became the model for the international system, a convergence of values shifting the security landscape from competition to cooperation among like·minded states. Britain's choices as a declining hegemon faced with a rising power created the model by which the United States shifted the paradigm of international order after 1945. The Anglo-American peace is thus key to understanding the constitution of the contemporary international system. Because the absence of centralized political authority did not force states to play competitive power politics, as realists would have us believe.[32]

Precursors

Much of the literature about U.S. history, especially that written by Americans, emphasizes the exceptional nature of the American body politic and the American experience as an international actor.[33] The United States' denomination of rights belonging inherently to individuals, and the opportunities America presented for individual initiative, did create a uniquely dynamic culture. But whether that translated into a different kind of great power is the question at issue;[34] liberals in political science and history argue that it did; political science realists and revisionist historians argue that it did not.

There is no doubt that America's domestic political creed has wide international appeal. There is also no doubt that America has frequently failed to live up to its ideals both domestically and internationally. A central challenge in recounting the American experience is creating a unified narrative that acknowledges both the breathtaking potential and the often disgraceful performance of our country. Walt Whitman captures the difficulty of summarizing American society in *Song of Myself*: "Do I contradict myself? / Very well then I contradict myself, / (I am large, I contain multitudes.)"[35] As a fingerprint of the culture, it sings; as explanation, it is unsatisfying.

Hegemons of the international order so far have all been empires: the taking and controlling of foreign territory for political or economic gain has been a constituent element of their power. The United States is no exception. Yet the term *empire* is a fraught and ignoble one in the American context.[36]

While the two are often conflated, *hegemony* is not synonymous with *empire*.[37] Adam Watson clarifies the difference being that "empire is the 'direct administration of different communities from an imperial centre,' and hegemony as the ability of some power or authority in a system to 'lay down the law' about external relations between states in the international system, while leaving them domestically independent."[38] By the very definition of the term, though, America has been an empire: it has taken territory to establish the state, incorporated territories by conquest, and even held suzerainty over territories not populated by its own citizens.

The scholarly literature on state power and hegemonic transition mostly averts its eyes from the messy subject of political culture.[39] Not only is culture difficult to quantify and weigh as an objective factor but, as Turkish writer Orhan Pamuk (himself a great practitioner of the art) has cautioned, "even the most intelligent thinker will, if he talks too long about cultures and civilizations, begin to spout nonsense."[40] Still, the political cultures of both Great Britain and the United States are undeniably important in why and how the transition of hegemony occurs. Analysis of other factors does not adequately explain why this transition, alone among all such transitions, was peaceful.

Direct comparisons of Britain and America at their zeniths of international power are surprisingly rare. Patrick Karl O'Brien and Armand Clesse's *Two Hegemonies: Britain 1846–1914 and the United States 1941–2001* explores the respective breadth of British and American politico-economic power. Virtually all of the contributors to *Two Hegemonies* also conclude that while significant differences existed in the breadth and type of power Britain and the United States had amassed at their zenith, their international behavior was similar.[41] But in seeking to compare the two countries' behavior at their respective heights of hegemony, the approach has only limited insight into the transition between British and American hegemony.[42]

Paul Kennedy's *The Rise and Fall of the Great Powers* is the canonical history of state choices as power waxed and waned; the United States figures prominently only in the least convincing part of the book, however. Kennedy makes a powerful argument about the economic determinants of state power and the parlous consequences of overextending international obligations; but spending patterns of America in its dominance show a dramatically decreased role for defense and international obligations as a state priority. Indeed, it could more easily be proven that the international order's most powerful contemporary states have allowed their international obligations to be crowded out by domestic spending.

Charles Kupchan's *How Enemies Become Friends,* like Kennedy's *Great Powers,* is a book that speaks to broad questions of state power.

Kupchan's argument relies heavily on Anglo-American rapprochement to make his case, and is therefore doubly important for situating the present study. He argues that Britain did not perceive America rising as a threat to Britain's interests, but that perception unrelated to the type of regime in either country. Yet he fails to explain why the detailed signaling of pacific intent on which his argument rests succeeded—or was even attempted—with America and not with other states. He also overstates the degree of enmity between the two countries (describing them as "implacable rivals for well over a century") and considers rapprochement between the two countries to have begun as an elite phenomenon that perked into public attitudes, and this seems to me exactly backwards.[43] His effort to demonstrate that political culture was irrelevant to rapprochement seems rather to prove just how important the similarities are between Great Britain and the United States that developed in the nineteenth century, and how much less consequential they seemed in the twentieth century when their common regime type became more prevalent in the international order.

Even though it has little to do with the United States, the most directly relevant book about the transition from British to American hegemony is Aaron Friedberg's *The Weary Titan,* which explores the realization and associated policy decisions by Britain of its declining relative power at the turn of the twentieth century. It is difficult to overpraise Friedberg's book; it is the definitive account of British retrenchment in the period from 1895 to 1905, rich with original sourcing and elegant in understanding.[44]

opposite

The account strongly supports Kennedy's thesis of imperial overstretch. Friedberg shows that while economists might predict expansion of the franchise would have resulted in greater welfare spending, what occurred instead was that, as Britain democratized, "the absolute bulk of the growth in spending was due to mounting defense costs."[45] Unlike those who pose realpolitik arguments, however, Friedberg brings in the cultural and political influences that shaped how British governments understood their decisions. Those influences suggest an almost maudlin wallowing in perceived weakness.[46]

They also demonstrate the extent to which Britain's decline relative to the United States had nothing to do with the United States. The two factors with greatest salience for Britain's overextension were technological progress that "reduced the effectiveness of Britain's winning naval weapon while exposing the previously secure part of its empire to attack on the ground"; and domestic choice to accept "virtual" limits on British power, such as opposition to conscription and a foreign policy that antagonized continental European states.[47] According to Friedberg, lacking the domestic discipline to develop internal consensus, to agree on and implement appropriate responses, the British chose to deceive themselves about the nature and magnitude of threats they were facing.

Yet by choosing so compressed a time frame, *The Weary Titan* misses earlier instances of behavior Friedberg ascribes to the British government as a means of managing hegemonic decline.[48] Extending the time frame of examination for British policies suggests many of the attributes were enduring features of British policy, not newly emergent responses to relative decline. In particular, concern about the costs of its policies, compromise to avert war, and seeking tactical alliances to resource specific problems are consistent elements of Britain's approach well before their power was challenged.[49]

In a way, the Anglo-American alliance could be seen to be the ultimate success of Britain's management of geopolitical position. The failures Britain experienced as other countries improved their relative position could be seen as conditioning Britain to bring about an American alliance that actually did cement Britain's dominant position. If Friedberg had extended the time frame of his study some, he could have captured Britain achieving the holy grail that had bedeviled its war planning from 1895 to 1905: manpower sufficient for their land war with European powers. Britain's leaders would not compel full conscription from the British population, feared too great a reliance on colonial reinforcements, and sought in vain for additional soldiers from alliance with Japan. Collusion with the United States eventually provided the men and money needed.

Two other books, straight histories, greatly informed the potential conflicts assessed in this study: Dexter Perkins's *A History of the Monroe Doctrine* and Bertha Ann Reuter's *Anglo-American Relations during the Spanish-American War.* Both books are detailed accounts of the diplomatic record, delightful reads, and essential guides to other source works. Their fine-grained examinations are important to understanding the choices two states made across an extended period of time in which one was the dominant power of the international order and the other a potential—and, in the end, successful—usurper.

Context

One challenge of utilizing crises rather than a continuous and unfolding narrative of history is ensuring that the crises are not taken out of context—selecting examples that are illustrative of the contextual pattern and not giving the crises too much emphasis relative to the evolving trends.[50] Crises more often simply punctuate changes rather than cause them. Not being a historian of the nineteenth century, I have felt those risks keenly and have included in this book a chapter based on the decades-long unfolding of national narratives, without which the convergence of British and American foreign policy perspectives is not persuasive. What follows are other detailed books relied upon for context.

Daniel Walker Howe's *What Hath God Wrought* is particularly important, serving as a gigantic tapestry into which all the various threads woven can be seen both in their specificity and in contributing to a complex pattern.[51] For the writing of the present book, Howe was the essential reference. His magisterial command of the vast expanse of early nineteenth century American history has helped me to keep in perspective what I believed I was seeing.

Kevin Phillips's *The Cousins' Wars* charts the many ways in which America created its sense of itself as a political culture in reaction to Britain, even though that country was its closest approximation. Phillips concludes his account with the American Civil War, when British political reformers believed liberalization in their own country depended on the success of Union arms—a telling reversal of aspiration from the American revolutionaries seeking their full rights as British citizens.[52] But that dramatic conclusion has Phillips stopping well before the United States surpassed Britain as a force in the international order. *The Cousins' Wars* also focuses predominantly on the challenge American revolutionary sentiments posed for Britain, and concludes that Britain brought itself to be more like America. The present study seeks also to understand the flip side: whether by taking on a larger role in the world—becoming an empire—American also became like Britain.

In *God and Gold,* Walter Russell Mead rollickingly provides an intellectual history of the common beliefs and practices transmitted from Britain to the United States.[53] He casts a much wider net than most historians, fishing in the murky waters of culture—and not just political culture—to ascertain the commonalities of Anglo-Saxon societies that have proven so successful in producing prosperity and power. *God and Gold* helps to calibrate the degree of similarity between the two societies even as the relative rates of change in economics and politics differed.

Mead projects forward that the qualities transmitted from Britain to the United States will continue to propel them ahead of challengers. This reconnects specific Anglo-American history to the broader lines of inquiry that instigated this search for an explanation of the only peaceful transition of hegemonic power in the history of the state system.

A peaceful transition from Great Britain to the United States would almost surely have been contested by violence without the cultural similarities the two countries shared in the nineteenth century. Yet it very nearly was violent in several instances even with those similarities, so the outcome is more contingent than a direct connection of political culture.

Safe passage required the mutual adaptation of the rising and dominant power to a common set of governing principles for their own societies and their international behavior. Their domestic principles set them apart from the rest of the international order and gave them common cause for the interlude of transition. Their power relative to each other mattered less than the cumulative power they exercised together. Once established as the hegemon, the United States became ambitious for systemic adoption of its domestic principles, something that separated its foreign policies from Britain; and as those principles became adopted, they reduced the incentive for a special relationship between Great Britain and the United States.

3

Theft on the High Seas: Monroe's Doctrine

The Monroe Doctrine

September 1821 Russia declares exclusive economic zone surrounding its Pacific holdings (including Bodega Bay and Sitka); the United States rejects it on the basis that "the American continents are no longer subjects for any new colonial establishments."

Summer 1823 Britain proposes joint action with the United States to prevent continental European powers from subjugating Spain's former colonies in the western hemisphere.

September 1823 The United States asks diplomatic recognition by Britain of newly independent Latin American states.

September 1823 British foreign minister George Canning secures reassurance from France that it will not reassert Spain's colonial claims.

December 1823 President James Monroe announces that the "American continents are . . . not to be considered as subjects for future colonization by any European powers."

1824 Russia withdraws its exclusive zone claims; Britain replies it "cannot acknowledge the right of any power to proclaim such a principle; much less to bind other countries to the observance of it."

1824–1898 The British Royal Navy enforces exclusion of other European powers from the western hemisphere.

The time immediately following the Napoleonic Wars has been described as "the most wretched, difficult, and dangerous in modern English history."[1] The end of wartime trading restrictions (which forced competition for British goods), reductions in military rolls, and advancing industrialization resulted in large numbers of unemployed for whom no provision was made by a political system responsive only to the interests of the most advantaged. The government continued wartime taxation levels and protected food producers with the 1815 Corn Laws, keeping prices high.

Yet amid this deep domestic discord, Britain was becoming the dominant power in the international order. Britain had emerged from the Napoleonic Wars strengthened relative to its continental European competitors, the other great powers of the international order. The threat of French invasion that had dominated British security concerns for the previous twenty years receded, leaving Britain with a national identity forged under arms and the lion's share of credit for diplomatic and military success.[2] The populist threat of the French Revolution had been beaten back by establishment powers on the battlefield and in the corridors of diplomacy.

Britain cooperated with Austria and Bourbon France in balancing power among European states at the Congress of Vienna, in the process gaining colonial possessions valuable as naval bases and cementing its global trading advantages. The mobilization of business, finance, and society that had made Britain's success possible could now stop subsidizing allies and turn toward prosperity.[3] Countries that had been conquests of Napoleon were reconstructing their domestic political order and repairing the damage to their territories. As a matter of political economy, Britain was the dominant power, able to set the rules of international commerce, by 1840; as early as 1823, Britain was able to constrain the international objectives of other powerful states and reach agreements that laid a firm foundation for even greater success.

Prior to 1823, American foreign policy consisted almost wholly of attempting to ensure that the rules of established powers were extended to the United States. The country's preoccupations were domestic in the sense of annexing or purchasing and dispensing land, subjugating native populations, struggling with the political and moral consequences of legal slavery, and establishing the respective powers of its branches and levels of government. Where the United States became involved internationally, its purpose was to prevent predations from entities that considered the country too weak to defend its interests: British trade restrictions and impressment of sailors from American flagged vessels during the Napoleonic Wars, and Barbary pirates' seizure of American ships.

The foreign policy announced by President James Monroe to the Congress in December 1823 therefore represents an enormous departure from prior practice. It also represents the squandering of an early opportunity for Anglo-American cooperation in foreign policy, an opportunity proposed by Britain well before that country had any foreboding of its relative power diminishing, and well before America showed itself a great power.

A joint declaration with the United States opposing European re-colonization of Spain's former holdings in the western hemisphere and committing to prevent interference with those territories would open them up for British commerce and restrain the alliance of Austria, Prussia, and Russia. Reaching westward across the Atlantic also held another advantage for Britain, as recalled by Foreign Minister George Canning in 1825: "the great danger of the time, a danger which the policy of the European System would have fostered, was a division of the World into European and American, Republican and Monarchical; a league of worn-out Govts. on the one hand, and of youthful and strong Nations, with the U. States at their head, on the other."[4] While not yet a threat to Britain, the United States represented the energetic future and held a political appeal for emergent states that the monarchies of Europe could not match. In proposing cooperation with the United States, Britain was looking to narrow the Atlantic divide and widen the channel between itself and continental Europe.

The American government seriously considered aligning itself with Britain right up until the president delivered his seventh annual message to Congress announcing what would become known as the Monroe Doctrine. America alone had recognized the independence of states emerging from Spain's collapsing empire and wanted British support—both diplomatic recognition and military force—because America's heft amounted to little on either count.[5] Time seemed of the essence in 1823: both Britain and America feared France supporting the Holy Alliance to regain Spain's American colonies. British reticence to openly recognize Latin American countries, rather than any compunction about associating with an undemocratic government, caused the Monroe administration to proceed unilaterally.

In announcing the policy, however, President Monroe gave full sail to a mixture of democratic ideology and national interest, asserting that "the American continents, by the free and independent condition which they have assumed and maintain, are henceforth not to be considered as subjects for future colonization by any European powers."[6] In its sweep and bravado, the Monroe Doctrine has few equals, especially since it was promulgated by a country that was not the peer of the states—Britain, France, and Spain—whose activity it sought to curtail.

Monroe's message marked a shift in American policy from a conception of itself as an extension of the European Enlightenment to something more fully belonging to the Americas. Daniel Walker Howe considers the Monroe Doctrine "the moment when Americans no longer faced eastward across the Atlantic and turned to face westward across the continent."[7] With Canning's offer, Britain enticed the United States to join the fellowship of European states, to tone down its revolutionary zeal and cooperate to balance the influence of competing European powers. With Monroe's proclamation, the United States declared it would not be a European-style power, but instead cast its lot with other revolutionary regimes, even going so far as to claim America's security reliant on their success. Catching the spirit of the president's message, Dexter Perkins titled a chapter in his canonical history of the policy "Monroe Hurls Defiance at Europe."[8]

One cannot help but sympathize with British exasperation with the United States in 1823. Having made a momentous offer, in terms incredibly generous to American pretentions, Canning was forced to watch as the Monroe government gained the political credit of

Britain's policy while relying on Britain's common interest in Latin American independence and the Royal Navy's might to enforce America's sphere of influence.

Overtures

As early as 1815, during the presidency of James Madison, Secretary of State Monroe instructed the U.S. ambassador to Britain, John Quincy Adams, to ascertain the attitude of the British government toward Latin American independence. When president in 1818, Madison sought his cabinet's advice on cooperative action with Britain in Latin America.[9] But these overtures need to be seen in the context of a relatively weak America navigating its way among much stronger powers, concerned principally with consolidating and expanding its continental domain. American foreign policy except toward Indian nations was primarily defensive in character before the Monroe Doctrine was promulgated. Spain's empire was collapsing; it was natural that the United States should be canvassing opinion about how countries would respond.

Nor was the United States flintily opposed to foreign entanglements.[10] As a member of Congress in 1785–1786, Monroe had supported an alliance with Spain to ensure free navigation of the Mississippi River.[11] Even Thomas Jefferson thought that if France controlled New Orleans, "we must marry ourselves to the British fleet and nation."[12]

The more relevant precursor to the Monroe Doctrine, the crisis that shaped attitudes of American government officials, was a dispute with Russia in the Pacific Northwest. In September 1821 the Russian emperor issued a proclamation forbidding foreign ships from approaching within 115 miles of Russian claims, declaring unilaterally an exclusive economic zone.[13] Russia not only had a trading outpost at Sitka but others as far south as Bodega Bay in the Mexican territory of Alta California, well south of the British and American shared sovereignty over the Oregon Territory. In rejecting the assertion Adams, now secretary of state, informed the Russian government "the American continents are no longer subjects for any new colonial establishments."[14]

European states encroaching on the Americas was not solely a Caribbean problem; Europeans were seen as competing for territory American settlers were already advancing into, and the U.S. government avariciously eyeing its own. European settlements were also seen as a longer-term demographic problem for the United States, complicating the country's political culture, as was evidenced during Congressional deliberations over the Louisiana Purchase.[15]

Reconquista

The American government had been solicitous of Europe's good opinion in 1819 because it was in the midst of negotiations with Spain for the purchase of Florida. Spain's decay and the advance of indigenous liberation movements in Latin America had both progressed so far by 1822 that the United States recognized the independence of several Latin American countries. It was alone in so doing, however, and was left exposed as continental Europe banded together to repress revolutionary activity in its own countries and throughout Europe. Even Britain had been party to the 1820 Troppau agreement to stamp out dissent by force. America was viewed with general hostility by those European governments because, as Dexter Perkins puts it, "the buoyant republicanism and the democratic faith of the people of the United States were a vast dissolvent which threatened destruction to the existing order."[16]

George Herring considers the prospect of the Holy Alliance's reconquest of Spain's colonies "the most serious threat to face the United States since the war of 1812."[17] Whether the British and American governments were right to fear incursions into the western hemisphere by the Holy Alliance, they clearly did in the summer of 1823.[18] France was on the march into Spain and had restored the Spanish king to power, which was seen by both Britain and the United States as a precursor to Spain, with Austrian, French, Prussian, and Russian backing, attempting to restore its American colonies. President Monroe envisioned the Holy Alliance starting in Latin America and progressing to the United States. In an early invocation of the domino theory, Monroe wrote to Thomas Jefferson that "we would view an interference on the part of the European powers . . . as an attack on ourselves, presuming that, if they succeeded with them, they would extend it to us."[19] Adams described President Monroe as alarmed about the threat "far beyond anything that I could have conceived possible."[20]

Relations between Britain and the United States had been warming since the 1818 agreement on joint sovereignty over the Oregon Territory. Secretary of State Adams had told the British he would welcome "to compare their ideas and purposes together, with a view to the accommodation of great interests upon which they had heretofore differed."[21] Britain unquestionably had an economic interest in preventing the exclusionary trade practices of other European imperial powers regaining hold in Latin America. And the United States, as the only country to have diplomatic relations with the newly independent countries of the western hemisphere and the only country in proximity to them, could be a valuable ally.

Belief that an imminent assault on Spain's former American colonies was being arranged by united continental powers was also the impetus for Foreign Minister Canning's overtures to the United States. He initiated discussion of joint action over the western hemisphere as France invaded Spain in August 1823 to overthrow the constitutional government, and repeatedly pressured the American ambassador for a reply because of the necessity of action.[22] When Canning could not get an agreement with the United States by mid-September 1823, he resolved the problem from Britain's perspective by negotiating a reassurance from France that it would not support any incursions to reassert Spain's claims in the western hemisphere.[23] When subsequently questioned by the American ambassador about Britain's sudden silence on joint action, Canning claimed to have defused the problem of Holy Alliance intervention, replying, "I flatter myself that neither you nor we shall have to lift our voice against any of the designs which were apprehended a few months ago."[24]

The Proffer

Thus, both the British and American governments clearly understood the problem of reconquest as urgent in the summer of 1823. The British government's concern about Holy Alliance action in Latin America can be measured by the extent to which it indulged American vanity in Canning's entreaties for common action. An August 16 conversation encouraging a joint declaration opposing intervention in Latin America can only be described as buttering up American ambassador Richard Rush:

> fully believing that the simple fact of our two countries . . . hold the same opinions, would, by its moral effect, put down the intention on the part of France, if she entertained it. This belief was founded . . . upon the large share of the maritime power of the

world which Great Britain and the United States held, and the consequent influence which the knowledge of their common policy, on a question involving such important maritime interests, present and future, could not fail to produce every where.[25]

That Canning was overstating America's moral, martial, and material influence in the world would have been obvious even to an American. Canning was, in fact, illuminating America with the ambient glow of Britain's power.

Canning went even further in stoking American pretensions in discussion with Ambassador Rush on September 18:

Was it possible [del] they could see with indifference their fate decided upon by Europe? . . . Were the great political and commercial interests which hung upon the destinies of the new continent, to be canvassed and adjusted in this hemisphere, without the cooperation or even knowledge of the United States? Were they to be canvassed and adjusted . . . without some proper understanding between the United States and Great Britain, as the two chief commercial and maritime States of both worlds?[26]

And Canning laid claim to a unique affinity between Great Britain and the United States: "Why then should the United States, whose institutions resembled those of Great Britain more than they did those of the other Powers of Europe, and whose policy upon this occasion was closely approximated to hers, hesitate to act with her to promote a common object, approved alike by both, and achieve a common good, estimated alike by both?"[27] It was an extraordinarily generous offer and an unusually generous estimate of America's potential role in the world—as a responsible stakeholder, if you will, a partner in interests and values to the hegemon of the international order.

Canning's flattery did not produce the agreement he proposed, however. The British government was willing to put in writing the shared principles of policy over Latin America, but hesitated to recognize the independence of Latin American states from Spain.[28] Recognition had become more problematic for Britain once France succeeded in reestablishing the Spanish monarchy.[29] But without Britain extending diplomatic recognition—formally and publicly breaking from the policy of the Holy Alliance—the American government feared Britain would not durably commit to a common approach.[30] It was a suspicion that turned out to have merit.

President Monroe and Secretary of War John C. Calhoun were inclined to take the British offer anyway. Adams was the cabinet member most concerned about British gambits; he alone continued to oppose the deal, because he feared the purpose of Canning's overtures was to get the United States to deny it had colonial interests in Latin America.[31] Adams, Monroe, and Rush were unaware of Canning's negotiations with France, but did rightly identify that Canning's urgency had abated, and they suspected they were being abandoned.[32]

Canning's pivot to France was the kind of shrewdness for which British diplomacy is justly famous. The American government was leveraging time for a commitment by Britain to recognize the independence of Latin American states, and such recognition would have been costly to Britain's relations with continental Europeans. Canning found an alternative solution to removing the urgency of decision by securing France's commitment not to intervene, sealed with the threat that Britain would recognize the new countries' independence if France used force to subjugate them or if Spain interfered with trade in the western hemisphere.[33] It was an elegant and low-cost solution; Canning was justified in crowing about it.

Although perhaps Canning ought not to have crowed to Ambassador Rush, since the exchange of diplomatic notes with France left the United States wholly alone in recognition of Latin American states and feeling it had been double-crossed by Britain. But the American government, too, was concealing its play. As late as November 1823, when the British ambassador pressed Secretary Adams for an answer to Canning's proposals, Adams claimed the American government needed more time because of the "paramount consequence."

Adams was not just dissembling: the Monroe government really did consider Canning's offer to be a monumental realignment of America's international role. Adams described the importance of the partnership Great Britain was offering as "a more permanent and harmonious concert of public policy and community of purpose between our two countries has never yet existed since the period of our independence," and "of such magnitude, such paramount consequence, as involving the whole future policy of the United States."[34]

President Monroe believed the formal alignment of the United States with Great Britain so important that he sought the counsel (and thereby to ensure the support) of former presidents Jefferson and Madison.[35] Jefferson's surprising advice merits quoting in full:

> Great Britain is the nation which can do us the most harm of any one, or all on earth; and with her on our side we need not fear the whole world. . . . Not that I would purchase even her amity at the price of taking part in her wars. But the war in which the present proposition might engage us, should that be its consequence, is not her war, but ours. Its object is to introduce and establish the American system, of keeping out of our land all foreign powers, of never permitting those of Europe to intermeddle with the

affairs of our nations. It is to maintain our principle, not to depart from it.[36]

Jefferson assessed that Britain was offering to underwrite the power and position of the United States in the western hemisphere, and recommended Monroe take the deal. Madison was likewise supportive, believing the alliance would deter challenges to American interests and noting that "there ought not to be any backwardness in meeting her in the way she has proposed. Our co-operation is due to ourselves and to the world; and whilst it must ensure success in the event of an appeal to force, it doubles the chance of success without that appeal."[37]

The Declaration

Secretary Adams continued to assert that without diplomatic recognition of at least one Latin American country by Britain, "we can see no foundation upon which the concurrent action of the two Governments can be harmonized," and he persuaded the president.[38] But the Monroe government undervalued the risks Britain perceived itself running in aligning with the republicanism anathema to all other powerful states.[39] In effect, the United States was asking Britain to not only denounce the countries whose international actions it had most to worry about but also to endorse colonial rebellion.

When Britain continued to finesse the issue, the United States acted unilaterally, using Canning's statement of principles for common action as the basis for President Monroe's statement of policy. But while the policy was Canning's, the language was Monroe's own, and so defamatory of European governments that Adams considered it "a summons to arms—to arms against all Europe, and for objects of policy exclusively European—Greece and Spain. It would be as new . . . in our policy as it would be surprising."[40] Adams's counsel almost surely resulted in Monroe dialing back from universal to regional application, asserting spheres of influence for Europe and the United States in the Old and New Worlds, respectively.

The other interesting objection to the declaration was raised by Attorney General William Wirt, who questioned whether the president actually had the backing of the American people to threaten war with all the great powers of Europe. Adams trumped the domestic political concern with one of foreign policy: "Suppose the Holy Allies should attack South America, and Great Britain should resist them alone and without our cooperation. I thought this not an improbable contingency, and I believed in such a struggle the allies would be defeated and Great Britain would be victorious, by her command of the sea. But, as the independence of the South Americans would them be only protected by the guarantee of Great Britain, it would throw them completely into her arms, and in the result make them her Colonies instead of those of Spain. My opinion was, therefore, that we must act promptly and decisively."[41] Fear of Britain cajoling allegiance from the weak and newly independent states of the western hemisphere was worth risking war with the strong and allied states of Europe.

President Monroe's seventh annual message to Congress is best remembered for the succinct policy statement "the American continents, by the free and independent condition which they have assumed and maintain, are henceforth not to be considered as subjects for future colonization by any European powers."

Monroe's declaration was more than a statement of support for fellow revolutionary governments, though; it also asserted that by the very nature of their governments, European states were a threat to America:

> The political system of the allied powers is essentially different in this respect from that of America. This difference proceeds from that which exists in their respective Governments; and to the defense of our own, which has been achieved by the loss of so much blood and treasure, and matured by the wisdom of their most enlightened citizens, and under which we have enjoyed unexampled felicity, this whole nation is devoted. We owe it, therefore, to candor and to the amicable relations existing between the United States and those powers to declare that we should consider any attempt on their part to extend their system to any portion of this hemisphere as dangerous to our peace and safety.[42]

The message also stated, "we could not view any interposition for the purpose of oppressing them, or controlling in any other manner their destiny, by any European power in any other light than as the manifestation of an unfriendly disposition toward the United States." A threat to any state in the Americas by any European state would therefore be considered a direct threat to the United States.

Responses

As late as December 1, 1823—the day before Monroe's message was conveyed to the Congress—Adams continued to mislead the British to believe cooperative action was still being contemplated. He told the British charge in Washington that "the United States would show by acts how cordially they concurred in the line of policy proposed to be pursued by Great Britain."[43] So it must have been a rude surprise in London to read the thunder of Monroe's denunciation, and of his relegation of Britain to the "old world" of Europe.

The most acidulous reaction was from Austrian chancellor Klemens von Metternich, who described the Monroe policy statement as something that "astonished Europe by a new act of revolt, more unprovoked, fully as audacious, and no less dangerous than the former [the American Revolution]."[44] His assessment of the threat posed by America claiming a vast geography for republican governance was that "if this flood of evil doctrines and pernicious examples should extend over the whole of America, what would become of our religious and political institutions, of the moral force of our governments, and of that conservative system which has saved Europe from complete dissolution?"[45] As befits a statesman of Metternich's reputation, he also saw opportunity: that American arrogance could bring Britain around to support Holy Alliance intervention in the Americas. In this Metternich was disappointed.

The Russian government, which had provoked the United States into developing a policy on European incursions into the Americas, was even more insulted. The Russian emperor instructed his ambassador "the document in question enunciates views and pretensions so exaggerated, it establishes principles so contrary to the rights of the European powers, that it merits only the most profound contempt. His Majesty therefore invites you to preserve the passive attitude which you have deemed proper to adopt, and to continue to maintain the silence which you have imposed upon yourself."[46] Russia did make some noises about challenging the doctrine, yet Monroe's declaration succeeded in attaining concessions from the Russians: the emperor withdrew his edict, acknowledged American territory commencing with the latitude lines of 54' 40" (which Britain would contest for another two decades), opened its ports and coastlines to American vessels, and committed not to impede American settlers.[47]

Adams was gentler in his reply to Foreign Minister Canning, noting that "for the effectual accomplishment of the object common to both governments, a perfect understanding with regard to it being established between them, it will be most advisable that they should act separately."[48] But this came after Canning already had news of Monroe's announcement.

Adams's response to Canning seems calculated to try and keep open the option of joint action in the future. He closed the note explaining that "should an emergency occur in which a joint manifestation of opinion by the two Governments may tend to influence the Councils of the European Allies, either in the aspect of persuasion or of admonition you will make it known to us without delay, and we shall according to the principles of our Government and in the forms prescribed by our Constitution, cheerfully join in any act, by which we may contribute to support the cause of human freedom and the Independence of the South American Nations."[49] But it is noteworthy that he speaks only of Britain and the United States working together to limit other Europeans, not working jointly in the Americas.

British Foreign Minister Canning's official reply was that Britain "cannot acknowledge the right of any power to proclaim such a principle; much less to bind other countries to the observance of it."[50] In Parliament, Canning boasted "I called the New World into existence to redress the balance of the Old" and purported that Britain's agreement with France ensured the independence of new states in Latin America, but it was not given much credence.[51] Monroe's statement did harness American political liberalism to the interests of British commerce, perhaps making their enactment more palatable to the countries of Latin America.[52]

Yet as Dexter Perkins concludes, "in its effects on the attitude of Canning, it stimulated rather than prevented a course of action inimical to the interests of the United States."[53] Not only were other offers of cooperation not forthcoming from Britain, but the British government began sowing questions with Latin American governments about American motives and cautioning other European leaders about the "ambition and ascendancy" of the United States.[54] Canning's actions in the aftermath of the Monroe declaration mark the first indication that Britain saw the United States as a rising power and its rise as a cause for concern and active prevention strategies.[55]

What assistance was actually entailed by the American declaration was unclear, and an issue of especial importance to the countries seemingly most affected by them: those of Latin America. When the Colombian ambassador asked for clarification, Secretary Adams said aid would be forthcoming only if "deliberate and concerted system of the Allied Powers to exercise force" were in evidence and there was "a previous understanding with those European Powers, whose interests and whose principles would secure from them an active and efficient cooperation."[56] Thus, America would carry out its aggressive proclamation only with the assistance of the British government.

That the success of Monroe's policy depended on Britain was true not only at the political level, but also—and even more fundamentally—in military terms. Britain's navy was the equal to those of all the other powers combined. Even with the advantages of propinquity, the American military was of such quality in 1823 as to cause doubt of successful operations beyond its own territory when confronted with the armies and navies of even one of the European powers. Paul Kennedy rightly concludes that "the *cordon sanitaire* which the Royal Navy (rather than the Monroe Doctrine) imposed to separate the Old World from the New, meant that the only threat to the United States' future prosperity could come from Britain itself."[57]

Britain's interest in free trade and navigation in the western hemisphere created the security within which the United States became a great power. Kennedy notes that "instead of having to divert financial resources into large-scale defense expenditures, therefore, a strategically secure United States could concentrate its own (and British) funds upon developing its vast economic potential.[58]

It is less clear that the American government advanced its interests by making such a grand statement about the superiority of republican governing institutions. The statement reinforced the resentments of European governments. Most of the new governments in Latin America were not successful, and Monroe's declaration incurred obligations future presidents struggled to limit American exposure to. Monroe could have construed the doctrine narrowly, applying it only to those territories contiguous to settled American territory or into which American settlers were moving. America would still have had the advantages of Britain's defense of the western hemisphere without having outlined an American doctrine. Indeed, the Monroe declaration may well have prevented the United States from having even greater support from the reigning hegemon of the international order.

In making such a bold statement, the Monroe administration showcased what America would become as a powerful state. It would assert the universality of its values and advocate the adoption of its domestic political arrangements. Monroe's declaration, then, can be seen as a regional claim to principles that would become universal as American power itself became universal.[59]

Adams congratulated himself, asserting that "my reliance upon the co-operation of Great Britain rested not upon her principles, but upon her interests."[60] And indeed, Britain's interests were so closely aligned with those of the United States in the western hemisphere that Britain upheld the Monroe Doctrine for fifty years with almost no contribution from the United States. Foreign policy interests were by 1823 beginning to push the United States and Britain into cooperation. But as the negotiations over what became the Monroe Doctrine demonstrate, that cooperation was transactional. And Monroe's declaration would make cooperation between Britain and the United States more difficult. If Great Britain could have found a way to achieve its interests without helping the United States after the Monroe declaration, it likely would have.

4

Parallel Latitudes:
Oregon's Boundaries

The Oregon Boundary Dispute

December 1845 President Polk invokes the Monroe Doctrine, seeks congressional authorization to annul the 1818 Anglo-American Treaty of joint occupation over the Oregon Territory.

Spring 1846 Britain dispatches thirty ships to the Caribbean, prepares for war in Canada.

Spring 1846 The Mexican-American War begins.

April 1846 Congress allows abrogation of the Anglo-American Treaty, but opposes war with Britain.

May 1846 President Polk offers compromise of boundary at the forty-ninth parallel.

The principles Monroe's declaration ringingly espoused were largely neglected in the foreign policy of the U.S. government. As secretary of state and then president, John Quincy Adams declaimed any responsibility for America toward the governments of the western hemisphere.[1] The challenge Monroe's declaration ostensibly posed to British hegemony was ignored, resulting in Britain involving itself freely in the hemisphere without repercussion—indeed, with encouragement—from the U.S. government.[2]

Even within the narrower confines of North America, Monroe's declaration was inoperative. When the doctrine was floated during 1824 negotiations over the Oregon boundary, the British government's response was a categorical rejection. Britain "considered the unoccupied parts of America just as much open as heretofore to colonization by Great Britain, as well as by other European Powers" and "the United States would have no right whatever to take umbrage at the establishment of new colonies from Europe in any such parts of the American continent."[3]

The subject didn't come up again for over twenty years, until James Polk campaigned for president, agitating for incorporating Oregon and large swathes of Mexico into the United States. In 1845, President Polk invoked Monroe's doctrine in challenging the rights of both Mexico and Great Britain to territory into which American settlers were steadily moving.[4] While demography would have solidified American control over those territories in a relatively short period of time anyway, Polk provoked war with Mexico and a near miss with Great Britain.[5]

Polk insisted that the Mexican government's inability to control the territory (in particular, to prevent depredations by the Comanche) amounted to a surrender of legitimacy. In the parallel case of the Oregon Territory (which included what is now the state of Oregon as well as Idaho, Washington, and parts of Montana and Wyoming), Polk argued that Britain, which long had trading outposts and settlers in the Pacific Northwest, was attempting to establish a new colony in violation of the Monroe doctrine. The United States made the first defense of its sphere of influence against Britain, rather than Spain or any of the Holy Alliance countries, in attempting to enforce the exclusion of European colonies in the western hemisphere.

Polk's challenge in Oregon resuscitated Monroe's sphere of influence but also its ideological underpinning: that people had a fundamental right to be governed democratically. Great Britain's leaders made a distinction between liberal government, which they considered they provided to their country, and democratic government, which they viewed as dangerously volatile and illiberal, the result of American "demagogues and non-entities."[6] Henry John Temple, Third Viscount Palmerston satisfied himself that "republics, where masses govern, are far more quarrelsome and more addicted to fighting, than monarchies, which are governed by comparatively fewer people."[7] Settlement policies by the U.S. government reinforced the concerns British governments had long held about expanding the franchise: the unprincipled land grabs and debasement of law through populist pressure and threats of violence were incompatible with the rules-based order Britain had established domestically and throughout its empire. The *London Times* considered Polk's challenge in Oregon "the clearest *causa belli* which has ever yet arisen between Great Britain and the American Union."[8]

By actually enforcing the Monroe declaration, the Polk administration sought to recant American adherence to the existing rules of the international order and assert a new standard that uniquely prejudiced claims in America's favor. If American policy toward consolidation of its "domestic" territories were to become American foreign policy, a rising America would be a serious challenge to

British interests in North America, the Caribbean, and even the Pacific. An international order in which representative government was allowed to trump claims of prior sovereignty, nationalism, or possession would be an American world order—if, in fact, it was order at all.

The long border dispute between the Oregon Territory and Canada was settled comparatively swiftly and without violence, though, in contrast to fifty years of American revisionist efforts along the Canadian border in the east. Smart diplomacy on the part of the British government strung the crisis along until America was already at war with Mexico, forcing the U.S. government into the strategic trap America had imposed on Britain in the War of 1812: pursuing claims in Oregon would entail fighting a two-front war. Britain's dispatch of thirty ships of the line to the Caribbean and preparations in Canada for war provided a timely reminder to the American government of the disparity in power between the two countries. America posed a demographic threat to Britain's claim, but Britain posed a military threat to America's.

Democratic politics in both the United States and Britain also tamped down the crisis. While Polk's assertion was widely popular during the election, discomfort of many of Manifest Destiny's ideologues with forcible accession, war with Mexico, and friction between North and South over slavery sapped support for sustaining a hard line over Oregon. With the overthrow of France's Bourbon Restoration fresh in their minds, British leaders had begun responding to pressures for greater political inclusion with the 1832 electoral reform; urbanization, the shift to industrial jobs, and crop failures focused attention domestically as worried politicians negotiated whether and how to reflect Britain's changing society in the nation's political structures.

The American challenge brought foreign policy ramifications into domestic policy. British reformers identified with the American creed, and hoped to incorporate elements of it as they remodeled Britain's governance; some even went so far as to support Polk's argument about the right to representative government for settlers in the Oregon Territory. The boundary crisis thus represented for Britain a satisfaction that its superiority of arms could easily subdue American claims, but also the unsettling demonstration that American ideology could reach into British society to affect support for Britain's foreign policies and even the character of Britain's domestic political arrangements.

Demagogues and Double Standards

The presidential election of 1828 is an important watershed in American history, marking as it does the passing of the founding fathers' generation. Both candidates were from the successor generation of politicians, but John Quincy Adams, Andrew Jackson's opponent in both the 1824 and 1828 presidential contests, was from the old school: a scion of the great founding family who was establishment bred, fed, and highly educated. He had been secretary of state for President Monroe, adroitly negotiating a weak America's interests to advantage against European powers. Adams was set against Jackson, the hero of the War of 1812's Battle of New Orleans, a frontiersman, and a man of the people. Jackson cast himself as the scourge of "a corrupt and abandoned aristocracy," an insult directed not at Europe but at the American political and economic establishment.[9]

It is Jackson, more than any previous American politician, who embodied the apprehensions Great Britain had about America and its growing strength.[10] He personified everything a rising American threatened: a bitter Anglophobe (as a child he had been imprisoned by British soldiers during the Revolutionary War), a victor in battle against British forces, and a purveyor of slaves and cotton.[11] As a militia leader in the First Seminole War he invaded Florida, resulting in its detachment from Spain.

The establishment's closing ranks around Adams decided the 1824 election, an outcome Jackson fulminated against as a corrupt bargain designed to exclude him from the electoral majority voters had delivered.[12] When Jackson triumphed in 1828, disestablishment of the Second Bank of New York and compounding economic errors of his presidency exemplified the rougher, more risk-tolerant, populist tenor of this new America.[13] So, too, did the unapologetic dispossession of Native American tribes as immigrant Americans pushed south and west. Other contemporaneous features of American politics, such as the increased tendency toward rioting and selective adherence to the law both by states and the federal government, also gave cause for concern to many—but not to Jackson, whose boisterous populism and territorial expansionism became the stock in trade of American politicians.[14]

Greed for land brought Monroe's declaration back into vogue. That Americans moving into Indian lands was a profound violation of the country's principles was never in doubt, even very early in the process. George Washington had been unequivocal: "Indians being the prior occupants possess the right of the soil . . . to dispossess them . . . would be a gross violation"; confiscation would "stain the character of the nation."[15] Yet even the towering respectability of Washington could not prevent settlers from doing so, and he was pulled into defending them in the Northwest Indian War. It would be an early iteration of a story repeatedly reenacted as immigrant Americans moved south and west across the continent.[16]

Britain, in fact, was still in possession of its thirteen American colonies when the pattern was established; after the 1763 Treaty of Paris, the British government by royal proclamation tried to prevent settlers streaming over the Appalachian Mountains and into the West. The proclamation was largely ignored, and Britain declined to prevent by force the violation of the king's will.[17]

The uniquely American contribution to the cycle of Indian dispossession was to marry greed for land with religious and political rationalization. During negotiations over the 1815 Treaty of Ghent (which ended the British-American War of 1812), Britain sought to extract promises of fair treatment for their Indian allies. American negotiators reaffirmed their government's commitment of "intending never to acquire lands from the Indians otherwise than peaceably, and with their free consent."[18] American negotiators pledged that their government "will not violate any dictate of justice or of humanity; for they will not only give to the few thousand savages scattered over that territory an ample equivalent for any right they may surrender, but will always leave them the possession of lands more than they can cultivate, and more than adequate to their subsistence, comfort, and enjoyment, by cultivation." Even in extending this earnest promise, the American government had already changed the terms of reference from Native Americans earning their livelihood through traditional means to the American government dictating that livelihood should be the cultivation of tracts of land and determining "an ample equivalent" to their need.[19]

Cognizant of the weakness of American arms and that time was working against them (with the Duke of Wellington's victory over Napoleon, Britain could now concentrate force in north America), President James Madison wanted to bring negotiations to a close.[20] The British had an interest in capturing American commerce within the British economic sphere, and thus were inclined to generous terms; but having observed the American government renege on numerous treaties with the Indians, Britain wanted greater confidence the Americans would honor the terms of the treaty. American negotiators at Ghent were at pains to distinguish between claims made against Indian tribes and the higher standard that would be set for territories controlled by European governments, and they assured Britain that claims against European states would be adjudicated within the accepted rules of the international order. Well before the rush of American settlers to the Pacific Northwest, the U.S. government had made an important distinction in the rules it would consider itself bound by. Promises of the Treaty of Ghent directed American settlement into Indian lands and away from the claimed territories of European powers, Spanish Mexico (before Mexican independence in 1823) and British Canada.

Extending the Area of Freedom

Britain and the United States shared sovereignty in the Oregon Territory from 1818 until 1846, an unusual arrangement made possible—and peaceful—by the vast expanse of territory being largely uninhabited.[21] Beginning in the late 1830s, ambitious Americans argued more boldly for "our Manifest Destiny to overspread the continent allotted by Providence for the free development of our yearly multiplying millions."[22] The architects of Manifest Destiny advocated an organic process of settlers voluntarily adopting American laws rather than advancing democracy by force of arms.[23] But weak and decentralized government was no match for local greed and racism. Manifest Destiny's grandiosity of purpose became a convenient rationalization for war with Mexico in 1846,

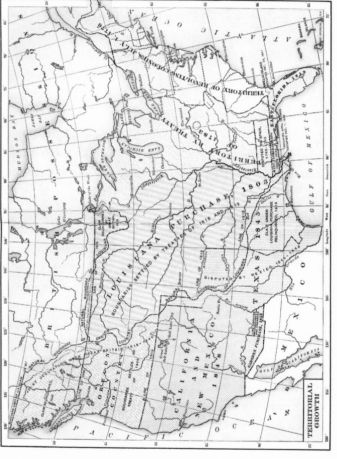

Source: Albert Bushnell Hart, ed., *The American Nation: A History from Original Sources by Associated Scholars*, vol. 26 (New York: Harper, 1907), 18. Digital reproduction from the private collection of Roy Winkelman, courtesy of the Florida Center for Instructional Technology at the University of South Florida.

netting not only Texas but also California and all of what would become the American Southwest.

The northern boundary of the Oregon Territory lay at fifty-four degrees, forty minutes of latitude. "Fifty-four forty or fight!" became a clarion call to annex all of the British claim in the Pacific Northwest up to the boundary of Russian territory in Alaska.[24] Even with a commitment to voluntary accession, Manifest Destiny would have been a threat to British holdings because of the revolutionary zeal many Americans had for advancing democracy. Mexico may have lacked the means to govern its territory, but Britain's governance was considered inherently objectionable—it was actually in argument over Oregon that the term *Manifest Destiny* came into usage.

John O'Sullivan, the journalist who coined the term and was for a generation one of Manifest Destiny's major proponents, argued for annexation of Britain's claims in the Pacific Northwest on the basis that Britain denied its citizens democratic governance and America must hold itself to "a higher law" than the norms of behavior commonly accepted among nations.[25] O'Sullivan advocated nullification of international law to advance the morally superior principles enshrined in the American domestic political compact—a very dangerous concept to Britain (and other nations).

Britain and its governance were at the center of the Oregon question for Americans. The *Illinois State Register* captured the animation of Manifest Destiny's adherents, noting, "What is it but a last final decision between those great principles of Monarchy and Democracy, as which shall take the firmest, deepest, widest foothold on the long coast of the Pacific? Divide by 49 and Democracy must crouch before Monarchy forever. . . . Will posterity—the sons of freedom— ever forgive a policy leading to such a result at this? They never will."[26]

But Manifest Destiny was not universally or uncritically accepted in American society, either; it was contentious even among those who sought a greater America.[27] The major political parties, which had been aborning since conflict between Jeffersonians and Hamiltonians but really crystallized during Jackson's political tenure, distinguished between themselves on the issue of expansion. Democrats (Andrew Jackson's party) stridently invoked Manifest Destiny as a political and religious obligation for America to spread its unique and exceptional virtues. Whigs excoriated expansion as a betrayal of American principles. Characteristic of Whig reaction is Robert Winthrop's ridicule of the claim to American exceptionalism that "I suppose the right of a Manifest Destiny to spread will not be admitted to exist in any nation except the universal Yankee nation."[28]

Manifest Destiny exacerbated long-extant tensions over slavery by raising the prospect of its expansion into new territories. Jackson's bold pledge that expansion was "extending the area of freedom" seemed to many self-evidently false given his support for slavery.[29] So much was Manifest Destiny hostage to the slavery question, and so deeply did slavery rend American life, that even Jackson hesitated to bring Texas into the Union during his term because the issues had become so entwined.

James Polk won the presidency in 1844, overtly favoring annexing Texas and Oregon (Congress preempted to bring in Texas before he took office). His inaugural address in March 1845 outlined his principles for governing prominently, which included "my duty to assert and maintain by all Constitutional means the right of the United States to that portion of our territory which lies beyond the Rocky Mountains. Our title to the country of the Oregon is 'clear and unquestionable,' and already are our people preparing to perfect that title by occupying it with their wives and children."[30]

When warned by his cabinet that he ought not to provoke both Mexico and Britain, Polk's answer was that "we should do our duty towards both Mexico and Great Britain and firmly maintain our rights, and leave the rest to God and the country."[31]

While Mexico was an easy mark for American territorial ambitions (Ulysses Grant considered the Mexican War "one of the most unjust ever waged by a stronger against a weaker nation"), Great Britain was not.[32] Britain had both force of law and force of arms to its advantage, and believed itself operating from a position of strength with regard to Oregon. The American government in 1815 had committed itself to upholding the existing legal order where territorial claims were contested with European governments, and it entered into an 1818 treaty of joint occupation and engaged in several negotiations with Great Britain over Oregon on that basis. But the military balance in both the Atlantic and Pacific also favored Britain. America's army had lost as many engagements as it had won against Indian tribes; its navy had been curtailed since the War of 1812 (although President John Tyler had made some improvements); and war with Mexico loomed, opening the prospect for imposing on the United States a two-front war of the kind America had forced on Britain in 1812.

America, though, had two even more practical advantages: settlers and the precedent of a straight line on a map. In 1840, only 150 Americans were residing in the Oregon; by 1845 there were five thousand Americans in the territory.[33] The Oregon Trail was quickly shifting the balance of possession from Britain to America. Had Polk not pressed the case, demography would have delivered Oregon into American hands anyway. Additionally, the Anglo-American Convention of 1818 had established the border as far west as the Rocky Mountains at the forty-ninth parallel, leaving only the Oregon Territory unadjudicated.[34] Having promulgated a straight border so far, the 1818 convention strongly prejudiced eventual completion of the border along the forty-ninth parallel as the negotiating saddle point.

Yet the British government repeatedly rejected that very proposal from several American administrations, emboldening American claims for annexation of British holdings along the Pacific Ocean all the way to the Russian territory of Alaska.[35] The Oregon dispute between Great Britain and the United States was as much over the harbors (to the north) and the inlet to the Columbia River (to the south) as it was over the territory itself.[36] For the United States, this sliver of littoral geography provided in Puget Sound the only safe harbors on the western coast of the American continent (the remainder belonging to Mexico in the south and Russia to the north of Britain's claims).[37] The Hudson's Bay Company, Britain's main representation in Oregon, believed (wrongly) that the Columbia River might prove navigable into the Canadian mainland, making a Pacific port important for reaching Britain's inland holdings, and the British government was also concerned with Pacific ports facilitating trade to China.[38]

Radicalism at Home and Abroad

Control over Oregon precipitated a crisis that is easy to imagine as a continuation of the so-called cousins' wars, with the British government fearing that "Canada was a hostage in American hands",[39] Britain attempting to hold a far-flung territory against an admittedly barely professional army but reinforced by militia with superior knowledge of local terrain and conditions; and settlers, seething with resentment of distant edicts, growing radicalized and melding into an American political identity. Yet the settlers along the Pacific

Northwest had no political grievance against the British government, which did not exercise governance so much as endorse the activity of the Hudson's Bay Company, and the company was (in contravention of instruction) welcoming and helpful to immigrant Americans arriving. What governance existed in the Oregon Territory grew organically out of the needs of settlers. The residents of the Oregon Territory did not see Britain as an abusive power—nor did the Indian tribes, who found the light footprint of British presence much less onerous than American acquisitiveness. Dispute over Oregon was precipitated in Washington, DC, not Washington, Oregon Territory.

The strident republicanism of America had always been an affront, but across seventy years it had evidenced little risk of catching on elsewhere. As Bertha Ann Reuter summarizes it, Americans were "people too radical either in religion or politics or both to live peaceably in their original home."[40] European states could thus export their problems to America.

In Britain there was a strong belief that democracy was "vehement, turbulent, over-bearing, and often overreaches itself."[41] Democracy was equated to rule by mob, something dreaded not only by British aristocrats but also its middle classes. Both of Britain's major political parties considered America "a concrete example of the sort of government they were trying to stave off in their own country, one where the common man ruled. They were hostile to its republicanism, fearful of its democracy, and especially threatened by these features because of its success."[42] Even among British liberals like Palmerston the belief was prevalent that "in the present state of our general education, political morality, and starving population," a republic was infeasible.[43] "We the people" connoted narrower confines in Britain: "'the People' were respectable, rational and generally propertied males, who demonstrated their civility in debating clubs, reading societies and formal radical organizations."[44]

Reform proposals were regularly rejected in the British Parliament from the 1760s onward, with restrictions on political organization and meeting being the government's response to agitation for greater representation. Opposition to political reform cannot be disconnected from the profound discomfort on the part of aristocracy for the effects of the industrial revolution in Britain; one of the major questions was whether to extend representation to inhabitants of the newly teeming cities of Birmingham and Manchester, both population behemoths due to work provided by their factories.[45] There was also a class element to the debate, with Britain's aristocracy not surprisingly being antirepublican while its lower classes wanted to adopt the political institutions that led to greater prestige and prosperity for their American counterparts.[46]

By 1830, attitudes had begun to change.[47] The destruction of Wellington's government by his intransigent defense of the political status quo showed the increasing power of public pressure: even though voting was circumscribed, the political system concerned itself with seeming representative.[48] That public pressure was resisted by the House of Lords, but not without public violence and agitation favoring a run on banks.[49] The 1832 Reform Bill was put forward with the American example paramount by its advocates, who argued that "if universal suffrage worked in America without democratic anarchy or perpetual revolution, who could deny the feasibility of a moderate ten pound householder franchise in Britain?"[50]

The 1832 Reform Bill reweighted electoral boroughs to account for Britain's burgeoning urbanization, registered voters for the first time, and substantially expanded the franchise to allow about

20 percent of English men the vote—but continued excluding participation for those without property. The effect of the reforms was thus modest, and public pressure did not abate.[51] Still, Britain was becoming, fretfully and slowly, more like America.[52]

Britain's foreign policy in 1845 remained principally concerned with great power relations, which meant managing the balance of influence on the European continent through the choppy waters of revolution in Belgium, the Polish uprising, the war for Greek independence, the succession crisis in Spain, and the civil war in Portugal. As Britain's foreign secretary, Lord Palmerston capitalized on domestic change for foreign policy advantage in 1834, arguing that Britain's natural allies were other constitutional states.[53] It was not America he spoke of; the international alignment suiting Britain's interests at that moment comprised states with legal constraints on the power of their monarch (France, Portugal, and Spain) and opposed to those without such constraints (China, Egypt, and Russia). As with the War of 1812 and the reconquest of the western hemisphere, America was an afterthought in Britain's actions.

Still, in advertising democratic constraints on power Britain considered divinely bestowed, Palmerston advanced the American argument that the nature of a state's domestic political arrangements was an important factor in foreign policy alignment. George Washington had cautioned his countrymen against permanent alliances because America stood alone in the world as a government of the people; Palmerston declared that the domestic political arrangements of states created natural alliances with those similarly constituted. While Britain's foreign secretary hadn't been speaking of America, America would be the country with which this eventually proved most profoundly true.

Compromise

Yet when President Polk provoked a crisis over the Oregon boundary in 1845, most sectors of British society opposed America's unquenchable thirst for land and unconventional doctrines for usurping title to it. Characteristic of elite British attitudes, the *London Times* responded to Polk's assertion as pretension:

> We are not accustomed to hear statesmen and rulers announce
> new principles of public morality, to demand insulation from the
> universal laws and sympathies of their kind, and in their place to
> erect a convenient system of original and axiomatic claims. . . .
> The Old and the New World are separated by much less distances
> than those that divide the constituent nations of each. If America
> is a world of its own, then also is each of the four conventional
> quarters of the globe. In fact there is no more reason why America
> should segregate itself from the universal system and universal
> code than any other quarter.[54]

The American ambassador in London believed even the British people were strongly opposed to Polk's aggressiveness over Mexico and Oregon, reporting back to Washington, "The newspapers, which I send by this opportunity, will convince you, if indeed any intelligent American Statesman at this time of day, needed such proof to convince him of that fact, that in this country, all the sympathies, both public & private are, on this occasion, and will be on any other, against the U.S."[55] America's example had a powerful hold on the imagination of reformers in Britain, though; for many radicals and Chartists, ideological solidarity superseded nationalism and they supported American claims to Oregon in order to advance democracy.[56]

An important economic argument was also beginning to be had in Britain about the costs of empire, with free traders arguing that colonies were a cost-inefficient economic undertaking.[57] Taxation and unproductive expenditure of empire were beginning to be considered in the balance against simply sustaining trade.[58] Britain and America had wide and deep trade and economic entanglement stemming from the Treaty of Paris (which ended America's Revolutionary War in 1783). Britain's economic interest in Oregon was predominantly trade—fur trade, specifically—and it was moving northward. Neither the Hudson's Bay Company nor, with one exception, British political leaders agitated for retaining Britain's long-standing position in negotiations over Oregon.

That exception, however, was Lord Palmerston (formidable in opposition), who had characterized the 1842 Webster-Ashburton Treaty that resolved several British-American boundary issues as "one of the worst and most disgraceful treaties that England ever concluded."[59] Refusing concession over Oregon became a point of honor difficult for either British political party to advocate as a result of Palmerston, who wrote of Polk's offer, "Their notion of the way of saving the honor of the party with whom they are dealing is as if the gentleman on the road after taking the traveller's purse should keep the sovereigns to satisfy his own claims and give back a shilling or two to save the wounded honor of the person with whom he was thus making *an equitable distribution* of the matter in dispute."[60]

The British government was more restrained than either Palmerston or Polk, not doubting its ability to succeed by arms but playing for time as the United States committed to war against Mexico.[61] Prime Minister Robert Peel encouraged third party mediation, which Polk refused on the basis that no monarchial arbitrator (and there were no other democratic governments to arbitrate) could possibly be fair to republican arguments.[62]

President Polk, like Monroe before him, ably used the public theater of democratic governing institutions to his advantage.[63] He countered the British slow roll by going again to Congress in December 1845 seeking authorization to withdraw from the 1818 Anglo-American Convention. He again paralleled the cases of the southern and northern borders, lyricizing the accession of Texas and outlining in great detail the history of negotiations with Britain over Oregon.[64] Polk declared that the joint occupation agreement would be "entirely annulled and abrogated" because "the extraordinary and wholly inadmissible demands of the British Government afford satisfactory evidence that no compromise which the United States ought to accept can be effected."

He invoked the Monroe Doctrine in outlining his policy:

> The American continents, by the free and independent condition which they have assumed and maintain, are henceforth not to be considered as subjects for colonization by any European powers. This principle will apply with greatly increased force should any European power attempt to establish any new colony in North America. In the existing circumstances of the world the present is deemed a proper occasion to reiterate and reaffirm the principle avowed by Mr. Monroe and to state my cordial concurrence in its wisdom and sound policy.[65]

In asserting its claims in Oregon, Britain was not establishing "any new colony in North America." Oregon was an established British territory, and America had validated the claim with joint jurisdiction between the two countries with the Anglo-American

Convention. Polk was making a sweeping assertion that America's interests negated Britain's.

Polk's proposal to Congress narrowed the geographic aperture of the Monroe Doctrine from the entire western hemisphere to territory Americans sought for settlement. But Polk expanded significantly the European activity over which the United States demanded a veto, going beyond Monroe's exclusion of new colonies to encompass any European "intrigue," a euphemism for efforts to capitalize on Mexico's cession of California. Dexter Perkins concludes that Polk's policy "out-Monroes Monroe."[66]

Polk congratulated himself, noting that "the civilized world will see in these proceedings a spirit of liberal concession on the part of the United States, and this Government will be relieved from all responsibility which may follow the failure to settle the controversy." He assured the Congress that extending American law to the Oregon Territory, fortifying the Oregon Trail, and "an adequate force of mounted riflemen be raised to guard and protect" immigrants to Oregon were all permissible within the treaty and should be undertaken. He closed by cautioning that "the national rights in Oregon must either be abandoned or firmly maintained. That they can not be abandoned without a sacrifice of both national honor and interest is too clear to admit of doubt."[67]

The Congress took a much more conciliatory view. John C. Calhoun, then in the Senate, had been Monroe's secretary of war and denounced Polk's use of the Monroe Doctrine in the Oregon negotiations, claiming President Monroe had not issued a general prohibition, but only one specific to the threat of Holy Alliance involvement in South America.[68] In any event, Calhoun argued, Monroe's policy had had no practical effect and should not be resurrected.[69] The Congress did eventually—four months later, in late April 1846—

approve the president's request, but only a much watered-down version and with assurances to Britain of the United States' desire that the countries should not come to war over Oregon.

President Polk was finding his position on Oregon less popular in government than it had been on the campaign trail, however—and becoming even less so once war with Mexico loomed. Not only would war in Oregon mean fighting in two places separated by thousands of miles—necessitating two separate armies and navies for the campaigns—but war in Oregon would give Great Britain reason to aid Mexico and to organize other European governments to intervene.[70] If that were to occur, Polk's invocation of Monroe would have failed, both in the immediate instance of Oregon and as a general guide for American foreign policy going forward. Perhaps most important, associating Oregon with the admission of Texas conjoined expansion with the centrifugal issue of slavery in American domestic politics.

The redoubtable newspaperman Horace Greeley editorialized that "all the gas of the Message about 'the balance of power' on the Continent, and our resistance to further European conquest and colonization is the paltriest fishing for thoughtless huzzas, worthy of a candidate for constable rather than of a President of the United States."[71] This coming from one of the most ardent disciples of westward expansion illustrates that the Manifest Destiny movement backed away from Oregon. Albert Gallatin, who had negotiated most of the relevant treaties with Britain, wrote a seventy-five-page essay opposing war over Oregon.[72]

While Polk talked tough, he made no military preparations for a conflict in Oregon.[73] Great Britain did, dispatching thirty ships and readying campaign plans for "offensive operations."[74] British military planners concluded that localized operations in Oregon were inadequate, since they left populated Canada at risk of American attack, and therefore advocated engaging American naval forces along the Atlantic seaboard and proceeding to a ground force campaign.[75] Report of Britain's preparations by the American ambassador reined Polk in; he fumed that the British government had "not altogether so pacific a character as the accounts given in the English newspapers had led me to believe."[76]

The denouement was great success for British coercive diplomacy: Polk acknowledged the legal bindings of 1815 and 1818, offered the British the compromise of delineation at the forty-ninth parallel, ceding them Vancouver Island and navigation of the Columbia River until expiration of the Hudson's Bay Charter, and a settlement was reached.[77] Polk sagaciously submitted the proposed treaty to the Senate for its consent in advance of his signature, reversing the normal order of business, so that he could claim to have acceded to the legislature's wishes rather than be seen to walk so far back from so strident a policy.

Intimations of Liberal Internationalism

In contrast to the 1823 announcement of the Monroe Doctrine, the crisis over the doctrine's rejuvenation in 1845 during the Oregon boundary negotiation was a satisfying victory for Britain over the arrogance and assertion of a rising America. Establishment British commentators exalted at the success, noting that "the prestige with which America and her institutions once undoubtedly enjoyed in many parts of Europe is rapidly fading away, as each successive post brings fresh evidence of her vices and her follies."[78] It was a moment to be savored: Britain's territorial claims had been sustained, America was put in its place, and the critique of democratic governance was validated.

Great Britain policing the Caribbean and Central and South America as free trading areas perhaps led the American government to overestimate its power in 1845; but it took just thirty British warships dispatched to the Americas to cause a recalibration, on the American side, of the two countries' relative power. Missouri senator Thomas Hart Benton, like many western Democrats unreconciled to the compromise over Oregon, bemoaned the essential truth: "why not march up to 'Fifty-four Forty' as courageously as we march upon the Rio Grande? Because Great Britain is powerful, and Mexico is weak."[79]

America's growing power indeed showed to better effect in the resounding victory over Mexico. Britain's government rightly commended itself for making a good deal at an opportune time: coming off the victory in Mexico, Polk might well have tried for all of British Columbia. By forcing surrender of all of Mexico's territories in Alta California and Santa Fe de Nuevo Mexico (what would become the states of Arizona, California, Colorado, Nevada, New Mexico, Utah, and Wyoming), Polk's war with Mexico cemented success of America's Manifest Destiny: those territories prised from Mexico would soon dramatically reshape the American West and give further jolt to America's rise.

America's burgeoning power showed also in the concerns that pushed the British government toward a negotiated solution over Oregon. During the Oregon Boundary Dispute, America had argued its national interests on the basis of a liberal—or at least liberalizing—international order wherein the claims of individuals superseded the rights of states. Britain suffocated that argument with a show of force in the Americas, but the growing appeal of individual liberties started to become visible in the policies the British government adopted and the justifications they made for those policies.

Lord Palmerston, the most uncompromising British opponent of Polk's policy, repudiated his prior criticism and welcomed the agreement, claiming that "in every quarter it will be learned with entire satisfaction that the unfortunate differences between this country and the United States have been brought to a termination which, as far as we can at present judge, seems equally favourable to both parties."[80] Palmerston's approval had less to do with the terms of the agreement than realization by his party that threats of war with the United States were bad politics, especially during a food shortage and with rising pressure from the disenfranchised for political influence.[81] The British prime minister announced the Oregon compromise, emphasizing both its democratic underpinnings and commonality across the Atlantic: "the majority of the people of the United States, and the majority of the people in this kingdom, wishing heartily all peace, the respective governments would be able to arrange this without going to war."[82]

British foreign policy would soon be consumed with the European revolutions of 1848, which Palmerston (though not Queen Victoria) celebrated as advancing the cause of constitutional governance and therefore potentially expanding the number of Britain's natural allies in Europe. The contradictions of British government attitudes about liberalization policy would be evident there, as well, with Palmerston opposing expansion of the franchise or extending to Ireland the political freedoms he advocated for Hungary, Italy, and other countries in Europe.

Britain's government was not, of course, wholly insensitive to public sentiment, although in the mid-nineteenth century it still lacked the feedback mechanisms for democratic governance, universal suffrage, and free media. But even as the British government lacked concrete information on public attitudes, those attitudes began to loom large in governing concerns.[83] In the early stages of the Oregon crisis, concern about public reaction prevented compromise, but as the British wrestled with domestic problems accommodation became more attractive.[84] Likewise, in the United States an aggressive policy was initially supported by the public but abandoned as tensions increased. The Oregon compromise actually undercut the argument of Britain's ruling establishment that democracy resulted in illiberal and erratic policies: in both Great Britain and the United States, the influence of public attitudes fostered compromise in 1845 rather than fomenting a push toward war.

In 1845 a rising America continued the effrontery that had exasperated Britain's government since the time of the American Revolution. Unlike earlier challenges in 1776, 1812, and 1823, however, by 1845 the United States was coming to be considered threatening by the British government. It was not that Britain lacked the diplomatic and military means to beat back America's challenges, but as the Oregon crisis gave tell, the United States portended danger for Great Britain less by the force of its arms than by the appeal of its ideology in British domestic policy debates.

Paul Cook concludes that, by 1848, "the United States came close to rivaling France and Russia as an object of British suspicion ... [because] its political morals were not based on European values as understood by aristocratic diplomatists."[85] Like no other power in the international order, a rising United States could turn foreign policy into domestic challenge; and a democratizing Britain was more susceptible to that influence than were more repressive states.

5

Domestic Threat: America's Civil War

The American Civil War

April 1861 Union blockade of Confederate ports.

May 1861 Britain declares its neutrality; Cassius Marcellus Clay's mission to London threatens to foment revolt in Britain.

November 1861 Union Navy confiscates the British ship *Trent* with Confederate envoys on board; the British foreign minister advocates declaring war.

December 1861 British and American governments both conclude that law supports the other's position; British prime minister Henry John Temple, Third Viscount Palmerston believes U.S. president Abraham Lincoln unable to compromise because of public opposition.

January 1862 U.S. government disavows responsibility for *Trent* seizure, releases envoys.

Autumn 1862 Britain diplomatic recognition of the Confederacy forestalled by inability of Europeans to cooperate, Union victories, and the Emancipation Proclamation.

As America became economically and politically stronger, other countries had opportunities to impede its rise. From 1861 to 1865 the United States was profoundly vulnerable to meddling from outside powers as the Union fought secession by the Southern states. The window of time from 1861 to 1863 was especially propitious for intervention, since Union armies were losing most engagements, and the North had not yet embraced slavery's abolition or become the industrial juggernaut it would as a consequence of the war effort.[1] In the space of two years at the start of the American Civil War, Britain had three ripe opportunities to intrude: an initial decision responding to the Union blockade, dispute over Union taking Confederates prisoner off the British ship *Trent,* and mediating a potential settlement between the North and South.

The British government clearly saw the possibilities of working against the United States in its time of crisis. In 1860 Britain was unquestionably the strongest state in the international order, holding 68 percent of the wealthiest continent's riches and a dominant military.[2] Britain had not only the means but also the motive. Prime Minister Palmerston noted that "if the North and South are definitively disunited and ... at the same time Mexico could be turned into a prosperous monarchy, I do not know any arrangement that would be more advantageous to us."[3]

The confluence of British interests in favor of recognizing the Confederacy was strong: appreciation by elites of the threat a rising America posed for Britain, politically and economically; economic complementarity of cotton-producing Southern plantations with

British industry; direct competition from Northern industries with British manufacturers and traders; a cultural attraction to the South on the part of British aristocrats; virulent anti-Americanism on the part of key political actors, as well as a broad cultural anti-Americanism among elites; and the savory delight of watching the United States rend itself asunder by the very argument Britain's North American colonies utilized in breaking from the British Empire.[4]

It would not have taken much in the early years of the American Civil War for Britain to tip the balance toward Confederate victory, either. Several options were available that incurred little risk of war or damage to Britain's strategic interests. Extending diplomatic recognition might by itself have been enough to definitively disunite America. The Union even gave the British government several legitimating opportunities in the way it crafted the blockade proclamation, the provocation of prisoners from the British ship *Trent,* and Union battlefield failures.

Yet Britain largely stayed out of the Civil War, declining to administer that devastating blow to American power and potential. The British government resisted not because it was intimidated by Union threats of war in retaliation, feared putting Canada at risk, thought the South would lose the war, was concerned with higher priority foreign policy problems, or could not—this early in the war—countenance aligning itself with a slaveholding Confederacy given abolitionist sentiment within Britain. It instead gave priority in its policy to preserving the international rules it had established involving intervention. Upholding the conventions that Britain as a hegemon had established and profited from created a strong incentive not to recognize the Confederacy until the secessionist states had established the fact of their independence and to abide by the

Union blockade in the meantime. As the international order's major maritime and trading state, Britain wanted to preserve the tool of the blockade for its own future use. As Peter Thompson has argued, it was more concerned with supporting international practices that would regulate the use of power than it was with the international distribution of power among states. In doing so, it was explicitly anticipating a time when the United States would become a great power.[5]

Britain's restraint was furthered by concern about the domestic repercussions of its foreign policy choices with regard to the United States. Historian Ephraim Douglass Adams posits that "the great crisis in America was almost equally a crisis in the domestic history of Great Britain itself."[6] Aligning Britain with the Confederacy risked aggravating two worrisome issues for the British government domestically: disaffection among urban workers still without political representation in Britain, and the deepening hostility of British immigrants in America. On both these counts, the United States was uniquely able to reach into Britain's domestic debate, and during the Civil War it actively did so.

In 1861 democratization in Britain had not much progressed since the 1832 reforms. The government feared stoking resentment among residents of major urban centers, since property requirements still prevented them voting—only one in twenty-four Britons were enfranchised.[7] Industrial workers, the newly urbanized and economically productive lower classes, were not among them.[8] British prime minister Palmerston considered affiliation of an aristocratic British ruling class with a plantation protoaristocracy in the American South to risk imperiling his ability to prevail in Britain's own domestic debate about political participation—a delegitimation by association. He feared domestic pressures not for a change of government between political parties but for a change in type of government from a narrowly construed franchise of landed gentry to a more expansive participation by aspiring political forces—or worse, a revolution of the kind continental European powers had been forced to suppress in 1848.[9] Acting against the Union required weighing foreign policy advantage against risk of domestic damage, a calculation that America—because of its more participatory form of government—was uniquely able to impose.

The American government posed the threat of domestic insurrection in a second way, as well: secession by Ireland and Scotland. Secretary of State William Seward's "spread eagle nationalism" was unrestrained in seeking ways to inflate the cost to Britain of intervening.[10] Palmerston was concerned about the effect of "the exiled Irishmen" making impossible cooperation between Britain and the United States.[11] At the height of tensions between the two nations, an American diplomatic envoy publicly alleged that British support for the Confederacy could be matched by the United States with actions internal to Britain.[12]

While many states harbored political and religious exiles, America's policy of citizenship and broad political representation gave British émigrés direct influence in government policies not replicated by other powerful countries. Immigration patterns created a strong affiliation by family as well as ideology between Britain's working class and the industrial American North. Kevin Phillips estimates that, by 1860, 90 percent of migration from England, Ireland, Scotland, and Wales was to the American North.[13] This represented a significant shift from the earlier immigration flow to the culturally more familiar South. Irish Catholics were more sympathetic to the Southern cause, but large numbers of them also served in the Union Army, often comprising whole units. (One reason for hostility to the North was the high casualty rate those Irish units suffered.) English, Welsh, and Scottish immigrants were staunch Union backers, like their German counterparts. All of these communities might become conveyor belts of insurrection back to home countries—if the United States were able to "weaponize" them.

Involving itself in the severing of a state would set an inherently dangerous precedent for an empire, and the British government excelled at avoiding precedential trouble. Severing a state to which so many disaffected Britons had emigrated for political, religious, and economic opportunity amplified the possibility of negative repercussion: failure in America might convince the disaffected to force change at home rather than move to where change was occurring. Playing a weak hand rather well, the government of President Abraham Lincoln, at arm's length, threatened it would promote secessionist movements in Ireland and Scotland if Great Britain made any diplomatic or military move supportive of the Confederate States. Support for insurrection in Ireland and Scotland was nothing new—the French made a habit of it with Scotland—but the immigrant composition of the United States reduced the stain of foreign support because it contained such strong linkages to the domestic.

The Civil War was the point at which American power came to be perceived as more than an abstract threat to the existing political order. The political liberties and economic opportunities afforded European immigrants in the United States turned out to be a powerful and unique foreign policy advantage: who the United States was as a domestic political culture served in 1861 to constrain the foreign policy choices of the hegemon of the international order.

A Plenitude of Reasons to Act

In 1861 Britain's rulers had considerable discomfort with America as a revolutionary power—not because America was at that time exporting its revolution but simply because of the ideology America represented: it was the rabble of every other country empowered by the franchise. Americans broadly understood and celebrated themselves in the same terms. As the *New York Times* crowed in 1862, "our friends—and there could be no grander tribute paid to the genius of the republic—are the dumb masses."[14]

A huge part of the story, both of American rambunctious pride and European concern, was the result of immigration. As Kevin Phillips nicely states it, immigration to America "made the British Isles safe for England." They could export their disaffected, and "Receiving much of this dispersal made the United States a notably different English-speaking, great world power: more democratic in its politics, more egalitarian in its culture, and more revivalist rather than traditionalist in worship. The new republic became a mecca for discontented populations from Catholic as well as Protestant Europe.[15] The flip side of exporting troublemakers was that Britain's American cousins did not have much stake in the status quo back in Britain—those who did would not have emigrated. Predictably, British attitudes toward America also cleaved along class lines. As described by the U.S. minister to Britain, Charles Francis Adams, "the great body of the aristocracy and the commercial classes are anxious to see the United States go to pieces. The middle and lower class sympathize with us."[16]

Palmerston, Britain's prime minister, exemplified this disdain for America in all its political, economic, and cultural dimensions.[17] The archive holding Palmerston's papers explains that "the widely held contemporary image of him was of the staunch defender of Britain, who would uphold old England's glorious fame and would use any means to achieve this."[18] Palmerston's hostility toward the United States was deep and of long standing: he had been defense minister during the War of 1812, advocated the shelling of Baltimore and the burning of Washington, DC. He ruminated with satisfaction in 1855 that "a British force landed in the Southern part of the Union, proclaiming freedom to the blacks would shake many of the stars from their banner."[19]

Palmerston also argued for policies that slowed the geographic and economic growth of the United States so that it didn't become a rival.[20] Intimations of an inclination to disrupt America's rise are frequent in Palmerston's correspondence. Indeed, if the measure of America's growing prominence is an increasing preoccupation with it on the part of British policy makers, Palmerston's correspondence suggests that the United States had arrived in 1861, when Palmerston assured Queen Victoria that "Great Britain is in a better state than at any former time to inflict a severe blow upon and to read a lesson to the United States which will not soon be forgotten."[21] America was not yet a genuine challenger to Great Britain's military prowess, economic productivity, or diplomatic reach, but it was no longer an afterthought in British strategic thinking.

Prime Minister Palmerston may have been exceptionally wary of America, but his attitude was by no means unusual in Britain's ruling class. Members of Palmerston's cabinet were also advocates of intervening in the American Civil War: William Ewart Gladstone, the up and coming man in liberal politics, overtly advocated for it, and Palmerston's government had lots of company in cheering progress by the U.S. South. By 1860 there was a general sense of America as an emerging rival and concern about retaining Britain's advantages over it. British reformer Richard Cobden estimated that three-fourths of the British House of Commons would vote in favor of actions by Britain to "dismember" the United States.[22]

For mid-nineteenth-century Britain's rulers, America represented the threat of universal white male suffrage. The boisterous sea of liberty (as Thomas Jefferson nostalgically termed it in 1820) may have suited the rough, frontier character of a nation in thrall to Jacksonian democracy, but it was seen as threatening to established societies and powerful governments in the international order. America's founding fathers had started out as British citizens and in many ways aspired to full citizenship and acceptance by British law and society. American democracy had early on been so tightly circumscribed, and the social mores so close to those of Britain, that America's rulers were perhaps more similar than different from their British counterparts.[23] Radicalization of the "moderates" among the founding fathers (John Adams and George Washington are illustrative) was the result of the American realization that Britain would not accept equality under British law for its colonists.

With the passing of the founding fathers from the political scene, America's policies became more assertive. America's leaders considered the War of 1812 fraught with danger; within a decade, John Adams's son was declaiming the Monroe Doctrine as a caution against British incursion into America's sphere of influence. The rise of the Jacksonian tide in the late 1820s looked very much to British eyes (at least the eyes of the ruling class) like the mob coming to power. By and large, the British viewed America as "an empire-seeking nation of hypocrites and elevated the South as the last bastion of a preindustrial paradise."[24] The hope by political leaders in the North that expanding the franchise and admitting new states to the Union would dilute the political power of the slaveholding South was perceived not as smart attenuation of the central problem in American democracy but as allowing the unfit to govern.

And by the 1850s, mob rule was also what Britain's rulers considered their central domestic political challenge. The country was in the crush of social and economic change engendered by its industrial revolution; political leaders were debating the extent to which the great migration of population from the countryside to cities should be absorbed into political representation. Britain's aristocracy had argued its case to be the ruling class as the producer of economic value. Newly urbanized Britons understood themselves in those same terms and agitated for the vote.

Palmerston and much of the British political establishment disapproved of expanding the voting franchise, and the United States was frequently held up as the threat it would unleash. Gladstone, Palmerston's treasury secretary, justified his exclusionary view of the franchise on the basis that "the natural condition of a healthy society is that governing functions should be discharged in the main by the leisured class."[25] In an 1862 speech Gladstone contrasted Britain's "improving class relations" in their political system to the breakdown of "what may be called American democracy."[26] As Bertha Reuter sums up, "those who dreaded the approach of democracy were quick to see in the American war a proof of its weakness and futility."[27]

Palmerston believed that "in the present state of our general education, political morality, and starving population" a republic was infeasible.[28] Britain's opposition to democracy was not simply political; it also had a pessimistic economic basis. In the words of sympathetic biographer E. D. Steele, "Palmerston did not think it possible for government and society to better significantly the lot of those in the lower reaches of the working class," requiring social hierarchy to prevent anarchy.[29]

Animosity among the British ruling class toward America was not merely confined to aristocrats and politicians but also had deep cultural roots. Charles Dickens was representative of literary Britain in considering America "more barbaric than the native cultures it subjugated."[30] His hostility toward America was part outrage at its pretensions to political liberty while countenancing slavery, and part fear of revolution at home: the protests represented in Dickens's novels typically have no political motive for their violence and are instead "products of a mindless, bestial mob manipulated by evil conspirators and psychological misfits, all actuated by personal grievances."[31] The commonality among Britain's political and cultural elite was its disdain for American enfranchisement of those mobs.

Even the beneficiaries of economic mobility, Britain's new economic elites from the industrial revolution, granted the vote in 1832, had reason to oppose the Union.[32] The Northern economic model was a threat to British industry, representing as it did direct competition in manufactures. As the United States industrialized (with important contributions from theft of British companies' intellectual capital), it chipped away at Britain's advantage in factory-produced goods domestically and exported to markets lagging in the advantages of mass production.[33]

The economic case for British intervention is often overstated, however. During the 1840s and 1850s, the British and American economies were complementary: British investments fueled trade between the two countries, increasing incomes through both the magnitude of activity and economic specialization. Union tariffs and blockage of Confederate ports did impose enormous economic hardship in 1860, when one in five British jobs were directly attrib-utable to cotton.[34] But the British economy had a stroke of luck with good harvests, adapted quickly to increase manufacturing of woolens and linens, and benefited from reduction of American merchant shipping and increases in production of coal and war munitions. Peter Thompson shows that during the American Civil War, British per capita income rose 14.1 percent, and the price of bread decreased 14.3 percent.[35] Palmerston did not consider the economic motive sufficient, writing of intervention that "the want of cotton would not justify such a proceeding."[36]

Foreign policy in the time of Great Britain's hegemony tended toward accommodation rather than warfare, as Paul Kennedy has emphasized,[37] and that tendency resulted partly from leaders' shrewd accounting of warfare's costs and partly from the restraint imposed by only partial democratization of Britain's domestic po-litical structures. John Clark concludes that this held back an other-wise interventionist British government in most instances because "whatever the benefit of war to the merchant classes, the politically predominant landowners were required to foot the bill as tax-payers."[38] But the attitudes of both merchants and landowners aligned with respect to the American Civil War: both favored rec-ognition of the Confederacy, and both supported the Palmerston government, thereby giving a strong impetus to intervention.

The Possibilities

Britain had a choice of several potential means to advance its inter-ests at America's expense. The British government could have di-rectly intervened to assist one side or the other, rendered ineffective the Northern blockade by refusing to comply with it, armed the combatants, taken advantage of American preoccupation to redraw the boundaries of British Columbia, or encouraged Indian tribes to rebel along America's frontiers.

It is, however, important not to overstate Britain's willingness to involve itself in the American Civil War. Overt intervention without provocation would have been a pricey and unpopular undertaking so soon after the Crimean War and the Sepoy Mutiny had humbled the ruling class and cast some doubt on the force of British arms. The magnitude of the American Civil War was daunting, too: the 23,000 casualties during the single day of the Battle of Antietam were more than the entirety for Britain during the Crimean War. Foreign Minister William Russell, addressing the American issue in Parliament to give the Palmerston government's first statement as hostilities commenced, allayed concern that Britain would involve itself overmuch, claiming that "we have not been involved in any way in that contest by any act or giving any advice in the matter, and, for God's sake, let us if possible keep out of it."[39]

No consideration was given to military challenge from Canada requiring the Union to fight a multivariate war, with an offensive campaign of preventing secession on one front and a defensive campaign protecting itself from invasion on the other. Even talk of reinforcing Canada was thought unnecessary in Britain, with Secretary of State for War George Cornewell Lewis batting down Palmerston's suggestion to that effect in early 1861 by pointing out that "the Washington government is violent and unscrupulous, but it is not insane, and with the 'belligerent' in the South to deal with I can hardly think that they will wish to make an enemy of the principle maritime power in the world."[40]

Low-risk and low-cost means would need to be available for influencing the war's outcome in the direction of British preferences if the nation were to intervene. Several possibilities were extant:

Britain might have refused to legitimate the Union tactic of block-ading Southern ports. It had naval power sufficient to the task; at a minimum, it could have easily driven up the cost to the Union of maintaining the blockade. British commercial vessels did brisk trade running the blockade from the West Indies, but involvement on the part of the Royal Navy to protect ships flying a British flag would have been an insurmountable obstacle to maintaining the blockade and justified both privateers and navies following suit. This option was unattractive to the British government because of the concern that it might set a precedent that could be used to the detriment of its own far-flung possessions.[41] Britain's long-standing advocacy of maritime blockades played to its own strength; calling the legality of a blockade into question could then be utilized handily by Russia and others against Britain's holdings, increasing the muscle required to sustain them. Having ennobled its own in-terests in law (an approach America would mimic greatly to its ad-vantage later), Palmerston's government was loath to undercut that law by breaking the Northern blockade.

An Internal Affair

Much less straining on the public purse, and not precedential, would have been to tip the scales against the Union without actually be-coming involved in the war. There, too, Britain had opportunities, the ripest being simple recognition of the Confederacy. All that was required was a government declaration; the government could even savor the satisfaction of pointing out that the Southern states argued for their independence on the same grounds the thirteen colonies that originally constituted the United States had made against a benevolent ruling power. While Secretary of State Seward insisted that America would declare war in those circumstances,

Secretary of State for War Lewis had rightly assessed the limitations of Union arms to fight simultaneously the Southern insurrection and the hegemon of the international order.

Two other lesser diplomatic gambits were also available that could confer legitimacy on the Southern cause: meeting with Confederate envoys, and offering to mediate between the warring parties. Where the rule setter of the international order saw fit, other nations would follow, so Britain's choices were particularly important to the Union cause. Great Britain flirted with all of these means—recognition, unofficial support, and mediation—in 1861–1862 as it determined its policy course.

Neutrality. Secession of Southern states after Lincoln's election in 1860, and imposition of a Northern naval blockade of Southern ports in April 1861, necessitated a decision by the British government whether to accord diplomatic recognition to the Confederacy. Under the maritime laws Britain had established internationally, nations at war imposing a blockade had the right to search ships thought to be in violation. The United States—which was now piously calling on all nations to honor this right to search—had been the main opponent of multilateral treaties according the practice.[42]

The Lincoln administration, like so many American presidential administrations before and since, was trying to simultaneously achieve contradictory objectives: to impose a blockade that required acknowledgment of the Confederate States as belligerents and to deny political recognition to the Confederate States. The choice of a blockade opened the door to recognition, because technically countries "closed" their own ports but "blockaded" foreign ports. The language of the blockade proclamation was also problematic, since Lincoln's description of the Confederate States as belligerents (rather than insurrectionists) also conferred eligibility for international acknowledgment.[43]

If Britain recognized the confederacy, it could have found itself at war with the Union. Affording diplomatic recognition to the Confederacy would not necessarily have made Britain a party to the conflict, though. Both Palmerston's cabinet and the British Parliament steeply discounted the risk of a Union attack on Canada in retaliation.[44] Recognition would not have complicated Britain's relations with continental European powers, most of which were either indifferent to the conflict or antagonistic toward the North. It would have dented Northern manufactures, kept Southern cotton available, and kept shipping busy—all things that were advantageous to Britain's economy. The support of abolitionists in Britain had been compromised by the American president disavowing slavery as the cause for war (and the continuing presence of slave states among the Union).[45] Recognition would have certainly prolonged and very likely decided the war's outcome on Britain's terms by keeping the South economically viable, a substantial diplomatic accomplishment.

If Britain declared its neutrality, it would be consenting to restricted commerce with the South and also granting the North the right to stop and search British vessels. These were big concessions from the hegemon of the international order, especially given the reliance of British industries on cotton imports from the Southern states. Neutrality had three advantages, however. First, it reinforced the legitimacy of blockades as a tool of warfare, something Britain often resorted to and wanted to build international support for the right of in order to reduce the requirement for enforcement. Second, it satisfyingly turned back on the United States at least the sting of interference, which the United States had irritated Britain with during the Canadian insurrections of 1837.[46] Third, it permitted Great Britain to continue its commerce with the Union, from which Britain imported 40 percent of its wheat.[47]

And Great Britain did choose neutrality. The Queen issued a straightforward injunction, stating, "We do hereby strictly charge and command all our loving subjects to observe a strict neutrality in and during the aforesaid hostilities, and to abstain from violating or contravening either the laws and statutes of the realm in this behalf or the law of nations in relation thereto, as they will answer to the contrary at their peril." The proclamation did not establish equivalence between the warring parties, describing secessionists as "certain States styling themselves the Confederate States of America." In practice, the neutrality declaration would prevent British citizens from overtly assisting the South and dramatically strengthen the Northern embargo.[48] Yet Americans in both the North and South considered the British proclamation of neutrality advantageous to the Confederacy.[49] The *New York Herald* called for retaliation against Canada; Secretary Seward threatened that any further action would precipitate an American declaration of war.[50]

Showing the political proficiency that had made him a successful New York politician, Seward gave both the Lincoln administration and the U.S. ambassador in London distance from the most dramatic and public threat made in response: that the American government would foster revolution in Britain.[51] The American ambassador to Russia, Cassius Marcellus Clay, set off a tirade of anti-American sentiment in London by ominously challenging, "Is England so secure in the future against home revolt or foreign ambition as to venture, now in our need, to plant the seeds of revenge?"[52]

Crisis. The United States pressed even more arrogantly six months later at sea, exercising the embargo's right to search the British mail ship *Trent*. Finding Confederate envoys to Britain and France on board, the American captain took them prisoner in an unprecedented interpretation of people as dispatches (that is, mail).[53] As a strictly legal matter, the British government determined the Americans had grounds, with Palmerston writing that

> much to my regret, it appeared that, according to the principles of
> international law laid down in our courts by Lord Stowell, and
> practised and enforced by us, a belligerent has a right to stop and
> search any neutral not being a ship of war, and being found on the
> high seas and being suspected of carrying enemy's despatches;
> and that consequently this American cruiser might, by our own
> principles of international law, stop the West Indian packet,
> search her, and if the Southern men and their despatches and
> credentials were found on board, either take them out, or seize the
> packet and carry her back to New York for trial.[54]

The *Trent* crisis was, however, not principally a legal matter, but a political one, and public attitudes were enflamed in both Great Britain and the United States by seizure of the Confederate envoys.[55] Britain demanded the envoys' release, reparations, and an apology from the American government.

War was considered likely (and privately threatened) by both countries.[56] General Winfield Scott, the hero of the Mexican-American War who had retired to Paris, returned home to offer his services for war against Britain.[57] The British government rushed reinforcements to Canada and the fleet in preparation of an anticipated attack by up to fifty thousand Union soldiers.[58] In Britain,

Foreign Minister Russell cautioned Prime Minister Palmerston that Americans were "very dangerous people to run away from" and twice advocated calling Parliament together for the announcement of war.[59]

The Lincoln administration said nothing publicly of the crisis—not as jubilation spread across the North, nor when Congress commended the naval captain, nor in response to the British, nor even in the president's annual message to the Congress. Privately, in the weeks before the British government could get word to Washington officially demanding the prisoners' release, Lincoln considered two options: proposing arbitration or trading the prisoners for British acknowledgment of this precedent governing all future cases (bringing British maritime practice into line with standing American policy). But he discarded both; in his judgment, law was on the British side.[60]

Palmerston understood Lincoln was, to a greater degree than other nations' leaders, at the public's mercy: "It is difficult not to come to the conclusion that the robust hatred of England which animates ... almost all the Northern newspapers will make it impossible ... to grant our demands."[61] Union attorney general Edward Bates attested to Lincoln's reluctance even in late December "to acknowledge these obvious truths ... the main fear I believe, was the displeasure of our own people—lest they should accuse us of timidly truckling to the power of England."[62]

Public attitudes in Britain were shifting toward accommodation, however. Charles Francis Adams, a man not unacquainted with the volatility of public sentiment, considered it extraordinary that "the current which ran against us with such extreme violence six weeks ago now seems to be going with equal fury in our favour."[63] Lord Russell's wife confided that "whatever may have been the first natural burst of indignation in this country, I believe it would be ready to execrate the Ministry if all right and honourable means were not taken to prevent so fearful a calamity."[64] As Lord Russell himself conveyed to Palmerston in mid-December, "I do not think the country would approve an immediate declaration of war. But I think we must abide by our demand of a restoration of the prisoners."[65] Instructions issued to the ambassador in Washington were each more palliative than the previous.[66] Palmerston even professed a willingness to settle along the lines Lincoln had considered too disadvantageous to Britain: "I should be very glad to make a treaty with the U.S., giving up our pretensions of 1812 and securing immunity to persons not in arms on board neutral vessels or to persons going bona fide from one neutral port to another. This would be a triumph to the U.S. in principle while the particular case would be decided in our favour."[67] The crisis was resolved in January 1862, with U.S. minister to Britain Adams informing British foreign minister Russell that the captain had acted without instructions, which Russell accepted as adequate in lieu of an apology, and the envoys were released to Britain.[68]

Holding out so long and refusing to apologize was a strikingly flinty Union position, given the risks acknowledged "to go to war with England now is to abandon all hope of suppressing the rebellion."[69] Seward's official response brazenly claimed the prisoners would be "cheerfully liberated" since "we are asked to do to the British nation just what we have always insisted all nations ought to do to us."[70]

Public attitudes were an asymmetric American advantage in the negotiation, understood by the British to constrain Lincoln's ability to compromise while weakening intransigence by Palmerston. Adams ascribed the changed British position to the weight of "the quiet and religious citizens of the middle classes" coming to bear on the government, and wrote to Seward, "I am inclined to believe that the happening of the affair of the *Trent* just when it did, with just the issue that it had, was rather opportune than otherwise."[71] By bringing pro-American public opinion into play with the British government, the *Trent* made more difficult any recognition of the Confederacy. Confederate agents in London also came to the conclusion that "the *Trent* affair has done us incalculable injury."[72] The British press retrospectively considered the effort "about the most worthless booty it would be possible to extract from the jaws of the American lion."[73]

Mediation. Lincoln's government had been optimistic it could capitalize on British public sentiment to occasion reconsideration of Britain's neutrality policy, but within six months the confluence of economic duress in cities dependent on cotton, and agitation by Southern sympathizers in Parliament, instead forced the Palmerston government to beat back legislation advocating mediation between the North and South. Worse for the Union, subsequent Confederate successes on the battlefield and European politics tempted the Palmerston government to reconsider mediation in autumn of 1862. Diplomatic historian Ephraim Douglass Adams considers this "the most critical period in the entire course of British attitude toward the Civil War."[74]

Britain's government had never believed the Union could succeed in suppressing the rebellion. When in February of 1862 the Union outlawed the slave trade, the British ambassador thought President Lincoln was shoring up Republican sentiment in advance of concessions to the South; at other times Union victories were interpreted as giving Lincoln enough success to allow the fact of Southern independence to be acknowledged.

The only Union war efforts that gave Britain pause were the government's ability to raise so large an army, and the development of iron-sided warships. The ships did not prompt revision of estimates about the war's outcome (the Union *Monitor* and Confederate *Merrimack* fought to a near draw), but they portended "the commencement of a new era in warfare, and that Great Britain must consent to begin over again."[75] Prime Minister Palmerston worried about this potential in the context of a rising United States: "Only think of our position if in case of the Yankees turning upon us they should by means of iron ships renew the triumphs they achieved in 1812–13 by means of superior size and weight of metal."[76]

Union war efforts, though, were mostly failing in the eastern theater, giving impetus to European mischief and encouragement to Confederate envoys.[77] The Confederates stressed they were seeking neither aid nor intervention but simply factual recognition that they had met the international legal standard of having maintained their independence.[78] Foreign Minister Russell stalled by questioning the permanence of Southern independence (Britain had never recognized a revolution while it was underway), from which the Confederates concluded that Britain "desires an indefinite prolongation of the war, until the North shall be entirely exhausted and broken down."[79]

In fact, however, Palmerston, Russell, and Gladstone favored mediation, which would have the consequence of according the South diplomatic recognition. As Russell wrote to Palmerston in mid-September 1862, "I agree with you that the time is come for offering mediation to the United States Government, with a view to the recognition of the independence of the Confederates. I agree further that, in case of failure, we ought ourselves to recognize the Southern States as an independent State."[80] Russell developed a proposal for armistice between the North and South: cessation of the blockade, accepting separation between the two sides as the basis for mediated negotiation for peace.[81] France and Russia would be approached to act in unison. Timing, not policy, was at issue, with Russell noting that "we must allow the President to spend his second batch of 600,000 men before we can hope that he and his democracy will listen to reason."[82]

The European angle made manageable Palmerston's concern about war with the Union; he noted in a letter to Russell that "if the acknowledgment were made at one and the same time by England, France and some other Powers, the Yankees would probably not seek a quarrel with us alone, and would not like one against a European Confederation. Such a quarrel would render certain and permanent that Southern Independence the acknowledgment of which would have caused it."[83]

Lincoln's administration tried unsuccessfully to forestall the British offer by hinting that a proclamation of slave emancipation was forthcoming, something that would unite British public opinion in supporting the Union. The British government considered the limited terms of emancipation offered to be of slight importance other than as proof of the irreconcilable bitterness between North and South.[84]

The Union was saved by the inability of Europeans to cooperate. Neither Russia nor France shared Britain's urgency about lifting the blockade, and Britain could not sustain their focus. Britain had hoped its support for France in Mexico would be repaid with support regarding America; instead, success in Mexico had made France ambitious to conquer the entirety of that country. France offered a mediation plan different from Britain's, and Russia declined to participate.

Public attitudes had not much played in the mediation, it being an internal government debate. Gladstone's pressure on his colleagues in the cabinet to recognize the confederacy and his public speech commending Jefferson Davis for creating a new nation were not popular, despite partiality for the South.[85] Public hostility was widespread as details of the government's mediation proposal became apparent, the *London Times* asserting in an editorial that "we do not see our duty or our interest in going blindfold into an adventure such as this."[86]

Frames of Reference

Five main explanations are generally advanced for why Britain did not intervene in the American Civil War: the need to protect Canada, strength of abolitionist sentiment in Britain making an alliance with the South unacceptable, preoccupation with empire, public war-weariness, and concern about allying itself with the losing side. None gives a persuasive explanation for the British government's decisions in the years 1861–1862.

One could argue—and British prime minister Palmerston did—that any conflict with the Union put Canada at risk. In 1861 Palmerston advocated dramatically strengthening the garrisons in Canada and the Atlantic coastal fleet, the commanders having concluded that Canada was not defensible against American assault.[87] The prospect was steeply discounted within his own cabinet; typical of attitudes was Secretary of State for War Lewis considering it "incredible that any Government of ordinary prudence should at a moment of civil war gratuitously increase the number of its enemies, and, moreover, incur the hostility of so formidable a power as England."[88] Parliament refused Palmerston's request for reinforcements to Canada in 1861.

The prime minister also worried that failing to keep the Confederate States in the Union, the North might attack Canada.[89] For this he had sound basis, as Secretary of State Seward had privately advocated the Union engaging in a foreign war to stimulate patriotic unity.[90] The provocation of the *Trent* affair raised a real prospect for war between Britain and the Union—not because the British were concerned that America would declare war, but because Britain itself would need to provoke war on a point of honor. The *Trent* affair won Palmerston support for reinforcements to Canada and the squadron along North America's Atlantic seaboard, but British war plans hinged on naval bombardment of Union port cities rather than defense of Canada. The affair left a residue of resentment in the British government that gave rise to subsequent mediation proposals; concern about Canada, however, had subsided.

The strength of abolitionist sentiment in Britain is often accorded wide sway in explanations of why Britain refrained from an act it otherwise manifestly considered in its national interests. British political sentiment had become increasingly internationalist in the nineteenth century, taking interest in injustices occurring outside its own borders. Britain had led the world in outlawing the slave trade at the turn of the century, the first among Western nations to do so, and abolished slavery throughout most of the British Empire in 1833, the holdings of the East India Company being subjected a decade later. It was a justifiable source of pride among Britons.[91] And Britain had been the motive force behind the Declaration of Paris, which outlined the responsibility and rights of belligerents. There was enough inconsistency in application, however, for the policy to be "opportune and strategic" rather than strictly principled.[92]

Recognizing the Confederacy need not have required Britain to support the South's "peculiar institution," either. As the debate over mediation shows, even with the Emancipation Proclamation being developed in the fall of 1862, the British government did not consider slavery to be squarely in the center of Union war aims. Diplomats made the case that the proclamation was an exigency of war, designed to aid Northern arms rather than a full embrace of slaves' freedom. And before 1863 President Lincoln himself had been limber in trying to keep abolition of slavery from being perceived as a central Union war aim; corralling Northerners behind the aim of national union was difficult enough without the divisions slavery stoked among them. Lincoln tried unsuccessfully in 1862 to use the prospect of emancipation to forestall mediation; the British government was not dissuaded. The confederacy's British advocates argued that even if Britain were complicit in the creation of a slave state, it could condition its relations to necessitate eventual emancipation. Howard Jones considers that "the move both for and away from intervention had little to do with moral sentiments about slavery."[93]

The third argument advanced for not intervening in the American Civil War is that of higher priorities: Britain had an empire to maintain, was already consumed with those challenges, and could not divert political attention or build support for even a welcome opportunity. The Palmerston government was operating in the shadow of Indian mutiny; busy occupying Canton and Peking; evincing an understandably greater concern about French land power and invasion of Lebanon precipitating the collapse of the Ottoman Empire; and enmeshed in effecting the war of unification in

Italy, Russia suppressing Polish rebellion, and Germany taking Schleswig and Holstein from Denmark. In terms of effect on the international order, Britain was understandably more concerned about developments in its imperial holdings and on the European continent than those within the United States.[94] The number of international concerns were evident in August 1861, as Palmerston's secretary of state for war appraised him, "I do not like the look of things in Hungary. I am more afraid of mischief from that quarter than from America."[95]

But if the press of other business was dispositive, why should Britain concern itself at all with the American war? Britain could have declared its neutrality and been done with the subject; instead it concerned itself intensively in developing mediation proposals, debating bills in Parliament, and assessing the prospects of lifting the Union blockade. The Palmerston government also did not lack appreciation for how much recognizing the confederacy would aid Britain's hand in dealing with those imperial issues. It thought it had traded support for France in Mexico for French support of mediation to end the blockade. Both Palmerston and Gladstone acknowledged that recognizing the Confederacy would give Britain and France common cause, denting the unification movement in Italy and Germany's designs on the continent—not a bad take for a small wager.

The fourth argument, war-weariness, does injustice to the British public. The long shadow of the Crimean War colored attitudes, of course, but public attitudes during the initial recognition debate and especially the *Trent* crisis demonstrate a judicious public moved to martial action but then reconsidering.[96] The British—and even the American—public showed during the crisis commendable judgment as the press of issues turned their attention to the prospects of war. Palmerston gave more than he took in understanding the greater relative pressure a fully democratic American leadership was subject to than was a partially democratic Britain. The Palmerston government fretted that public pressure on Lincoln would be too great for any compromise, yet Lincoln was able to concede on the *Trent*, even though the taking of Confederate envoys was the only sliver of success in the war effort. After the *Trent* affair Palmerston was able to prevent the 1862 Parliament bill from passage that would have required his government to mediate between the North and South, even as British cities suffered from the economic effects of the Union blockade.[97] In fact, debate over whether to intervene in the American Civil War demonstrated the fallacy of British elites' belief that the public could not be trusted with the maintenance of liberal policies.

Finally, decisions about whether to recognize the confederacy in 1861–1862 were in no way freighted with concern that association with the South would tie Great Britain to a losing party in the conflict. Quite the contrary; at no point did the Palmerston government believe the North could prevail in the war. Just before the North's victory at Antietam, Palmerston recorded his view that it was "in the highest degree unlikely" that the North could suppress the rebellion.[98] Secretary of State for War Lewis shared that view as he weighed concern about Canada:

> It is clear that the Northern states are bent upon giving the Southerners a severe lesson, even if they cannot subjugate them, and make them submissive members of the Union. They leave vigour by two defeats, one serious and disgraceful, and they will now use all their efforts to repair their losses, and to attain some successes. Their eyes will be turned southward, not northward,

but they are reckless and unscrupulous, and it would be most unwise of us to tempt them to hostilities by the appearance of unguardedness.[99]

At the time Britain considered mediation, Robert E. Lee's Confederates were running rings around the Union capital and carrying every engagement. The parade of ineffectual generals commanding the Army of the Potomac—the theater of war most closely watched by audiences both domestic and foreign—would continue until 1864 when Lincoln nominated Ulysses S. Grant to overall command of the Union Armies. Palmerston and his cabinet believed the South would wrest its independence by force of arms from the North, and that sentiment prevailed in the British government well after the Gettysburg campaign in July 1863.

Upholding the rules of Britain's hegemonic order was a primary concern: reserving intervention to beat back revolution, expanding the reach of the Declaration of Paris and reinforcing belligerent rights weighed at crucial times in British policy.[100] In determining neutrality and handling the *Trent* dispute, the precedent Britain's choices would set heavily influenced policy to bring practice into line with the rule it wanted binding on the United States. With the declaration of neutrality, Britain sustained its policy of not recognizing belligerents that had not materially established their independence and forestalled any retributive acts that might encourage insurrection in Canada, Ireland, Scotland, or Wales. In the *Trent* dispute, Britain sought to bring the United States into alignment with practices of the Declaration of Paris on behavior toward belligerent nations. Both cases illustrate how Britain, now securely the strongest power of the international order, sought to translate its military and commercial power into rules that, consistently followed by the major powers, would make the sustainment of British power less costly and likely of longer duration as other countries, like the United States, became more powerful.

But international order is seldom the sole concern—even of great powers. Domestic politics were the crucial factor in Palmerston's considerations about whether to involve Great Britain in the American Civil War. America was unique as a foreign policy problem because choices about it could resonate back to Britain's own politics. The collapse of the Ottoman Empire might create headaches (and opportunities) for Britain's foreign policy, but there was little risk of the British public demanding to be governed as Ottoman sultanates governed or dispensing with their British citizenship to become Ottoman—with nationality being conjoined with ethnicity, such a thing was hardly even understood as a concept. The success of America could result in more Britons choosing to become American, furthering the United States' rise as a challenger and increasing its animosity toward Britain. The collapse of America would be felt with resentment by British subjects in England, Ireland, Scotland, and Wales as the end of their democratic aspirations—and not just abstractly, but concretely, with immediate effects on their own families.

The affinities of the newly urbanized industrial workforce in Britain had a cultural attraction to the dynamism, opportunity, and political enfranchisement of an industrializing American North. Attitudes were mixed early in the war, but they solidified after canny encouragement from the Lincoln administration, which sent ships of food for relief of unemployed British workers.[101] President Lincoln also wrote to workers' organizations encouraging common cause. As a result, even textile workers in Manchester—those most economically affected by the embargo—were staunchly opposed to the Confederacy by 1864. Lincoln's fostering of that sentiment capitalized on Palmerston's fear that his foreign policy choices regarding intervention in the American Civil War would reverberate back inside Britain.

As U.S. minister to Britain, Adams repeatedly characterized the American war as an internal insurrection, something Britain itself was concerned with because of the possibility for parallels with British subjugation of Ireland, Scotland and Wales. The furor over Ambassador Clay's threat that America would stoke rebellion within Britain shows the resonance that policy toward America could have in complicating Britain's hold over those territories. Debates over whether to become involved in the American Civil War show the first glint that the composition of another nation's people had the ability to affect Britain's governance of its own. The predominance of bloodline in determining nationality for other countries of the international order gave the United States a unique advantage, one that was coming to salience in building and sustaining American power as a dominant force in the international order.

In other words, what the United States was as a political culture effectively limited the foreign policy choices of the hegemon of the international order in the 1860s. America's immigration policy, social mobility, and inclusive political rules prevented the British government from making a choice that would have been disastrous to the Union.

Denouement

The social upheaval both Britain and the United States were experiencing in the nineteenth century brought democratizing pressures into both political systems. The economics progressed faster in Britain with its pioneering of the industrial revolution, but class structure and settled territory limited social mobility. Politics galloped ahead in the American circumstance, with the passing of the generation of founding fathers, the opening of the West, and wishful efforts on the part of Northerners that admitting new states could diffuse the political power of the South and put slavery on a path to extinction. Slavery not only discredited America's claim to a higher creed than other countries not constituted as democracies but also deformed the economic progress of the United States, incentivizing plantation cotton in the South.

The Civil War smashed that degraded and degrading model, freeing up more productive uses of land, people, and capital in ways that catapulted the United States into prosperity and international prominence. As Bruce Porter concludes in *War and the Rise of the State,* "Appomattox thus represented not only the defeat of the South but the defeat of the whole Southern economic and political system, and the triumph of a state-fostered industrial and financial complex in the North."[102]

More fully living up to its values of political and economic liberty served America's interests. As Palmerston declining to recognize the Confederacy demonstrates, America's values served to constrain the choices of its international adversaries by using the aspirations of their own citizens against them. Palmerston's decision not to intervene in the American Civil War by recognizing the Confederacy, and that Confederacy's subsequent loss in its bid for independence, permitted the Union—the United States—to continue rising.

That Southern economic and political system was close in spirit and organization to Britain's landed aristocracy; its failure to defend itself against the more roiling representative political organization and efficient industrialization marshaled by the Union was portentous of America's surging potential. The South's loss was, in a way, representative of the limits of Britain's political and economic model when placed in direct competition with that of the United States.

Lincoln had also demonstrated an incipient ability to reach into British domestic affairs. It is often thought that the composition of the American body politic, consisting as it does of immigrants from so many lands, is a vulnerability in foreign policy—that, for example, German immigrants would harbor affinities for their land of origin and become disloyal during the world wars. The argument was taken to shameful extreme with the internment of Japanese Americans after Pearl Harbor. What has received less attention is the extent to which America's immigrant fabric is a threat to other countries because of familial connections. That is what Palmerston feared, and what Lincoln stoked, and the result was an important inhibition on the most powerful state of the international order.

Palmerston's decision had important domestic consequences internal to Britain as well. One of the major concerns restraining the prime minister's temptation to intervene in the Civil War was that association with the Confederacy would increase domestic support in Britain for expanding the electoral franchise. He did not anticipate that the success of the Union would have a corresponding effect, but it did. As Kevin Phillips argues in *The Cousins' Wars,* "instead of Americans circa 1775 seeking the rights and liberties of Englishmen, the interaction had come full circle: Englishmen were looking to the cousins' wars to secure them the rights and liberties of Americans."[103] H. C. Allen emphasizes that "there is no doubt that the Northern victory greatly facilitated the passage of the reform bill of 1867."[104] Change in electoral law made Britain more like the United States in political participation and eventually in spirit, contributing significantly to the convergence of political attitudes between the two countries in the coming thirty years.

The British novelist Anthony Trollope, who was traveling in America at the time, offered one epitaph of the tensions during America's Civil War:

> These people speak our language, use our prayers, read our books, are ruled by our laws, dress themselves in our image, are warm with our blood. They have all our virtues; and their vices are our own too, loudly as we call out against them. They are our sons and our daughters, the source of our greatest pride, and as we grow old they should be the staff of our age. Such a war as we should now wage with the States would be an unloosing of hell upon all that is best upon the world's surface.[105]

The sense of Great Britain and the United States being like each other, countries whose people and whose fates were intertwined, had begun taking root.

Ironically, given his concern about the further democratization America represented, Palmerston would come to be seen as the politician that brought Britain into the democratic era. Upon his death, the *Times of London* described his solicitousness of public opinion: "Lord Palmerston bowed to this deity, recognized its power, and used it as he could."[106]

6

Manifesting Destiny: Defining the Nation

THIS CHAPTER DIFFERS from others in this volume because it does not focus on a singular event or crisis between Great Britain and the United States but instead attempts to grasp the two societies' sense of themselves as they underwent hugely disruptive political, social, and economic changes. Governments make snap decisions; they have the capacity to change directions swiftly and need to make choices when events present themselves. But societies typically do not; their reconsiderations are unspooled hand over hand, slowly, as ideas take hold and become part of a collective consciousness. Understanding that process is tricky. It is also important. Societies' communal understanding shape their reactions to events, and in societies with representative governments, it defines the government's range of choice.

In 1870 the reversal of station between Great Britain and the United States was still some distance in the future, but the perceptual shift between hegemons was already taking place.[1] Henry Adams wrote of the time that "the revolution since 1861 was nearly complete, and for the first time in history the American felt himself almost as strong as an Englishman. He had thirty years to wait before he should feel himself stronger."[2] America grew stronger, bigger, and flintier, hardened by the Civil War and wresting land from Indian tribes. Britain became pervasively pessimistic about its economy, less persuaded of the benefits of empire, more attentive to the improvement of its domestic possibilities.[3] Occurring independently but nearly simultaneously, the changes made America an empire and Great Britain a democracy.

The Union's grim determination to prevent Southern secession and ennoblement of that effort in abolishing slavery removed a principal disparagement tarnishing America's republican ideology. British elites continued to have a (mostly justified) sense of cultural superiority over America, but in the 1870s, those elites begin to realize the consequences of American dynamism: the United States as a rising power, one that would challenge Britain's dominance. G. Lowes Dickinson, traveling in America at the time, typified British anxieties in concluding "the two things rubbed into me in this country are (1) that the future of the world lies with America, (2) that radically and essentially America is a barbarous country."[4] The British political leaders likewise felt America rising; Benjamin Disraeli commented in 1872 that America was "throwing lengthening shades over the Atlantic," creating "vast and novel elements in the distribution of power."[5]

Electoral reforms were transforming Britain in the same time frame, the debate marked by conscious rejection of American modes. Even those who favored expanded political participation in Britain feared democracy portended instability, corruption, and "public passion"; those who wanted to preserve a narrow, elite franchise viewed democracy as a threat to liberal governance. The slow pace of political change and strong preservationist sentiment in Britain contrasted sharply with American risk tolerance and innovation, attitudes prevalent in economic as well as political debates. The two societies did not consider themselves congruent in the 1870s; the sense of sameness that would develop during the Great Rapprochement lay more than a decade in the future.

What the 1870s did encompass was Great Britain and the United States developing the defining mythologies of their political cultures. The United States would begin to overcome the schism between the North and South by adopting the conquest and settlement of the American West as its sense of itself. Great Britain soothed economic disruption and engendered patience among the disenfranchised by fostering a cultural veneration of continuity (that, conveniently for elites, preserved class distinctions). The national narratives contrasted starkly—American conquest, British contentment—and were by no means representative of all that was occurring in either society. But they were also compatible, allowing each country to lionize itself without challenging the other's sense of itself, and thus facilitated British acceptance of a rising America.

The Rush

The settlement of the American West was essential to the United States becoming a hegemonic power. Without the consolidation of territorial control under American governance, it is unlikely that America could have accrued the productive national wealth; the broad distribution of that wealth among its citizenry; the magnitude of economic resources in gold, coal, oil, land, and minerals to fuel industrialization; or the security that comes from stable borders and social cohesion to produce the behemoth of political and economic power that America would become in the twentieth century.

Before the Civil War, westward expansion was central to the hope of a more perfect union, both in terms of the direct abolition of slavery and in breaking Southern dominance of the Congress (perversely ensured by the counting of slaves as three-fifths of a person for apportioning legislative representation). The weight of the South in the legislature foreclosed remanding the problem in law at the federal level, but the incorporation of new states from the West portended a diluting of the Southern chokehold that might make the problem amenable to solution. That it would be achieved by wronging Native Americans was, to the extent such considerations were weighed in the moral balance, a lesser evil.

In the mid-nineteenth century, America struck gold, both literally and figuratively. Westward migration that had taken on the respectability of a national cause with Manifest Destiny became a stampede with gold strikes in California and the Dakotas and silver in Nevada. The westward rush was fueled and reinforced by government policies and public-private partnerships to create transportation infrastructure and encourage settlement. In the aftermath of the Civil War, another wave of migration ensued as former slaves and free blacks fled violence and the failure of Reconstruction, whites fled Reconstruction's partial successes, and others fled economic failure of businesses profitable only with slave labor or simply wanted fresh starts.[6] The westward expansion reinforced America's sense of itself as a country where anyone could make his or her way and find fortune.[7] It gave the country a new and unifying national narrative after the Civil War.

The reunited United States came roaring out of the war with large-scale transfer of capital from the plantation South to more productive applications; an even more mobile labor force; and industries developed from wartime innovation, primed from wartime production, and fueled with bountiful natural resources. A million veteran soldiers returning to the labor force had won a war using railroads, steamships, and telegraphs, their leaders able to move and coordinate great armies. Now an industrial primacy of arsenals, engineering works, and logistics would be freed up for civilian use. Innovation in weaponry had burgeoned: rifles, metal cartridge bullets, iron-clad ships, and torpedoes. The U.S. Navy expanded sixfold to 671 ships at war's end, 237 of them steam powered, and forty of them iron-clad.

Winston Churchill, in his *History of the English Speaking Peoples,* acknowledged the economic importance of a changing America but was dismissive of the political importance of the movement west, writing that "from the end of Reconstruction until the closing decade of the century American politics lacked interest."[8] He was mistaken. Not only was the economy primed, but the state itself had changed as a result of the war and had put the changes to use in the West. America was transformed from a loose confederation into a nation-state, with politicians seeing the opportunity war presented for social change: homestead legislation, land grant colleges, the transcontinental railroad, admission of new states, empowered industrial capitalism, capital itself redistributed from the South to the North and West, re-creation of a national banking system, and finally, an end to the divisive political problem of slavery.[9]

America had never been more dynamic, and the country unquestionably saw itself in grander terms after the Civil War. Having passed through the fiery trial, there was a religiosity in America's vision of itself tracing forward into settlement of the West. Walt Whitman declared America "a new empire, grander than any before."[10] Herman Melville imagined the country had "empire in her eyes."[11] The empire America conquered would be that of its native inhabitants in what would come to be considered its domestic lands.

Many of the apostles of American expansionism attribute the country's growing strength to becoming a major sea power and eschewing land wars.[12] In this characterization of shrewd choice, America is seen to model Britain's maritime strategy. The assessment seems brazenly at odds with the actual experience of America (and of Britain, for that matter).[13] Looking back on the nineteenth century Alfred Thayer Mahan may have seen a maritime nation, but from the French and Indian War in 1754, what would become the U.S. Army was fighting Indians, and Americans were consumed with questions of territorial security from Indian threats. Sea power may be an inherently better strategic choice for preserving and extending a state's resources, but it is only possible as strategy when territorial security allows the luxury of focusing on sea power. For America, that territorial security came about by forcing Indian tribes off their lands.

President Andrew Jackson's aggressive dispossession of land from Indians in the 1830s had coincided with the rise of populism in American politics. It also traced the fault line between those Americans living in safety and those settling the frontier: the removal policy was deeply unpopular in New England, supported where people were exposed to Indians.[14] And the political power of the frontier was rising with the admission of new states, federal need for the metals and minerals being mined, and continued settler expansion.

The separation of federal and state powers further aggravated the schism between presidential policies and local attitudes, as very often federal treaties promised land that states refused to hand over to Indian control.[15] The policy cleaved along another uniquely

American fault line during the Jackson administration, with the president declining to enforce the Supreme Court's decision that Georgia must comply with federal treaties governing relations with the Cherokee.[16] Thus, part of the explanation for how a republic so constituted could persist in such flagrant violation of its beliefs across such an expanse of time comes from the separation of powers in the American system of government, a jealousy and conflict unique to its design of preventing government tyranny.

After Jackson, though, the previous policy equilibrium was restored, in part because the attention of the nation was riven by conflict over slavery and the gathering storm of the Civil War. Secession of the Southern states removed federal troops from the West and increased competition for skilled soldiers and militia.[17] Before the Civil War, the professional army was spread across the states and territories; with the advent of war, troops were recalled east, and localities were required to raise volunteers to protect emigrant trails and mail delivery. America's best soldiers were fighting each other, not Indians. The diluting of talented soldiery was especially felt in the Southwest, where plains tribes pushed the frontier back more than a hundred miles. After the war the federal government refused to allow former Confederate states to raise militia, even in response to brutal raiding by the Apache and Comanche. In 1871 the line of settlement had not yet returned as far west as before Southern secession.[18]

The toughness and resourcefulness of the Americans who settled the West would come to embody how America mythologized itself; illustrative is General George A. Forsyth's description of laundresses who worked on army posts as "good, honest, industrious wives, usually well on in years, minutely familiar with their rights, which they dared to maintain with acrimonious volubility."[19] Reading diaries and letters from those settlers, it is amazing to witness the hardships they endured, the near constant peril they found themselves in from starvation, attack, and exposure to the elements. Unlike the pilgrims who sailed for Plymouth confident their God would provide, the Americans who moved westward knew providence could well be indifferent to their fate—"Indian country" is emblematic for danger.

Despite the danger (or for some, because of it), the magnetism of opportunity in the West proved compelling. And the magnitude of westward migration is staggering. In 1848 there were roughly 157,000 people in the California territory: 150,000 Native Americans, 6,500 people of Spanish or Mexican descent (known as Californios), and 7,500 or so nonnative Americans; within two years, an additional one hundred thousand Americans came.[20] And not only Americans; by the mid-1850s, more than one-third of Californians were foreigners.[21]

It is, however, a mistake to believe that Americans ebbed steadily west, encroaching on an expanding propinquity of land. Before President James Polk brandished California gold during his fourth annual message to Congress in 1848, traders transited the plains and there existed a rind of American population along the Pacific coast also slowly moving eastward to fill in the middle of the country. In addition to prospecting for gold, missionary avocation, flight from violence over slavery in the border states or from civil war military service, the desire of Mormons to be beyond the reach of American government, the chance to start anew unknown, and later parceling of land free for settlement all contributed to the strength of the current, pulling prairie schooners across the plains.[22]

War Paths

Indian resistance to these incursions was constant. From 1768 through 1889, the American army fought "943 actions in twelve separate campaigns and numerous local incidents" against the continent's prior inhabitants.[23] As Fairfax Downey notes, "from 1866 to 1892 there was not a year, and hardly a three months, in which there was not some expedition against the Indians in the vast regions west of the Mississippi, and between the Canadian and Mexican borders."[24]

The American government and its army were less supportive of the settlers than one might imagine given how much government policies encouraged settlement. Buffalo Bill Cody, awarded the Medal of Honor for his scouting with the army, said "every Indian outbreak that I have ever known has resulted from broken promises and broken treaties by the government."[25] Many in the professional army agreed with that view; more often than not, they blamed settlers for causing massacres. The federal army was throughout the Indian Wars generally critical of the policies of state and territorial governments and hesitant to enforce them or cooperate with militia engaged in them.[26] General William Tecumseh Sherman, commander of the army, rejected settler demands for protection on the Texas frontier in 1871, commenting that "they expose women and children singly on the road and in cabins far off from others, as though they were safe in Illinois . . . such actions are more significant than words."[27] His meaning: that settlers were reckless, responsible for their own trouble.[28]

While weapons technology advanced significantly during that time period, the fiercest of the Indians also had access to some of the best weapons—in many instances they were better armed than the

American soldiers they were fighting.[29] Soldiers were provided with single-shot muskets, mostly front-loading, making nearly impossible any reloading while on horseback (a distinct disadvantage in Indian country). As an economy measure, soldiers were also not issued ammunition for practice firing. The army was often simply outgunned. It was also largely untrained for this kind of war—George Custer's Seventh Cavalry was famous for its hunting expeditions, yet its soldiers were barely proficient, and certainly not the peers of their native opponents. American Indians, as S. C. Gwynne notes, "were warlike by nature, and they were warlike for centuries before Columbus stumbled upon them."[30] This was particularly true of the tribes on the western plains, who had so elegantly mastered the military technology of the time before industrialization and knew of the baleful experience other tribes had had with Americans.

It is an essential, and essentially American, truth that the federal government was too far removed from local concerns to craft workable solutions. Throughout the Indian Wars there was an enormous gap between the policy of the American government and the views of those Americans living in Indian country. The War Department was continually hobbled for funds and chose policies for efficiency rather than effectiveness; it long held the belief that "if the Indians could be induced to keep the peace, forts and war would be unnecessary."[31] The policy foundered time and again when it was settlers, not Indians, who refused to keep the peace.

The federal government was finally pushed into "solving the Indian problem" in President Ulysses S. Grant's second administration.[32] That solution was an overt renunciation of peace policies, development of a more proficient Indian fighting army, relentless prosecution of a military campaign against the tribes, and decimation of Indian livelihood.

President Grant had initially supported what we would now describe as a culturally sensitive approach to the problem of violence between Native Americans and immigrant settlers. He sought to minimize conflict, supporting "any course toward them [Native Americans] which tends to their civilization and ultimate citizenship," ordering military commanders to prevent settler incursions onto Indian land, accepting responsibility for Indian welfare on reservations, establishing educational and medical programs—even symbolizing the policy by appointment of the first Native American commissioner of Indian affairs. Military commanders were subordinated to "Indian agents," government civilians purportedly caring for Indian interests. What in contemporary parlance we call "whole of government operations" were in vogue for managing the Indian problem: departments to work in seamless coordination, each contributing its bureaucratic strengths and sharing the burden of a well-modulated and adaptive policy.

The more nuanced strategy did not, however, reduce spectacular incidents of violence that hardened public attitudes even in the cosseted east. The Modoc War on the California-Oregon border resulted in the killing (during peace negotiations, no less) of the only general officer during a hundred years of Indian warring. The Sioux at Little Big Horn massacred Custer's Seventh Cavalry; Grant considered this to be Custer's own fault, but the public would not be assuaged.

The peace policy was discredited as much by failure of the Indian agencies as by violence. The magnitude of corruption experienced throughout the Indian agencies has seldom been equaled; its revelation was devastating to liberal reformers' hopes for a humane resettlement of Native Americans. From the nation's capital, the government had crafted a grand strategy it was incapable of implementing. Faced with the collapse of more sophisticated strategies than enforcing compliance, and the public outcry after Custer's massacre, Grant changed course, subordinating the Indian agencies under military control and ordering the military "to subdue all Indians who offered resistance."[33]

This instruction finally got the Army serious about the Indian Wars. The change from dashing romanticism of the frontier to its conquest is epitomized by the transition from Custer, with his long golden hair and fringed buckskins, writing memoirs for publication about life on the plains, to Ranald Slidell Mackenzie, a severe, unpopular commander who defeated the Apache, Cheyenne, Comanche, Kiowa, Sioux, and Ute, and who had a fearsome mix of intellect, adaptability, and the brutal arithmetic of industrial age warfare.[34]

In the end, though, it was less the American army than American society that destroyed the Indian tribes. As Mackenzie's boss, General Philip Sheridan, testified in 1873 when hunters were killing buffalo by the million,

> These men have done more in the last two years, and will do more in the next year, to settle the vexed Indian question, than the entire regular army has done in the last forty years. They are destroying the Indians' commissary. And it is a well known fact that an army losing its base of supplies is placed at a great disadvantage. Send them powder and lead, if you will; but for a lasting peace, let them kill, skin, and sell until the buffaloes are exterminated.[35]

And they did. U.S. Indian policy was directly a function of its democracy; America was not only a government that was illiberal in the nineteenth century but Americans were an illiberal people. The

West became American only with the decimation of Indian ways of life. Population tables tell the story most dramatically: white settlement in Wise County, Texas, dropped from 3,160 in 1860 to 1,450 in 1870 as Indians took advantage of the removal of troops for the Civil War and prohibition of militia during Reconstruction to drive settlers out of the territory; but in 1880, five years after the end of the Indian Wars in the area, it had surged more than tenfold, to 16,601.[36]

The large-scale destruction practiced by Americans as they moved their domestic frontier westward to the Pacific Ocean and filled in the middle of the continent with immigrant Americans is even more brutal than colonial practices by the British in India (even in the aftermath of the 1858 rebellion), Europeans throughout Africa, the Portuguese and Spanish in South America, and all of the above in Asia. For Europeans, the purpose of empire was to harness indigenous inhabitants for the economic gain and political control of an external power. What is exceptional about the closing of the American West is that the policy was not merely conquest of indigenous inhabitants but their extermination or deportation to free the land up for settlement by immigrant Americans. What comes to be the defining mythology of America is more closely akin to British and Dutch settlement in South Africa; the central difference is that American settlers working their own smallholdings could subsist independent of indigenous labor, whereas those working the gold and diamond mines and large plantations of Europeans in Africa could not.

How, then, did the settlement of the West become an overwhelmingly positive cultural mythology for Americans?

Illiberal Democracy

Every American president from George Washington forward until the decimation of Indian freedom sought to find some solution that did not affront the collective national conscience; none succeeded. As Robert Remini explains, "by shunting them off to the wilderness where they would no longer threaten the safety of the United States or hinder its westward and southern expansion, Americans felt they could resolve the problem of the Indian presence in a humanitarian manner that would not conflict with their Christian conscience or moral sensibility."[37] America developed a conscience-easing policy of resettlement and turned its eyes from the actual effects.

The rush to the West was not inevitable or natural in the sense of it occurring freely in nature without recourse to human action. Westward expansion was the product of explicit and intentional government policies: the distribution of government lands at no cost to the public provided they domiciled on and made productive use of the dispensation for at least two years; public-private part-nerships incentivized (again with free land, but also bond issuances and enabling legislation) to create transportation and communica-tion infrastructure; federal statute conveying to the title holder of property the mineral rights to the land (one reason America had a gold rush but other countries didn't is that mineral rights remained with the government in other states); and the establishment of land grant colleges to foster and disseminate scientific knowledge of ag-riculture to newly agrarian citizens. As Walter Russell Mead amus-ingly points out, westward expansion is proof that "Americans have always wanted their government to give them free stuff."[38] The ex-pansion of America across the continent from the Atlantic Ocean to the Pacific was the result of government action that rewarded in-dividual initiative.

Government policy was also a central element in the failures that characterize America's westward expansion and in explaining how a society so dedicated to the universality of its values could fail so miserably to accord them to the country's original inhabitants. No American government favored outright extermination. But as Dan Elbert Clark argues, because of "the confusion of attitudes, prerogatives and interests among those who sought to formulate and execute that policy, the results were as disastrous and unjust to the Indians as would have been a deliberate and acknowledged program of conquest and extermination."[39]

This glaring inconsistency of government policy therefore necessitates explanation for a country that believes itself called to and emblematic of a higher moral standard. How could so important an endeavor be allowed to go so far wrong for such an extended period of time?

After Abraham Lincoln's death, policies for occupation and reconstruction of the American South became much more punitive, and the failures of those policies further hardened attitudes in both the North and South. With so much still entangled in the unfinished business of forcing the Union back together, depredations against Indians never received the attention in their time that slavery has in the American imagination. African slaves were held in physical bondage, forced to labor under close supervision, beaten and killed for underperforming, and sold as property irrespective of the bonds of matrimony and parentage; their suffering is unique in the American experience and much to be lamented. But Native Americans, too, suffered horrifically at the hands of both the American government and American citizens, and the taking of their lives, livelihood, and freedom nearly as completely did not at the time—and does not in our time—receive the attention those sins deserve. Native Americans were dispossessed and suffered forced indenture and the taking of children from their parents as a matter of policy well after the Civil War had settled the immorality of those practices against African Americans; they persisted against Native Americans into the twentieth century in California.[40] Perhaps Americans look differently upon the Indian experience because Indians offered armed resistance, whereas America had little experience of slave revolts.[41] Moreover, slaves were purchased as property and therefore subjugated from the start, whereas tribes had to be brought under control.

Americans view themselves as members of a frontier society, individuals braving all manner of difficulty for the opportunity to have something of their own: pioneers carving wealth out of wilderness; people banding together in citizen militia for protection the government could not provide, and decisively defeating worthy adversaries on the battlefield; and bringers of law, community, and religious faith to lands that had not known any of those blessings.[42] Manifest Destiny, the doctrine that claimed Americans had a sacred responsibility to spread their values across the vastness of the West, would become not only the nation's domestic policy but would also form the basis also for America's engagement with the world.

Native Americans are objects rather than subjects of that victor's narrative, however. The land was vast, but inhabited by hundreds of thousands of people organized into political communities. In some instances those communities were malevolent, in some benevolent, but in nearly all cases they were as democratic as the American body politic, and in some cases much more so.[43] The American West was inhabited by cultures reverent of nature and a creator "great spirit," some practiced rituals of communion, generally believed themselves in possession of a religion, rather than in need of one.[44] Their religions were in the main categorizable as deist, putting them within the spectrum of the American founders' beliefs. Their economies were hunting and gathering the abundance around them, farming where necessary, and trading for manufactures, much as the economies of most Americans on the frontiers.

That the American and Native American societies became incompatible is a tragedy, but it was not an inevitability, which makes the choices that produced such an outcome all the more tragic and important, especially for a political culture that lays claim to universal principles of human dignity and political representation. Even more so that the decisions were not made in haste, but taken *seriatum* and with forethought across decades. The repeated pattern was settlers rushing to homestead up to and beyond the perimeter of (scant) government-provided security, settlements made on land deeded to Indian tribes by treaty, raids by Indians intended to drive settlers off and reclaim their lands, settlers howling for government protection, and eventually the government acceding. The decisions that were taken to move Indians off their traditional lands and, eventually, make them wards of the state were forced by restive American settler populations on the federal government.[45] Theodore Roosevelt gave a typically clear-eyed summary of the Indian Wars in his book *The Winning of the West*:

> The frontier was pushed westward, not because the leading
> statesmen of America, or the bulk of the American people, foresaw
> the continental greatness of this country or strove for such
> greatness; but because the bordermen of the West, and the
> adventurous land-speculators of the East, were personally
> interested in acquiring new territory, and because, against their
> will, the governmental representatives of the nation were finally
> forced to make the interests of the Westerners their own.[46]

The government was complicit in bad outcomes because it consistently formulated policies that were unworkable and aggravated the likelihood of violence, whether by sending insufficient military forces to police the roads and settlements, not restraining new settlements, or allowing gross corruption in the Indian agencies to despoil tribal communities and collapse Indian confidence in the American government upholding its word.

Where Indian policy was concerned, America was an illiberal democracy well into the twentieth century. Between 1789 and 1838 (and therefore only accounting for the move geographically through the Midwest and in time through the administration of Martin van Buren) more than 81,000 Native Americans were forcibly relocated from their land; the American people largely supported those removals.[47] American political culture throughout the period was characterized by government acting on the will of the majority; the maturing of American democracy to fully embody the protection of minority rights lay well in the future.

Westward expansion provided a turning of the American kaleidoscope, bringing into view both momentousness of the country's potential power and the momentum to attain it. The constituent colors and shapes of America took on a new pattern with the conquest of the territorial west. The Wild West was a place of limitless horizon and pervasive risk; embracing that risk would be the defining choice of American political culture. Hundreds of thousands of people ran those risks for nothing more than opportunity. From the distance of contemporary safety, it is genuinely shocking how much Americans put at stake to attain what was, for most of them, very little.

An accurate portrait of America rising needs to come to terms not only with what was gained by American settlement of the West but also with what was lost. Gained was a country of continental expanse, social and economic mobility, breathtaking tolerance for turbulence and risk, wealth creation on a scale not previously imagined, an abiding belief in the necessity and righteousness of armed force, ennoblement of the individual crafting his or her own fate in a harsh wilderness, urbanization of the industrial revolution balanced by rural landowners, and the genius of the founders' political structures accommodating both in the respective houses of Congress.

What was lost—if indeed, it was ever truly possessed by immigrants in America—was the upholding of the political creed that all men are created equal, that they are endowed by their creator with certain inalienable rights, and that among these are life, liberty, and the pursuit of happiness. These truths were not self-evident to many Americans that flooded into the West in the second half of the nineteenth century. Nor was it true to their experience once there. The majoritarian democracy practiced in America since the rise of Andrew Jackson would migrate west where force was law. Justice was a luxury that for immigrant Americans typically followed far in the wake of settlement, and hasn't ever really followed for Native Americans. By dispossessing Indian tribes in the rush westward, America became an imperial power at home, fighting wars that consolidated the country's territory under control of immigrant Americans.

A Land of Settled Government

Both Britain and America were consumed with domestic upheaval in the second half of the nineteenth century: America with Reconstruction and the westward expansion, Britain with urbanization and demands for greater political representation.[48] In both America and Britain, the mythology adopted into political culture was at dramatic odds with practice. For Americans, the incongruity was between a republican creed newly burnished by abolition of slavery and the decimation of Indian tribes. For the British, the incongruity was between the rapidly modernizing economic and technological powerhouse of their society and a political system dominated by the least dynamic elements of that society. Both societies made virtues of societal choice on these issues in crafting their national stories.

The American and British experiences of the 1870s were not wholly unconnected, either. The Union's Civil War victory and bitter experience of Reconstruction in the South accentuated the need for a defining national narrative in binding the country back together, and America found that narrative in westward expansion. For Britons, the Union victory increased pressure for electoral reform, industrialization and its associated urbanization generated new wealth the class hierarchy struggled to accommodate, and decisions about how far to proceed with democracy—how much to emulate or differentiate from America—were crucial in shaping British national identity.[49]

The 1832 Reform Act had still excluded 85 percent of adult men because of property requirements. Proposing an expansion of the electorate to include skilled workers brought down the government of Prime Minister John Russell in 1866, yet the strength of momentum toward reform is reflected in the conservative government that replaced Russell quickly introducing an even more reformist bill.[50] The Representation of the People Act 1867 doubled the electorate by including heads of household and townspeople (although not in proportion to their numbers), enfranchising an additional million Britons but retaining an absolute majority of aristocracy and gentry in the House of Commons.[51]

The political disruption of economic change weighed much more heavily in Britain than in America. Arnold Toynbee has described the industrial revolution as "a period as disastrous and as terrible as any through which a nation has ever passed."[52] Political and cultural elites recoiled from the dislocation of urbanization chosen by so many to gain the material advantages that tenant rural life did not offer them. British aristocrats not generally being men of industry, they lacked faith the economy could genuinely improve the lot of the working class, even as that lot was dramatically being improved.[53]

In Britain's defense, the social upheaval of the nation's industrialization drawing hundreds of thousands of people off the land and into squalid tenements was a daunting social challenge, even before mixing in the stultifying effect of class privilege. British political theorists worried the public had a natural tendency toward radicalism, society thus in need of a "safety valve" like that which available land in an expanding western frontier provided America.[54] Charles Dickens's novels provide a window into Britain's societal upheaval, and also capture its "typically Victorian middle class dread of democracy."[55]

There were also serious concerns, even among British reformers, about whether expansion of the franchise would produce democracy—and the American example featured prominently as illustration of Britons' fears about corruption, especially in urban locales where the expanding national franchise would net the largest pool of voters. British elites defended political exclusion—an illiberal political structure—on the argument that it alone permitted liberal governance, by which they meant a farsighted international policy and prevention of corruption domestically.

In coming to terms with the social upheaval caused by economic change, Britain was seeking to be "untouched by the baser tendencies of the time," in contrast to American enthusiasm for progress in all its vulgarity and unruliness. America represented what aristocrats and intellectuals feared Britain becoming: "a giant, unrestrained replica of the nineteenth century English middle class."[56] The makers of manners were not only repelled by the grasping materialism on display in America but also considered it politically dangerous.[57]

British elites understood that the status quo was unsustainable, however: it was simply too unrepresentative, revolution all too imaginable a consequence. The consuming political question in Britain throughout the latter half of the nineteenth century was how to accommodate a rapidly changing society. The argument for expanding the franchise was explicitly to stave off revolution.[58] This British elites did as slowly as possible, carefully attenuating the excesses they perceived occurring in America, France, and other unruly societies.

Politicians were assisted in the effort by a culture likewise in thrall to a past in which the ravages of mass production and urbanization had not scarred consciousness. America celebrated social mobility; class hierarchy in Britain consciously sought to prevent it. Martin Wiener persuasively taps out the drumbeat of cultural rejection of modernity in Britain, from the arts and crafts movement hallowing the handmade to the Gothic revival in architecture and Pre-Raphaelite art, Alfred, Lord Tennyson and the "squirearchical romanticism" in poetry, Thomas Hardy's pastoral novels, colleges' emphasis on gentlemanly rather than scientific education, and economists and politicians shifting their frame of interest from material advancement and economic growth. The argument for consumerism—the availability to many of what previously was the prerogative of the wealthy few—was lived in Britain but not made there.

But if, as Wiener argues, a "pastoral retreatism" took hold among British elites in this time frame, the effect was outrun by democratization.[59] The Third Reform Act in 1884 would propel Britain even further toward commonality with the United States, allowing 60 percent of adult British males to vote.[60] Social strictures would prevent Britain being wholly democratic until after the First World War, but the effects begin to be felt in the 1870s: elites recoiled from the new world dawning, but could not restrain the growing demands for representation.

Condescension by British elites toward American "culture" (for they determined overwhelmingly that America lacked its essential ingredients) was ubiquitous in the 1870s.[61] The dominant cultural myth formulating in America with the settlement of the West was an egalitarian republicanism. The inward focus of both societies in the 1870s would prevent the United States from attempting to reach into Britain's domestic politics for foreign policy advantage, as the American government had in the Oregon Boundary Dispute and during the Civil War.[62] But America was now central in British thinking: it had become the glaring symbol of the modernity that British elites were defining themselves in opposition to.

Where Americans cultural icons noticed, they often agreed with British descriptions of the country as greedy and grasping. Mark Twain perfectly captured the criticism recast as pride in his *Roughing It*:

> It was a splendid population—for all the slow, sleepy, sluggish-brained sloths staid at home—you never find that sort of people among pioneers—you cannot build pioneers out of that sort of material. It was that population that gave to California a name for getting up astounding enterprises and rushing them through

with a magnificent dash and daring and a recklessness of cost or consequences, which she bears unto this day—and when she projects a new surprise, the grave world smiles as usual, and says "Well, that is California all over."[63]

America's natural allies were those Britons agitating for greater opportunity, and they were growing in number and importance across the late nineteenth century. What British elites had long feared of America as a revolutionary power proved true—not because of America's actions so much as the universality of its ideals.

The Weight of Empire

Political change in Britain was intimately intertwined with economic performance: if there had been greater confidence in the economy, British elites would have felt much less pressure to expand political participation. The 1870s were an especially fraught time economically in Britain, termed "the great depression" until devastation of the 1930s overtook that title. Britain's economy remained strong in the absolute sense: standards of living continued to rise, productivity continued increasing, and exports continued a strong showing.[64] Relative to the United States and Germany, though, Britain's economy slowed.[65] The innovator's advantage of early industrialization was dimming; with development of new industries occurring elsewhere and asymmetric advantages of trade protection and public financing accrued to others, domestic capital investment diminished.[66]

More noticeable to Britons, the economy slowed compared to the galloping pace of its improvement in the years 1850–1870. Britain began importing more in goods and services than it exported. The political effect of this change to the balance of trade was to collapse support for free trade.[67] Its economic effect was to reinforce patterns of trade within the British Empire (where tariff-free trade existed) and foster urgency to open new, unprotected, markets for British goods.[68] Yet even as trade patterns were strengthening within the empire and new colonies were eagerly sought, the costs of sustaining empire were called into question.

Parsing out when concerns about sustainability of empire become a dominant strain of argument in Britain is difficult. Great Britain in its hegemony seems always to have been concerned with its military vulnerabilities, the frailty of its diplomatic position, the possibility of others allying against it, and the risks attendant on its economy. Affordability was a constant preoccupation—Henry John Temple, Third Viscount Palmerston's treasury secretary had "pleaded for recognition of 'overextended responsibilities'" in the colonies and diversion of spending to social programs that would buffer the process of urbanization.[69] As Barry Supple argues, Britain has "a long tradition with the politics of national catastrophe."[70]

Perhaps British reconsideration of its empire began with the Indian Rebellion of 1857, and the increased state role in enforcement of commerce that resulted. The Sepoy uprising against the East India Company shocked British sensibilities and dissolved that canonical government-supported corporation the following year. What had been only a quasi-governmental outgrowth in India became fully imperial, and with time nineteenth-century economists and statesmen questioned the costs of so direct a governmental role.[71]

The 1870s do appear to be a turning point, however, when economists in Britain began to argue that the colonies were net losses and trade was no longer Britain's capital asset. As C. K. Harley and D. N. McCloskey characterize the debate, "from 1820 to 1870 the questions asked by the historian of British trade are variants of 'How did foreign trade make us rich?' From 1870 to 1914, they are variants of 'How did foreign trade make us poor?'"[72] Part of the answer is that social and political structures in Britain prejudiced economics toward food and raw materials by inhibiting spending on durable goods for consumers.[73] Britain's political and social choices interacted with its economic dimensions in ways that gave even greater impetus to political change.

Another important input into the debate about affordability of empire in the 1870s was the changing geostrategic balance. Not only was the numerator of the imperial equation (economic gain) diminishing but the denominator of the equation (cost to sustain) was increasing. Without an isthmian connection between the Atlantic and Pacific oceans, the span of Britain's imperial commitments required a costly three-ocean navy. While the Suez Canal opening in 1869 facilitated transit to India and set off a scramble by European powers for colonies in Africa, it also granted enormous advantage to whoever controlled its access, deepening British obligations in Egypt.[74] Railroads began to create reliable land transportation for the first time, portending a reduction in relative value of Britain's unmatched sea power to interdict transit and raising the cost of defending far-flung imperial possessions other countries could more quickly rush military forces to by rail.[75] Weakness of Islamic states from the Balkans eastward gave Russia opportunities to press British interests throughout the Middle East and South Asia while Britain also became reliant on Russia to check a unifying Germany's advances in Europe.

The same economic anxiety that fueled fears of revolution and reconsideration of empire in the 1870s also constrained British foreign policy more generally. A public perceived to be dangerously restive, a faltering economy aggravating that restiveness, and a political system only slowly responsive to demands for inclusiveness "did not"—in the words of the foreign minister, Edward Stanley, Fifteenth Earl of Derby—"lend themselves to a 'spirited' foreign policy."[76] He outlined a passive British foreign policy to Parliament in 1866, asserting that "it is the duty of the Government of this country, placed as it is with regard to geographical position, to keep itself upon terms of goodwill with all surrounding nations, but not to entangle itself with any single or monopolising alliance with any one of them; above all to endeavour not to interfere needlessly and vexatiously with the internal affairs of any foreign country."[77] When pressed by France for assistance countering Germany in 1874, Derby believed "nothing is so unpopular in England: and reasonably so"; the balance of power on the Continent, he added, "may not in the slightest degree concern our interests."[78] The British government would make a virtue of its domestic and economic bindings, celebrating a policy that kept aloof from the machinations of other great powers.

Trajectories

In the second half of the nineteenth century, Britain and America refined their sense of self in reaction to change, taking up descriptive versions of their national stories that became widely accepted; both countries adopted defining narratives that would carry well into the future. America accepted an imperial mind-set, and Britain a (cautiously) democratic one. And although their attitudes toward each other were antagonistic, America was becoming more like Britain internationally, and Britain more like the United States domestically.

Whereas America manufactured its first sense of itself during the American Revolution in opposition to Britain, its Civil War and

westward expansion turned the nation's attention inward for definition. Britain, too, turned inward in the late nineteenth century; its
chosen mythology became a reaction to America. American illiberalism reinforced British concern about democratic governance; the
corruption spectacularly on display in the politics and business of
westward expansion practices of the time were a potent argument
for opponents of greater enfranchisement in Britain. Political elites
in Britain sought, and achieved, a slow-moving democratization
without the corruption or majoritarian tendencies of America.[79]

American illiberalism also reassured the British government that
Americans were not so politically exceptional; they, too, differenti-
ated between "subjects of the crown" and "colonials."[80] The distinction was crucial in determining whether the United States would
be a continued force for disruption internationally, the position congruent with its political creed and prior behavior, or a potential
partner for Britain as America ventured out into the world. The
British government also perceived emerging similarities of perspective: America was becoming economically advanced enough that
its industries would push, as British industries did, for an open-door
policy on trade.[81] The force of American power might be harnessed
to British interests. The trajectories of America and Britain were
thus set to intersect in the late nineteenth century, a rising America adopting the cast of mind of an empire as Britain looked to share
the obligations of upholding one.

7

Mission Creep: The Venezuelan Crises

The Venezuelan Debt Crises

1894 Venezuela appeals to the United States for protection against Britain under the Monroe Doctrine; President Grover Cleveland advocates arbitration.

March 1895 British ultimatum to Venezuela for debt repayment; Britain occupies the Venezuelan port of Corinto to collect customs.

June 1895 Cleveland determines that the Monroe Doctrine prevents only colonies, not conflict.

June 1895 British prime minister Robert Arthur Talbot Gascoyne-Cecil, Third Marquess of Salisbury refuses arbitration; the United States responds with a furious rebuttal, "Olney's twenty-inch gun," asserting the right to dictate terms of European involvement in the western hemisphere.

December 1895 President Cleveland receives unanimous congressional support to enforce the Monroe Doctrine; Britain agrees to American arbitration and offers a general Anglo-American treaty.

1897 Congress rejects the Anglo-American treaty.

1899 An arbitration commission endorses British claims.

1901 Britain eliminates U.S. threat from its military plans, withdraws forces.

1901 President Theodore Roosevelt affirms the United States will not object to European uses of force in the western hemisphere, provided European states do not acquire territory.

1902 Venezuela defaults; Britain, Germany, and Italy blockade Venezuelan ports after consultations with the United States.

December 1902 Venezuela arrests British and German nationals; Britain and Germany evacuate their citizens, fire on Venezuelan forts; the United States begins Caribbean naval maneuvers.

December 11, 1902 The United States delivers Venezuelan arbitration offer, rejected by Germany.

December 19, 1902 Germany accepts arbitration; both Britain and Germany continue blockade of Venezuelan ports.

January 1903 Germany bombards Venezuelan civilian targets; Britain disavows, European powers agree to generous debt forgiveness and repayment terms.

Spring 1903 Court of Arbitration allows preferential repayment to countries that had used military force.

December 1904 The Roosevelt Corollary commits the United States to "exercise of an international police power" for collection of European debts in the western hemisphere.

Twice within the space of a decade, falling on either side of the Spanish-American War, Venezuela attempted to call in America's marker to prevent colonial predation from European countries. In 1895 the government of Venezuela was subjected to aggrandizement by Britain that would have closed it off from the mouth of the Orinoco River. In 1902 the government was punitively assaulted by Britain and Germany, its ports blockaded for remuneration of debt. In both instances Venezuela appealed to America for protection under the Monroe Doctrine. And in both instances, the American government aligned itself with Great Britain against a country American policy had been designed to harbor.

The 1895 Venezuelan debt crisis has been obscured in popular history, overshadowed by the bombast of the Spanish-American War only three years later. Yet it represents *anagnorisis* for a rising America, that moment when the country realized and asserted its power. It also represents *anagnorisis* for Great Britain, when the hegemon of the international order reassessed its strategy toward a rising America.

The Venezuela crisis was a diplomatic dispute in which America had little interest and a settled, passive policy. As events unfolded, the dispute took on totemic significance, resulting in a dramatic expansion of American claims and subsequently its international obligations. Nelson Blake asks, "How did it happen that caution so abruptly became rashness?"[1] It happened because the event gave cause for a rising America to reconsider its relative power and confidently assert itself. Fearful about the economy's ability to generate jobs after the closing of the American West and anxious for an isthmian canal to connect its continental expanse, the United States took an increasing interest in Latin America. Dismissiveness from the Salisbury government provoked President Cleveland away from his inclination to "to avoid a doctrine which I knew to be trouble-some" and instead invoke and expand James Monroe's proclamation, demanding an American right to dictate the outcome of any dispute between European and Latin American governments.[2] The crisis was the direct result of a rising power and an established power navigating their changing heft relative to each other.

More surprising than the American assertion of its newfound strength is Great Britain's acquiescence to—indeed, even embrace of—it.[3] Whereas Prime Minister Salisbury began the 1895 crisis flatly denying the United States had any superior claim in the western hemisphere, less than a year later he announced in the House of Commons that "we are entire advocates of the Monroe Doctrine . . . you will not find any more convinced supporters of it as a rule of policy than we are."[4] The ground had shifted in Anglo-American relations.

Great Britain ceded the sovereign right to exercise its political, economic, and military power in the western hemisphere, acknowledging an American sphere of influence along its periphery. Britain acquired several assets in the exchange, however. It was in 1895 dealing with not just one upstart rival, but three: America, Germany, and Russia. The Americans undertook to prevent all European powers from closing off enterprise in Latin America, a useful shifting of responsibility from the British perspective. The blithe confidence with which America had risked military conflict with the hegemon demonstrated it would see off lesser powers, and thereby protect British interests in commercial access.

There emerged in between the two Venezuelan debt crises a sense of solidarity for Britain and America not evident earlier.[5] The two crises therefore illustrate in sharp relief how much changed between 1895 and 1902. In 1895, Britain's choices were the result of strategic

and diplomatic readjustment rather than accession to public sentiment or enthusiasm for an American partner in the world.[6] There
were similarities of circumstance, to be sure: the two countries'
economies both felt pinched, and both were at a stage of industrialization that underscored the perceived importance of international
trade and investment. But as Christopher Layne concludes, "the
British did not welcome the rapid expansion of American power;
rather, they reconciled themselves to something they could not
prevent."[7]

The two countries acknowledged in resolving the 1895 crisis that
their interests in shaping the international order dovetailed. In 1895,
the two countries reached a common understanding on the structure
and content of the international economy outside the British Empire (although Britain's practice of preferential trading among its
colonies would continue to rankle the United States). Negotiations
over Venezuela produced concordance between British and American views on the issues of diplomacy, military intervention, political
economy, and also segued into a general arbitration agreement between the United States and Britain. The two countries disavowed
military force as a means for resolving their disputes and established a mutually agreed-upon institutionalized process of settlement, a profoundly unusual restraint between a hegemon and a
rising power.

By 1902 the British and American governments showed themselves friendly to each other, hostile to Germany, and indifferent
to the rights of lesser countries like Venezuela. Just how much
had changed in the Anglo-American relationship since 1895 is evident in the very different treatment accorded by Washington to
Great Britain and Germany in their joint assault on Venezuela for
debt default. Britain partnered with Germany, was responsible

for the choice to impose a military rather than pacific blockade, and even commanded the naval forces of both countries, but easily managed to dissociate itself from actions that provoked American concern. Britain routinely informed Washington on Germany's actions and intentions, taking credit for Germany's willingness to consult Washington in advance of military operations and eventually for agreeing to arbitration of the dispute. Britain received inordinate credit from Washington for accepting arbitration a few mere days in advance of Germany. Roosevelt's December 1902 ultimatum was specific to Germany, not to the joint command. The president would write Alfred Thayer Mahan, "I feel very differently toward England from the way I feel toward Germany."[8]

While the Anglo-American relationship would retrospectively be explained as the inevitable product of a common cultural heritage, and even race, in real time Germany would be essential in demonstrating the two countries' likeness to each other. As Henry Adams credited it, "the sudden appearance of Germany is the grizzly terror which in twenty years effected what Adamses had tried for two hundred years in vain—frightened England into America's arms."[9]

The closing of the 1902 dispute would catalyze a further expansion of American claims under the Monroe Doctrine. When the Court of Arbitration verdict accorded preferential payment of debts to countries that had brought force to bear, Roosevelt feared it would incentivize European military adventurism in the western hemisphere. He committed the United States instead to provide "international policing" with the Roosevelt Corollary. Prime Minister Salisbury, in his 1895 rebuttal of Richard Olney's treatise, had presciently argued that to accept the American formulation of the Monroe Doctrine "would have imposed upon the United States the duty of answering for the conduct of these states, and consequently the responsibility of controlling [them]."[10] That was exactly the result of the 1902 Venezuelan crisis.

Declinists

Economic pessimism came to America in the 1880s. As had been the case in Britain during the 1870s, the idea gained traction that the domestic economy could no longer produce work sufficient to the population. Westward expansion being complete, it could no longer serve the safety valve function of siphoning off excess labor; Walter LaFeber even argues that labor unrest in the east "highly dramatized the fact that the great American frontier no longer attracted, but even repelled the discontented of the nation."[11] Debates over trade and monetary policy became central in American national politics, defining the political parties: Democrats favored free trade, Republicans stridently opposed it.

So central was trade that in 1887 President Grover Cleveland, a Democrat, spent his entire third annual message to Congress advocating tariff reductions. He argued the government was building excessive surpluses by its tax on imports, thereby creating "a hoarding place for money needlessly withdrawn from trade and the people's use, thus crippling our national energies, suspending our country's development, preventing investment in productive enterprise, threatening financial disturbance, and inviting schemes of public plunder."[12] Cleveland argued that American industries were strong enough to bear competition, wages could be sustained, and tariffs hurt consumers.

It was a remarkable education in economics. It was also a political disaster. In the 1888 election Democrats lost control of both houses of Congress, and Republican Benjamin Harrison gained the presidency, building a coalition of industrialists and factory workers and proclaiming a mandate for continued tariffs. The Tariff Act of 1890 (called the McKinley Tariff for its progenitor in the Congress) established rates as high as 50 percent across thousands of products.[13]

Public disaffection with the economy flipped the Congress back into Democratic hands that same year, with Republicans losing fully half their seats in the House; by 1892, in an election fought almost entirely over tariffs, Republicans also lost the presidency (again to Grover Cleveland).[14] Although the 1893 congressional hearings were a veritable parade of manufacturers' appeals for continued protection, by 1894, Congress was dismantling tariffs—only to see Republicans sweep back to control of the federal government in 1896 with the architect of the 1890 tariffs as president.[15] The seesawing of political power in America in the 1890s illustrates the deep public disaffection with economic stagnation. Political ground shifted from tariffs to monetary policy in 1896 (whether to challenge the gold standard with silver, which was being mined in great supply in the United States), but the fight was still over how to pull the American economy into greater prosperity.

Foreign and economic policy were fundamentally conjoined; concern took hold that American farmers and manufacturers produced more than the nation could consume, and therefore foreign markets were increasingly necessary for economic and political reasons. The United States was also becoming a source of foreign investment to other countries, especially lesser-developed countries. As in Britain, the "proponents of empire were economic nationalists," seeking to maintain protection of domestic markets while forcing open markets abroad.[16] These similarities of economic condition began to bring British and American foreign economic policies into alignment.

Great Britain figured prominently both as villain and model in American economic debates. Success of the Cobdenite movement to repeal Britain's Corn Laws in the 1840s had made that country the international order's leading advocate and practitioner of free trade. The United States, while an avid consumer of British investment to fuel its economic development, stringently protected its domestic industries. As the U.S. economy matured, the two economies came into direct competition.

Richard Cobden's argument that free trade and nonintervention would create both peace and domestic prosperity had its American counterpart in the policies of the Cleveland administration, whereas for Republicans in the 1880s and 1890s Cobdenite policies were seen as a British conspiracy to stunt American economic development and prevent it becoming an international competitor.[17] What Republicans saw to emulate in the British example was coercively opening underindustrialized markets to manufactured goods and investment.[18] But tariff barriers to U.S. market access and increased competition from America in foreign markets made a strong case for preferential access to British goods within its empire in order to capitalize on the advantage of political control.[19] Britain favored an open-door trading policy outside its empire, advantageous terms of trade within it; but Britain's policy of imperial preference gave the United States an economic as well as an ideological opposition to Britain's empire.

What Africa and China were experiencing of Europe's intrusions the western hemisphere seemed also destined for in the 1890s. Skirmishes between European and American commercial interests had been occurring for several years before the Venezuelan debt crisis, with the United States helping Brazil fend off a French-supported monarchist coup and countering British commercial interests in Nicaragua. Central America was of particular interest to the United States because of its utility as a canal site.

Fiat Law

Britain's 1895 dispute with Venezuela began with a little privateering: in 1839 an explorer commissioned by the Royal Geographic Society drew a map delineating the border between Venezuela's 1830 Spanish inheritance and Britain's 1814 Dutch bequest of Guyana. On neither side of the demarcation was a claim buttressed by the traditional means of population, but the Orinoco was Venezuela's riverine highway, the disputed territory was mineral rich, and Britain laid claim to both. Contestation in 1844 by Venezuela produced a British offer to cede the Orinoco headwaters, but that offer was not taken up (a failure important to understand in the context of Venezuela only beginning to coalesce into a state, its capacity for governance limited and practice often sporadic). Agreement in 1850 for neither side to encroach on the disputed territories settled the matter for nearly forty years.

Britain's reassertion in 1886 of its right to the whole sweep of the surveyor's map precipitated Venezuela breaking off relations, freezing the conflict diplomatically for another seven years while both sides moved to fortify their claims.[20] It was in this context that Venezuela first appealed to the United States for support.[21]

President Cleveland favored free trade and arbitration of international disputes, and so opposed imperialism that he had refused to proceed with his predecessor's annexation of Hawaii.[22] It was his policy not to interfere in commercial disputes. With regard to the Monroe Doctrine, he described himself as "quite willing if possible within the limits of inexorable duty, to escape its serious contemplation."[23] Domestic opponents, including Henry Cabot Lodge in the Senate, were caustic about the passivity of his foreign policy; Cleveland seemed indifferent to their criticism.[24] In December 1894 he advocated arbitration of the Venezuelan dispute, his influence sufficient to produce a congressional resolution of support in February 1895. And there the matter might have rested, an ineffectual appeal by a disinterested third party, had the Salisbury government not landed marines to occupy the Venezuelan port of Corinto.

Great Britain had issued Venezuela an ultimatum in March 1895, which went unanswered, determining the Salisbury government to take by force customs receipts to satisfy its claims. While consistent with British practice elsewhere, American commentators rushed to alarm about British "encirclement" of the United States.[25] Lodge thundered, "If Great Britain is to be permitted to occupy the ports of Nicaragua and, still worse, take the territory of Venezuela, there is nothing to prevent her taking the whole of Venezuela or any other South American state. If Great Britain can do this with impunity, France and Germany will do it also . . . the American people are not ready to abandon the Monroe doctrine, or give up their rightful supremacy in the Western Hemisphere. On the contrary, they are as ready now to fight to maintain both, as they were when they forced the French out of Mexico. They are not now, and never will be willing to have South America, and the islands adjacent to the United States, seized by European powers. They are resolved that the Nicaraguan canal shall be built and absolutely controlled by the United States . . . The supremacy of the Monroe Doctrine must be established and at once—peaceably if we can, forcibly if we must."[26] The Venezuelan government appealed for support, but Cleveland held to a narrow interpretation of the Monroe Doctrine that only prevented colonies, not punitive action.[27] Prime Minister Salisbury (newly returned to power) reversed course and refused third-party adjudication, prompting Secretary of State Richard Olney to defend a policy both the president and the Congress had endorsed.

"Olney's twenty-inch gun," as he called the démarche, was a twelve-thousand-word assertion of the legal right for the United States to dictate the terms of settlement in any disputes between European and Latin American powers.[28] Olney described the Monroe Doctrine as settled international law (which it was not), and went much further to claim that "the United States is practically sovereign on this continent, and its fiat is law upon the subjects to which it confines its interposition."[29]

Where the Monroe Doctrine had been specific in limiting American interest to the establishment of European colonies, Olney and therefore Cleveland expanded the application to any involvement of a European state in the western hemisphere. Not only were Europeans not free to colonize the western hemisphere, but they could undertake no involvement without American approval.

From a British perspective, Cleveland's expansive interpretation was clearly unacceptable, just the latest in the string going back to the Oregon Boundary Dispute in 1845 of unilateral U.S. attempts to create new rules for the international order prejudiced to American advantage. As Joseph Chamberlain pointed out, "Great Britain is an American Power with a territorial area greater than the United States themselves."[30]

Moreover, it had to be exasperating for Britain to have America arrogantly, after fifty years of the Royal Navy preventing European establishment of colonies in the Americas, make Britain out to be the arriviste power. As a measure of just how much more powerful Great Britain still was compared to the United States, Britain's Naval Defense Act of 1889 committed to a major military buildup in order to meet the "two power standard" that the Royal Navy must remain at least equal to the forces of the next two navies combined.[31]

The British government didn't even bother replying to Olney's exhaustive treatise. Instead, Salisbury ratcheted up demands on Venezuela and dispatched more guns in reinforcement. Reports swirled in the American press of military preparations by Britain to take over Nicaragua.

Just how much the dispute had become about America's stature is evident in Secretary of State Olney's follow-up to Salisbury, where he noted that

> the seeming if not intentional contumely with which the statement of our position on the Venezuelan boundary question was received by the British Foreign Office . . . seemed to be explicable only on the theory that we had no policy such as we claimed to have; or if we had it, that we had no right to it; or if we had, that we had neither the spirit nor the ability to defend it.[32]

The Salisbury government belatedly and curtly replied that "the Government of the United States is not entitled to affirm as a universal proposition, with reference to a number of independent States for whose conduct it assumes no responsibility, that its interests are necessarily concerned in whatever may befall those States, simply because they are situated in the Western Hemisphere." Salisbury flatly denied the United States had claims superior to Britain's in the Americas.

Salisbury's brush-off provoked President Cleveland to put in play the unique American foreign policy advantage of public support.[33] In December 1895 Cleveland requested congressional authorization to "resist by every means in its power as a willful aggression upon its rights and interests the appropriation by Great Britain of any lands or exercise of governmental jurisdiction over any territory which after investigation we have determined of right belongs to Venezuela."[34]

Cleveland's message to the Congress made a sweeping case that enforcement of the Monroe Doctrine was actually "important to our peace and safety as a nation, and is essential to the integrity of our free institutions and the tranquil maintenance of our distinctive form of government." He compared the doctrine to balance-of-power politics tended so carefully by Europeans on their continent, asserting an American right to establish a balance of power favoring itself in the Americas. He replied to Salisbury's charge that the Monroe Doctrine was not "founded on the general consent of nations" by asserting it didn't need to be—that principles which have "peculiar if not exclusive relation to the United States" were adequate justification for America to act.[35] The United States would not be bound by the laws Britain had established in the international order; it would be a law unto itself.

It was a claim so outrageous that Britain's chancellor of the exchequer confidently proclaimed that when the "case of Great Britain . . . was laid before the people, either on this side of the Atlantic or on the other, the result would be happy, peaceful, and honorable to both parties."[36] He was mistaken. Legislation supporting Cleveland passed without a dissenting vote in either house of Congress.[37] American newspapers shrieked threats of war. Nor was baying for confrontation the unique province of newspapermen and the public; America's leading political figures engaged in it with gusto. Theodore Roosevelt described himself as "having fun making jingo speeches," and seemingly half the politicians in America were publishing aggressive tracts trying to capture patriotism as the exclusive province of their political party. American generals were quoted estimating that with ten days' preparation Canada could be taken from Britain.[38]

The American ambassador in London was so surprised by the dramatic change in policy that he asked the president for clarification. Cleveland indicated a complete reversal of his earlier view:

> I am entirely clear that the doctrine is not obsolete, and it should be defended and maintained for its value and importance *to our government and welfare,* and that its defense and maintenance involve its application when a state of facts arises requiring it. In this state of mind I am positive that I can never be made to see why the extension of European systems, territory, and jurisdiction, on our continent, may not be effected as surely and as unwarrantably under the guise of boundary claims as by invasion or any other means.[39]

And Cleveland ascribed his change of position to Britain's "intensely disappointing" response to American calls for arbitration.

There are no indications from within the Cleveland administration or in the frothy public commentary of any concern about war with Britain. Cleveland sounds at ease confronting the world's strongest military power:

> Instead of threatening war for nor arbitrating, we simply say inasmuch as Great Britain will not aid us in fixing the facts, we will not go to war but do the best we can to discover the true state of facts for ourselves, with all the facilities at our command. When with all this, we become as certain as we can be, in default of Great Britain's co-operation, that she has seized the territory and superseded the jurisdiction of Venezuela—that is a different matter.[40]

There was concern on the part of the British, however. Britain's commerce, navy, and attention had been pulled away from the Caribbean and toward Asia and now, in weighing whether to run the risk of confrontation with the United States, preservation of Canada was by far the main British interest in the Americas.[41] Whether the Monroe Doctrine permitted a continuing British colonial hold in Canada was much debated in the American press. Whereas in 1861 the British government could dismiss out of hand an American threat to Canada, by 1895 the British government was seriously concerned about the balance of military power in North America, fearing an assault on Canada or a stalemate that would play to America's economic strengths in undercutting Canada.[42]

The British military was concerned that America's large internal market and autonomy from foreign trade "rendered it virtually immune from even the most complete naval blockade," rendering irrelevant Britain's main military advantage.[43] Still, the British military concluded its existing garrisons and naval power were adequate for North America—and "small local squadrons" sufficient to deal with an American attack.[44]

Salisbury's effort to put America in its place backfired: rather than intimidate the rising power, his condescension precipitated Cleveland committing to a much more assertive policy. The British government appears to have been shocked by the virulence of American reaction.[45] Arthur Balfour, Tory leader in the House of Commons, described American hostility as "simply incredible."[46]

Salisbury's strong approach also smoked out the existence of a much fonder attitude about America than had previously been apparent. Britain's continued democratic reforms in 1884–1885 were making public sentiment a more prominent element in policy calculations. An American newspaper appealing for peace messages from Britain received hundreds—including one from the Prince of Wales saying that "we earnestly trust, and cannot but believe, that the present crisis will be arranged in a manner satisfactory to both countries, and will be succeeded by the same warm feeling of friendship which has existed between them for so many years."[47] Three hundred fifty four members of the British House of Commons signed and sent to their American legislative counterparts an appeal for a general treaty of arbitration.[48] Americans were left with the impression that Britain considered war between the two democracies to be fratricide.[49]

Cleveland had undertaken no military preparations for war with Britain in conjunction with his brazen announcement, and he had no time to subsequently: the British government quickly acceded not just to arbitration but to American arbitration. Salisbury had entered into the argument with Olney believing American threats were not serious; after Cleveland's address to Congress, he reconsidered.[50] Salisbury remained personally opposed to negotiations over Venezuela, but "the hard-headed realism of the school of professional politicians and strategists headed by Salisbury" surmounted his objections.[51]

The *London Times* bemoaned that by agreeing to arbitration, Britain "has set up a precedent which may in future be quoted with great effect against herself, and she has greatly strengthened the hands of the United States Government."[52] It was, however, unquestionably a popular move. In February 1896 Salisbury reported to cheers in the House of Commons that "all danger of a rupture of relations between the two nations be entirely removed."[53]

The arbitration tribunal produced twenty-three volumes of evidence and testimony, concluding in 1899 with a boundary dramatically favoring British interests.[54] The commission's findings were surprising—especially to the Venezuelan government, which had enlisted American political help and had reason to believe based on Cleveland's message to Congress and the unanimous passage of legislation forcing creation of the commission that Americans had taken its side of the argument. While Venezuela was hard done by, getting only terms Britain had offered in 1844, both the British and Americans considered the agreement a great success.[55]

Concurrent with accepting arbitration over Venezuela in January 1896, the Salisbury government proposed a broader bilateral treaty of dispute arbitration enshrining the practices of British-American cooperation. The Venezuela crisis caused Britain to understand arbitration as a shield against the volatility of American public attitudes and policy; the British sought to constrain by legal proceeding and international tribunal the enthusiasms to be feared where democracy ruled.[56] The Olney-Pauncefote Treaty of 1897—brought to conclusion two years faster than the Venezuela negotiations—was lauded by both governments as a new dawn of like-minded internationalism.

The Congress, however, did not agree, refusing its consent to ratification.[57] British strategy toward America had shifted, and with democratization in Britain so had public attitudes, but American public attitudes did not yet align. Anglo-America was yet awhile in the future. But the Pauncefote treaties (first with Richard Olney, and then John Hay) were a defining moment in the hegemonic transition, because Britain surrendered a claim to the Panama Canal and with it a major role in the Caribbean.

Even before American attitudes shifted, the British government reconfigured its defense plans to eliminate the United States as a potential foe.[58] In 1901 the British government determined its military requirements had become unaffordable. As part of a major military reorientation, Britain excluded the United States from those countries whose navies Britain must match with its "two power" standard and withdrew its squadrons assigned to North America, the South Atlantic, and the West Indies.[59] Reconsideration of America in British military planning was both a recognition of the closer political bonds between the two countries and an acknowledgment that the United States had become too powerful for Britain to contain. Britain's first lord of the admiralty described the defense of Canada as "absolutely hopeless." His recommendation to the government if confronted by America was to "use all possible means to avoid such a war . . . it seems an utter waste of time to prepare for it."[60]

Default

Venezuela figured a second time as British-American relations were being reconfigured at the turn of the twentieth century. This time Britain would be caught between the blossoming opportunities of a new kind of relationship with America and the obligations attendant on its continental and commercial policies. It would, again, play a weakening hand extraordinarily adroitly. Britain not only sustained its cooperation with Germany but also maneuvered Theodore Roosevelt's America into becoming paymaster of debts by countries of the western hemisphere to European businesses. And all this while basking in the growing affection of the American public.

Britain achieved by diplomatic elegance a repudiation of the meaning of the Monroe Doctrine.[61] The doctrine had sought to shield the western hemisphere from the commercial activity and political structures European colonies would impose. Roosevelt's Corollary instead subsumed responsibility for political order and commercial predictability from Europe to the United States. In order to prevent European military actions in the western hemisphere, America would conduct them in Europe's stead.

The achievement was only possible on the basis of a fundamental shift in attitudes on the part of the American government. Whereas previously it had presupposed European influence to be a hindrance in development of societies and states in the western hemisphere, the experience of liberation movements caused hopes for democratic governance in newly independent former colonies—that is, all of Central and South America—to founder. The American experience governing Cuba brought to light how thin the veneer of educated elites was and how thick the needs in newly independent countries for basic building blocks that created and sustained free societies. Low literacy levels, weak institutions, inexperience by indigenous leaders at governance, underdeveloped civil societies, class structures ingrained by European colonies, predatory capitalism, resource-rich territories, and civil wars had the predictable result of caudillo governments in much of the region.[62]

The Monroe Doctrine when operationally taken up by the United States created a problem of moral hazard by shielding those caudillos from the consequences of their international behavior. Before President Cleveland wielded his expanded Monroe Doctrine in 1895, countries of the western hemisphere were at constant risk of bombardment and occupation by European powers. Britain and France, in particular, were militarily superior and able to enforce their political and commercial will (as Mexico found to its sorrow in both 1838 and 1861–1863).

Theodore Roosevelt had expressed concern that hemispheric countries would use Monroe as a shield behind which to behave commercially irresponsibly—while vice president he memorably wrote that European countries should "spank them" for it and stated flatly in his 1901 presidential message to Congress that "we do not guarantee any state against punishment if it misconducts itself, provided that punishment does not take the form of the acquisition of territory by any non-American power."[63] That this was contradictory to his Mahanian advocacy of American dominance of the Caribbean and Central America does not appear to have troubled Roosevelt.

It is doubtful that the caudillo governments in Argentina, Brazil, Bolivia, Colombia, Ecuador, El Salvador, Guatemala, Honduras, Mexico, Paraguay, Peru, and Venezuela were actually encouraged to reckless commercial behavior on the basis of a thinly effectuated promise by an unproven American guarantee, especially after Roosevelt's message to Congress. Nonetheless, it was potentially a useful argument for those governments.

And it was taken up by Cipriano Castro, the caudillo of Venezuela, in 1902. Seizing control of the government amid a civil war, Castro argued the European firms were owed by the deposed government, not his, and ignored, by British count, seventeen separate government entreaties for reparation. As was the international practice of the time, governments did the gunboat bidding of their prominent commercial houses. Britain and Germany (with Italy chasing the parade) issued an ultimatum to Venezuela demanding it accept arbitration of its debt; receiving no reply, they joined forces to blockade the Venezuelan ports until their companies received satisfaction.

Britain and Germany did respect the standard President Cleveland had established for the Monroe Doctrine in 1895: they consulted with America in advance and assured the Roosevelt government they were only interested in debt payment, not extending their political or economic influence into Venezuela. Great Britain and Germany acknowledging the need for American approval satisfied President Roosevelt as consistent with Monroe; he reiterated his opposition to any territorial claim but was otherwise encouraging of the European action.

Gunboat Diplomacy

Roosevelt credited himself with a canny insurance policy: a big stick to back up the parameters he established for European action. He would write of the crisis, "I assembled our battle fleet under Admiral Dewey near Porto Rico for 'maneuvers' with instructions that the fleet should be kept in hand and in fighting trim and should be ready to sail at an hour's notice."[64] Admiral George Dewey, having stared down the German fleet in Manila Bay a few years earlier, would have made a pointed statement to both Britain and Germany.[65]

The 1902 Venezuela crisis was less over Britain and Germany's initial blockade than Germany's subsequent belligerence.[66] A squadron of eight British and four German ships operating jointly under British command made short work of Venezuela's navy and were in command of the harbor. Venezuelan leader Castro retaliated by arresting two hundred British and German citizens in country. Both countries landed forces to evacuate their nationals, then bombarded Venezuelan fortifications.

That same day the American government forwarded to Britain and Germany the government of Venezuela's offer to submit some of the contested debts to arbitration. Both Britain and Germany considered the Venezuelan offer unsatisfactory, but Britain agreed in principle to arbitration, while Germany initially did not. Although the lapse between British acquiescence and German was only a few days, the British government played the difference to great advantage.

It was in the temporal space between Venezuela's December 11 proposal for arbitration and Germany's December 19 acceptance that Roosevelt's threat of war is said to have occurred. Roosevelt claimed to have issued an ultimatum to the German ambassador, threatening war if Germany did not accept arbitration within ten days.[67] Whether or not Roosevelt was personally involved, or threatened war, his administration did certainly encourage the European powers to desist hostilities against Venezuela and accept arbitration.[68]

On December 18, the administration announced that Dewey's fleet would remain in the Caribbean. Secretary of State John Hay warned Germany's ambassador the Congress might direct the president to enforce the Monroe Doctrine.[69] Hay's feint would have been obvious to anyone knowledgeable of American politics, as Roosevelt was very much in command of both his party and the Congress on foreign policy. The German government was, however, not adept at gauging democratic politics in America, and uncomfortably exposed by Britain, so it consented to arbitration.

Both Britain and Germany continued their blockade while negotiations were underway with Venezuela, an understandable precaution to ensure enforceability of any decision given Venezuela's previous inattention to British and German entreaties. In late January an incident between Germany and Venezuela escalated, with Germany bombarding Maracaibo's fort and nearby settlements, killing a score of civilians.[70] The British government quickly assured Washington it had been done in contravention of British instructions to the joint fleet's commander.

Public reaction in both America and Britain was swift, loud, and negative—Britons questioned why their government was allied with Germany, and Americans called for enforcement of the Monroe Doctrine. Britain's King Edward VII, who had brokered the Anglo-

German agreement (with his cousin, Kaiser Wilhelm II) even questioned judgment of the secretary of state for foreign affairs, Henry Petty-Fitzmaurice, Fifth Marquess of Landsdowne in having entered into it. Britain and Germany (and also Italy) quickly folded, agreeing to generous debt forgiveness and repayment terms negotiated by America's ambassador in Caracas, and the blockade was lifted.

The crisis says as much about mutual distrust by Britain and America of a rising Germany beginning to operate aggressively in the western hemisphere as it does about the changing nature of relations between Britain and America. Roosevelt's recollection of the crisis was that "the United States was on the verge of war with Germany,"[71] but not with Britain—even though Britain comprised the majority of the striking force, was acknowledged to be in command of operations, and had seized an island at the mouth of Venezuela's Orinoco River, making it guiltier of violating the Monroe Doctrine than was Germany. It was Britain that insisted on a military blockade of Venezuela's harbor; Germany agitated for a pacific blockade that would permit Venezuela to retain its navy.[72] Yet in the crisis, Roosevelt asked, "[D]on't they [the Germans] know that they are inflaming public opinion more and more here? Don't they know that they will be left alone without England?"[73]

And England did abandon Germany. In Parliament, the government promised its actions were "in no way an infraction of the Monroe Doctrine . . . and that no nation in the world had been more anxious than England to assist them in maintaining that doctrine."[74] Prime Minister Balfour stated British policy unequivocally and publicly: "We welcome any increase of the influence of the United States of America in the Western Hemisphere. We desire no colonization, we desire no alteration in the balance of power, we desire no acquisition of territory. We have not the slightest intention of interfering with the mode of government in any portion of that continent. The Monroe Doctrine, therefore, is not really in question at all."[75]

Roosevelt and Secretary of State Hay certainly received information from the British about friction within the coalition and Britain's greater willingness to accept arbitration: Foreign Secretary Landsdowne was telegraphing that Britain was willing to accept arbitration but Germany was not. Doubtless British officials were painting Germany with excess; but while Britain would certainly have had reasons to exaggerate its differences with Germany and blame any actions Americans disliked on their coalition partner, Germany did enough on its own to further American suspicions.[76]

The American government would have well remembered and still resented the German challenge during the Spanish-American war only three years earlier. Germany's "temporary" occupation of Kiachow Bay in China was looking permanent. A year before the crisis, Germany had sent a warship off Venezuela's coast and threatened "temporary occupation of our part of different Venezuelan harbor places and the levying of duty in those places."[77] Germany was also active elsewhere in the Caribbean, firing on Haitian rebel craft and drawing a rebuke from the U.S. State Department. And the German ambassador in Caracas talked loudly and often of the benefits of a German naval base in Venezuela. German attitudes were dismissive of the Monroe Doctrine as a "non-binding monologue," and even after the Spanish-American War, Germany's government seemed not to recognize just how much American military power had increased.

Roosevelt clearly believed the Germans only agreed to arbitration and restraint because of the looming presence of Dewey's fleet. Admiral Dewey also believed the naval maneuvers were consequential, recording with satisfaction in his journal that their effect "on foreign powers, particularly at the present moment of the demonstration against Venezuela of so powerful and mobile a fleet in the Caribbean it can only be considered as a work redounding immensely to our naval and national prestige."[78] Britain was perceived as acting in friendly concert with the United States, and Germany only complying at threat of military force.

The Inversion

The Venezuelan crisis dropped one more shoe in the spring of 1903. The Court of Arbitration (that the American government had insisted the parties refer the conflict to) decided that those countries that had used military force to extract Venezuelan agreement deserved to be the creditors of first resort.[79] Preferential payment to countries engaged in hostilities seeming to incentivize that behavior, the Roosevelt administration worried the decision portended much more active gunboat diplomacy from European powers. It is in this context that Roosevelt's corollary to the Monroe Doctrine came into being, with the president acknowledging to his secretary of state Elihu Root "to say 'Hands Off' to the powers of Europe . . . sooner or later we must keep order ourselves."[80] In order to prevent Europeans taking military initiative in commercial disputes in the western hemisphere, the United States committed to taking preventative military action on behalf of jilted creditors.[81]

In Roosevelt's casting, "the adherence of the United States to the Monroe Doctrine may force the United States, however reluctantly, in flagrant cases of such wrongdoing or impotence, to the exercise of an international police power." Since the war, Roosevelt had used Cuba as an exemplar of progress the rest of the western hemisphere ought to emulate. He also attempted to construe the corollary as a limited warrant: "We would interfere with them only in the last resort, and then only if it became evident that their inability or unwillingness to do justice at home and abroad had violated the rights of the United States or had invited foreign aggression to the detriment of the entire body of American nations."[82]

Roosevelt imagined the cases necessitating American military forces "necessarily few," and his examples were all drawn from humanitarian exigencies: Spanish atrocities in Cuba, massacre of Jews in Kishenef (modern-day Moldova, then part of the Russian Empire). His standard for intervention was "crimes committed on so vast a scale and of such peculiar horror as to make us doubt whether it is not our manifest duty to at least show our disapproval of the deed and our sympathy with those who have suffered by it."

The language Roosevelt used to express his limited warrant flies in the face of his stated presumption of limited application. He lived in the age of Manifest Destiny—his own life illustrated it—and to suggest a "manifest duty" was to make a sweeping claim. Americans of the day would have heard "manifest duty" as the international parallel of the domestic Manifest Destiny, a sacred obligation to bring places into religious and political light as Americans defined them.

That Roosevelt included in his listing a pogrom from Russia's empire also calls into question the limited warrant he claimed to be establishing. Bessarabia was far afield of the western hemisphere, yet the president of the United States considered intervention to punish violence against Jews in Kishenef among his limiting cases. Roosevelt contradicted himself about the breadth of application, seeming to embrace a worldwide application of humanitarian activism even while claiming to be limiting the principle.

In practice, American might was brought to bear not on the side of "principles of civil and religious liberty," as Roosevelt described, but on the side of European and American commercial interests.[83] America invaded the Dominican Republic the following year, administering its customs houses to the benefit of European creditors—the first of many American usurpations of sovereignty in the western hemisphere. Roosevelt's ostensible corollary actually inverted the principle established by the Monroe Doctrine: instead of shielding the western hemisphere from European involvement, Roosevelt extended American muscle to enforce European claims against the countries of the region.[84] It would be extended further by Roosevelt's successor, William Howard Taft, as "dollar diplomacy," a complete subjugation of republican ideals to powerful states' business interests.

The question arises whether Roosevelt's America was eager for that role—whether European actions gave a newly powerful America rationalization for what it sought to do.[85] That Roosevelt couched his dramatic expansion of American claims over the western hemisphere in humanitarian terms suggests a public hesitance to support the policy on other terms. Roosevelt was a canny politician, much given to jingoism, as his letters and speeches during the 1895 Venezuelan crisis attest. In announcing a major policy in his own presidential administration, he restrained those impulses, instead appealing to the universal values of protecting people from predatory governments, whether their own or foreign.

At the time of the 1902 Venezuelan debt crisis, Americans already had some experience of an activist foreign policy ostensibly based on advancing its values in the world: in between the two Venezuelan crises, the United States had liberated Cuba and the Philippines from Spanish rule. That experience was proving difficult and unsatisfying. Roosevelt's first message to Congress in 1901 had described the challenges of governance in each of the protectorates taken with the Spanish-American War. In reviewing the Philippines for the Congress, Roosevelt sounded plaintive: "We are extremely anxious that the natives shall show the power of governing themselves. We are anxious, first for their sakes, and next, because it relieves us of a great burden. There need not be the slightest fear of our not continuing to give them all the liberty for which they are fit."[86]

Three years later—in the same context, his annual message to the Congress, but now describing his corollary—Roosevelt sounded much more like his domestic political opposition than the advocate of an imperial America: "We have plenty of sins of our own to war against, and under ordinary circumstances we can do more for the general uplifting of humanity by striving with heart and soul to put a stop to civic corruption, to brutal lawlessness and violent race prejudices here at home than by passing resolutions and wrongdoing elsewhere."[87]

Moreover, Roosevelt's actions during the 1902 crisis were not the grandstanding he is often caricatured with (and, it must be admitted, his own words often give sail to). The breezy recklessness from the Spanish-American War was nowhere in evidence once he was responsible for war. In the previous Venezuelan crisis, Roosevelt had written to Henry Cabot Lodge that America should "let the fight come if it must; I don't care whether our sea coast cities are bombarded or not; we would take Canada."[88] As president, his choices were more cautious than those of Cleveland and Olney in 1895.[89]

Roosevelt did not make public pronouncements that raised the temperature of the crisis or undertake provocative acts that foreclosed exit ramps by either the Europeans or the government of Venezuela. What threat he or his administration made was made privately, with a window for German government consideration and leaving them an exit with dignity. He encouraged arbitration, condemned the gunboat diplomacy of both Britain and Germany, and used American military power to impose limitations on the stronger even while acknowledging the weaker party to be substantively at fault. Moreover, his political objectives in the crisis were conservative, setting boundaries of acceptable damage for what he considered justifiable European military force against a defaulting debtor—his threat against Germany was to restrain Germany.

Roosevelt undertook sensible precautions and military preparations to both signal American intent and position its fleet, utilizing the maneuvers to have a striking force within range should the Germans overstep agreed boundaries. But he did not brandish the fleet or provoke the British and German naval squadron. His demonstrative use of military force was not isolated from its intended use, but constituent for its potential use. The Caribbean maneuvers are actions more in line with the "quiet military measures" of Dwight D. Eisenhower during the 1958 Berlin Crisis than the fulminating Roosevelt of political cartoons and newsreels. In fact, Roosevelt's choices in 1902–1903 are the quintessence of speaking softly and carrying a big stick. Whatever Roosevelt may have said and written when not in a position of responsibility for taking the nation to war, whatever his reckless enthusiasm for war as sport, as chief executive he had a restraint and a delicacy of touch on international strategy where great powers were concerned.

This was less the case with less powerful states: the United States would exercise dominion over the Philippines for another half century; America would intervene thirty-three times in countries of the western hemisphere before another Roosevelt, Franklin, would pivot to his Good Neighbor policy during World War II. The trap expanding Monroe's Doctrine set for a rising America was establishing as America's responsibility the fitness of other countries to govern themselves. Lacking the building blocks of functional democracy, newly decolonized states in the late nineteenth century fell victim to domestic despots and ineffectual reformers. America was unwilling to let them loose until they were stable enough to prevent their resubjugation by European states. An external hand was not America's only option; it had prospered earlier with squalor in the western hemisphere and again with widespread European involvement in the western hemisphere. What had changed by Roosevelt's time was the American frame of reference: European involvement came to be seen as a greater threat than indigenous squalor.

Europeans were not more rapacious in their colonial and commercial quasi-colonial involvements than previously. Consciousness was changing in some European countries, though—and particularly in Britain, where campaigns against slavery and the barbarism of Belgian colonization in the Congo pioneered international activism. The 1902 Venezuelan crisis is partly of interest because Britain's sympathies lay with American attitudes but its commercial interests lay with Germany. Britain aligned itself uncomfortably with Germany, something the Salisbury government had a difficult time explaining to both king and country.

As Britain was becoming more democratic in its outlook, Roosevelt's America had become imperial in its outlook toward lesser-developed countries. The stridency of republican ideology that Britain so feared becoming the hallmark of American international policies had evaporated by the turn of the twentieth century. While Roosevelt professed a continued belief that countries should be democratically governed, he indulged the European condescension that countries that could not govern themselves to America's standard would be subject to U.S. military intervention. It seems not to have occurred to him that the Philippine insurrection was a natural, nationalistic reaction to American control; he dismissed the groundswell of violence to "local banditti and marauders."

Roosevelt understood economic opportunity to be essential for both pacification and political development in the Philippines. And he sought means of incentivizing businesses for "throwing them open to industrial development." His solution—a surprising one for a domestic campaigner against corruption and the untrammeled power of big business—was legislation granting preferential franchises to American businesses. The dynamic that would culminate in dollar diplomacy had its roots in Roosevelt's own advocacy.

In outlining his strategy for countering challenges to American control, Roosevelt explicitly used the devastation of America's Indian wars as his model, telling the Congress,

> Exactly as our aim is to give to the Indian who remains peaceful the fullest and amplest consideration, but to have it understood that we will show no weakness if he goes on the warpath, so we must make it evident, unless we are false to our own traditions and to the demands of civilization and humanity, that while we will do everything in our power for the Filipino who is peaceful, we will take the sternest measures with the Filipino who follows the path of the insurrecto and the ladrone.

Roosevelt took the worst of American instinct in domestic policy and made it the basis of American foreign policy toward the western hemisphere and the Philippines. The key to understanding this malignant use of "our own traditions" is that both with regard to native Americans and the peoples of countries Americans prised from Spanish rule, Roosevelt's attitude was the prevailing European attitude of the day: these were inferior races and cultures that must be forced to compliance with our superior standard. He delineated two categories of conflict: those between "civilized powers," which he considered diminishing in number, and "wars with barbarous or semi-barbarous peoples come in an entirely different category, being merely a most regrettable but necessary international police duty which must be performed for the sake of the welfare of mankind."

The legacy of the Monroe Doctrine was to align America with Europe and against those countries emerging as America had from colonial rule. Roosevelt set America up as judge for when countries could govern themselves. In so doing he made America into what it began its international involvement condemning. America had become a European power in foreign affairs, just as Britain had bet it would. At the very moment Salisbury's Britain was becoming dour about the costs and obligations of empire, Roosevelt's America relieved them in Latin America.

European Powers

The 1895 negotiations represent the beginning of an attitudinal change on the part of America's governmental establishment, the leading edge of the Great Rapprochement that would culminate in an intensely affectionate special relationship between Britain and the United States. In consenting to American arbitration, Great Britain conceded the principle of American primacy in the western hemisphere, and the American government quickly showed itself willing to support any solution that acknowledged the Monroe Doctrine.[90] If Britain did not welcome American power, it nonetheless turned it to incredible advantage. What Britain compromised in principle, it was compensated for in practice: utilizing soft power with an elegance seldom achieved by governments then or now, the British commissioners secured greater gains than they had been willing to settle for with Venezuela.

By taking American aspirations for an international role seriously, the British granted America that stature a rising power craved. In return, Britain got some measure of devotion from America. Britain had turned the trick of palliative agreement with the rising power, trading principle to achieve practical gain.[91] So successful was this British policy that Theodore Roosevelt would later describe his 1902 judgment, "I speedily became convinced that Germany was the leader, and the really formidable party in the transaction; and that England was merely following Germany's lead in rather half-hearted fashion. I became convinced that England would not back Germany in the event of a clash over the matter between Germany and the United States, but would remain neutral; I did not desire that she should do more than remain neutral."[92]

The British government saw the opportunity to shed its expensive maintenance of international order onto receptive American shoulders, hedging its bets against an assertive Germany, Japan, and Russia through the cultivation of an activist America. The rising power demanded stature and acknowledgment; once the hegemon granted that, broader cooperation became possible. An America with stars in its eyes wanted to be what Britain wanted it to be. And Britain manipulated that desire with admirable shrewdness and subtlety, an effective—and cost-effective—diplomacy for the record books on the management of a rising power. Britain luring

America into commonality of interest internationally sustained British power and a preferred British order far beyond the expanse of time that Britain's unilateral efforts could have.

Venezuela's 1895 and 1905 appeals were the first real tests of the Monroe Doctrine. The doctrine's intended effect, of shielding Latin America from European influence, backfired spectacularly. In the first instance, in 1895, the Cleveland administration traded Venezuela's territorial claims to secure Britain's adherence to the principle of United States supremacy in the Americas. In the second instance, in 1902, the Roosevelt administration undertook to underwrite European financial claims against Latin American states, dramatically expanding the writ of American intervention. The Roosevelt Corollary turned the United States into the enforcer of European investment in the fledgling states struggling into being in the western hemisphere. A stronger America showed its foreign relations indistinguishable from the British empire.

The crises notably served to establish new rules of order between Britain and the United States. The threat of war in 1895 changed British policy toward America, and with the change in policy came diplomatic opportunities to lock in a different kind of relationship. Arbitration over Venezuela also led to a broader agreement between Britain and the United States to resolve future disputes by arbitration. In committing not to resort to military force, the two nations established rules of international order unique to their relationship. These defanged for Britain the risk that a strengthening America would use its burgeoning military power to coerce British policy or economic concessions (provided, of course, that America honored its treaty obligations). While the Senate forced negating amendments on the canal treaty and rejected outright the arbitration treaty, the American government had elected a different kind of relationship with Britain than it had with any other country.

America becoming an empire was by itself not enough for the convergence between Great Britain and the United States as the hegemonic transition occurred. Britain's own continued democratization—in particular, in the reform bills of 1884-1885—was important in cementing the sense of sameness. Because while America became an empire, it never was comfortably so; the rhetoric of democratic societies was important in justifying policies, even for the outsize imperialism of Theodore Roosevelt. A democratizing Britain surely acted strategically, but also understood the opportunity—the comparative advantage it held over other countries—in creating a sense of commonality with a rising America. As H. C. Allen emphasizes, "Britons deliberately, persistently, energetically and even with a sense of urgency, set out to win the friendship of the United States."[93]

The effect is most visible in relief—in contrast to the German-American experience of the same time. The German government still seethed in 1902 that the Monroe Doctrine was "a species of arrogance peculiarly American and inexcusable."[94] Secretary of State John Hay thought "the jealousy and animosity felt toward us in Germany is something which can scarcely be exaggerated. . . . the Vaterland is all on fire with greed and terror of us."[95] Otto von Bismarck (who mostly ignored America in his policies as peripheral to Europe's machinations) expressed mystification at the bonds emergent between Britain and the United States that great power politics could not account for. It was the alignment of the United States with Great Britain that caused Bismarck to conclude that "the colonization of North America has been the decisive fact of the modern world."[96] The balance of power in Europe, so carefully manipulated by statesmen for centuries, had been upended by what looked to Bismarck to be a sentimental attachment that had no explanation and no place in the decisions of statecraft.

The change in American attitudes toward Britain is illustrated by the change in attitude of Richard Olney, author of the "twenty-inch gun" that brought the Monroe Doctrine into practice in 1895. Only three years later Olney would write,

> Nothing can be more obvious, therefore, than that the conditions for which Washington made his rule [of isolation] no longer exist. . . . There is a patriotism of race as well as of country—and the Anglo-American is as little likely to be indifferent to the one as to the other . . . that they would be found standing together against any alien foe by whom either was menaced with destruction or irreparable calamity, it is not permissible to doubt. Nothing less could be expected of the close community between them in origin, speech, thought, literature, institutions, ideals and in the kind and degree of the civilization enjoyed by both."[97]

8

Us versus Them:
The Spanish-American War

The Spanish-American War

1896 Spanish removal of Cubans to concentration camps begins, eventually resulting in the death of over one-fourth of Cuba's population.

December 1897 President William McKinley denounces Spanish extermination of Cubans but declares American annexation of Cuba would be "criminal aggression."

January 1898 Cuban riots against Spanish barbarity; McKinley sends USS *Maine* for potential evacuation of American citizens.

February 15, 1898 USS *Maine* sinks in Havana Harbor, 266 American casualties.

February 1898 Congress appropriates $50 million in defense spending; McKinley offers to buy Cuba from Spain, proposes arbitrated settlement.

April 1898 Peace initiative by Austria-Hungary, Britain, France, Germany, Italy and Russia rejected by McKinley.

April 1898 Congress passes the Teller Amendment precluding annexation or colonial control of Cuba.

April 25, 1898 McKinley declares war on Spain, Spanish forces in Cuba and the Philippines quickly defeated; although Britain is formally neutral, it provides material support to U.S. forces.

May–August 1898 Confrontation between U.S. and German naval forces in Manila.

1901 Congress passes the Platt Amendment, giving the United States unlimited political and economic authorities in Cuba.

What occurs between the first and second Venezuelan debt crises is, of course, the Spanish-American War. During that conflict the last essential element of a uniquely close British-American relationship fell into place: reciprocation of British affection by Americans. The sensing of sameness between Great Britain and America that began with the 1895 Venezuelan debt negotiations came to full flower as America ventured to fight the Spanish Empire and take imperial possessions of its own. Great Britain encouraged the expansion of American obligations beyond America's borders, firmly believing that American and British interests aligned. An America taking the training wheels off its engagement with the world was grateful for the encouragement.

The alignment of action by governments was enabled and buttressed by a reciprocal public sympathy. What was strategy for governments was sentiment for publics. Similarities of language, culture, and—notably—civil society made sympathetic portrayals accessible to broad publics. American and British publics for the first time gave each other's governments an assumption of righteousness not extended to others. Before the first Venezuela crisis and Spanish-American War, Britain and the United States jealously assessed each other's relative power; with the war came the erasure of those evaluations by the governments and the broad publics of both societies.

The two countries saw themselves as the two democracies advancing humanitarian rights and commercial openness throughout the world. Whether or not that is what Great Britain and the United States were, it is what they looked like and professed to each other. As the *New York Times* declared in the fall of 1898, "they and we are the joint representatives and guardians of a principle of government that no other nation even fully understands—the principle of orderly freedom which is the hope of the race."[1] The collective power of Great Britain and the United States perked into political culture in both countries as Anglo-America.

Storming San Juan Hill?

James A. Field argues that the worst chapter in almost any book on American history is the one covering the 1890s: simplistic readings of Alfred Thayer Mahan of an argument for a fleet to police the Caribbean once the Panama Canal had become a major thoroughfare then expounded into a grandiloquent justification for imposing American power everywhere, and an American public enthusiastic for empire, whipped into a frenzy by a sensationalist press.[2] And a caricature of America as Theodore Roosevelt: eager for adventure once the West was no longer wild, bombastically assured, imperialist by means of commerce and war.[3] The war with Spain, initiated by America despite no threat to America itself and resulting in acquisition of colonies both actual (Guam, the Philippines, and Puerto Rico) and virtual (Cuba) is, in this telling, a rising America's debutante ball. It is where America seized on the opportunity provided by a corroding Spanish Empire to introduce itself to the great powers of Europe and Asia as a force to be reckoned with.

And while there is some truth in the characterization, taking it as the dominant story line does injustice to both the hesitance with which Americans undertook imperial action in 1898 and to the humanitarian concerns that motivated so many in America and beyond in opposition to Spain's policies in Cuba.[4] What would come to be known as the Spanish-American War was not a war America instigated; it was an ongoing insurrection in which the United States reluctantly intervened to assist the success of indigenous people against colonial rule.[5] The American intervention in Cuba's war for independence was precipitated not by a frothy aspiration for global power but by public outrage over continuing depredations by Spain against the Cuban people and an act of sabotage believed committed by Spain.

Yellow journalism plays a central role in the rush-to-empire narrative, with William Randolph Hearst's apocryphal telegram about supplying the war making a star turn. While Hearst and Joseph Pulitzer's newspapers were unquestionably agitating for American involvement, there is scant evidence their efforts moved public opinion.[6] Nor was the American Congress seething for empire. As it had with earlier efforts to establish protectorates, Congress had declined to provide its consent for President McKinley's proposal to annex Hawaii.[7]

Relief for Cuba unquestionably had popular appeal in the United States. In 1896 Congress passed a resolution of support for the

Cuban people (ignored by President Grover Cleveland), and both political parties included Cuba in their platforms during the 1896 election, but the subject had not figured prominently. The contest between William McKinley and William Jennings Bryan was fought out on policies for economic recovery: tariffs and establishing silver as an alternative to the gold standard ("bimetallism"). McKinley considered talk of annexing Cuba "criminal aggression."

In Cuba, Spain faced what we now call an insurgency. In countering that insurgency its methods aggravated the problem by giving little attention to the legitimate grievances and desire for political representation—understood then and now to be essential to any enduring solution.[8] In an effort to restrict insurgent activity, the Spanish forcibly relocated Cubans from their farms and towns to densely populated internment camps, burning crops and decimating livelihoods in order to dry up political support and material assistance for rebel forces. Spanish war efforts were unspeakably brutal: both Washington and Madrid estimated the casualties from the *reconcentrado* efforts to number 400,000—a quarter of Cuba's population.[9]

That President McKinley was outraged by Spanish tactics is clear: he denounced them in his first annual message to Congress as "extermination" rather than "civilized warfare." Then, describing America's options, he said, "There remained only: recognition of the insurgents as belligerents; recognition of the independence of Cuba; neutral intervention to end the war by imposing a rational compromise between the contestants, and intervention in favor of one or the other party. I speak not of forcible annexation, for that cannot be thought of. That, by our code of morality, would be criminal aggression."[10] What McKinley recommended was patience and aid; the Congress assented.

Far from stampeding to Cuba, McKinley took a measured approach in both process and policy. He'd sent a personal envoy to Cuba to establish the facts of Spanish and Cuban actions, consulted with European powers and used the consensus of those countries as leverage to pressure Spain, and allowed José Martí and the Cuban rebels to raise some money and buy weapons in the United States but not stage attacks from Florida, basically using them as a lever to gain Spanish compliance for reform.[11] All McKinley asked for from the government of Spain was to allow the delivery of aid (in a grace note to make that assistance more acceptable, McKinley provisioned it through the Catholic Church), and some form of political autonomy for Cuba within Spain's control.[12]

Giving the Cuban rebels stature as belligerents in war rather than continuing to call them insurrectionists would legitimate countries openly providing weapons and supplies and also aid in undertaking diplomatic relations with their leaders. American evangelical and protestant churches agitated for involvement to throw off the yoke of Catholic Spain, business interests that didn't outright support an end to Spanish rule were losing confidence that Spain could restore a stable environment for commerce (Cuban-American trade estimated at $100 million per year had dropped by two-thirds), and many Americans of all denominations and professions saw parallels to America's own revolution in the Cuba Libre movement.[13] Assistance would have flowed thickly across the Florida Keys. And sources of support were not only American: the governments of Britain, France, Germany, and Russia, had all advocated recognition during the McKinley consultations.[14]

The Spanish government consented, not because of a change of heart but because of a change of government. The Spanish military in Cuba, however, refused to comply, and its continuing barbarity fomented riots. S. C. Gwynne nicely summarizes Spain's colonial approach in a different context, noting that "though they were not always cruel and incompetent, they were cruel and incompetent enough of the time to cause great problems for themselves."[15] One consequence of the January 1898 riots was President McKinley dispatching an American navy vessel to Havana in case Americans living there needed to be evacuated or business interests protected.[16]

In conjunction with dispatch of the USS *Maine*, McKinley ordered American fleets gathered in Hong Kong, Lisbon, Key West and the Gulf of Mexico readied.[17] At anchor in Havana Harbor on February 15, the *Maine* suffered a tremendous explosion and sank, with the majority of its crew, 266 sailors, going down with the ship. Even after the *Maine*, McKinley continued to believe the costs outweighed the benefits of involvement in Cuba; but he continued preparations for war.[18] McKinley requested the Congress to provide $50 million in military spending, which it unanimously provided on the same day.[19] Public attitudes were incensed when the navy concluded that a detonation outside the ship's hull—sabotage—had sunk the *Maine*.[20] The army, then totaling 28,000 soldiers, put out a call for volunteers, hoping to raise an additional 50,000; more than 220,000 Americans, including entire state and National Guard units, answered the call.[21] A prominent senator who had traveled to Cuba gave an electrifying speech to the Congress describing Cuban suffering.[22] A hundred Republican members of Congress caucused to consider joining the Democrats in an unrequested declaration of war. McKinley described the public attitude as "a perilous unrest among our own citizens."[23]

McKinley offered to buy Cuba from Spain, and proposed a comprehensive political solution of armistice, an end to *reconcentrado* efforts, and an American arbitrated peace negotiation.[24] He proposed American food and other aid to the Cubans "cooperating with the Spanish authorities, so as to afford full relief."[25] But he also gave the government of Spain only a forty-eight-hour deadline to accept, after which he would turn the matter over to the Congress—which even those inattentive to American politics would have known meant war. McKinley's approach looks to have been a strategy of buying time for Spain to reconsider its policies, coupled with domestic measures to coalesce the American public in support of war. He seems genuinely to have believed Spain would recognize its relative weakness against a stronger American military force operating close to its home bases.

Spain instead countered with a conditional cease-fire offer—if requested by the rebels of Spain's general in chief, who alone would determine the terms and duration—and tepid acknowledgment that Cuba's indigenous parliament could meet to develop peace terms, "it being, however, understood that the powers reserved by the [Spanish] constitution to the central government are not lessened or diminished." McKinley considered the Spanish proposal so vague as to the terms of settlement, and unresponsive to the humanitarian concerns about the practice of *reconcentrado,* as to not be serious. Austria-Hungary, France, Germany, Great Britain, Italy, and Russia undertook an eleventh-hour initiative, jointly delivering to President McKinley a letter appealing for peace. McKinley rejected their appeal.[26]

War Powers

President McKinley's war message asked that Congress "authorize and empower the President to take measures to secure a full and final termination of hostilities between the government of Spain and the people of Cuba, and to ensure in the island the establishment of a stable government, capable of maintaining order and observing its international obligations, insuring peace and tranquility and the security of its citizens as well as our own."[27]

The humanitarian motive was explicit and paramount in America's rationale for war. The message claims "the dictates of humanity" as both a universal obligation and also an especial one of neighboring countries toward each other: "it is no answer to say this is all in another country, belonging to another nation, and is therefore none of our business. It is specially our duty, for it is right at our door." Protecting American citizens and commercial interests in Cuba were acknowledged—but lesser—claims on American involvement, as were the threats posed directly to the United States by Spain, which "compel us to keep on a semi war footing with a nation with which we are at peace."[28]

McKinley's message did not sound clarion notes of American imperialism. He made no mention of the Monroe Doctrine as justification. He emphasized instead that, for American policy, the "primal maxim has been the avoidance of all foreign entanglements" and that across two presidential administrations, America had sought "an honorable adjustment of the contest between Spain and her revolted colony, on the basis of some effective scheme of self-government for Cuba under the flag and sovereignty of Spain."[29]

The policy did, however, anticipate the requirement of imposing a settlement on both Spain and Cuba. The request shied away from declaring Cuba independent because in case of intervention "our conduct would be subject to the approval or disapproval of such government. We would be required to submit to its direction and to assume to it the mere relation of a friendly ally."[30] McKinley reserved to American forces the determination of necessary action, independent of the views of Cuba's insurgents.

The declaration nonetheless sounds tender toward the aspirations of Cubans, saying, "Our people have beheld a once prosperous community reduced to comparative want, its lucrative commerce virtually paralyzed, its exceptional productiveness diminished, its fields laid waste, its mills in ruins, and its people perishing by tens of thousands from hunger and destitution."[31]

Nor was McKinley entirely strident about Spain: he commended its willingness to refer the *Maine* sinking to arbitration and admitted his administration had not taken up the offer. He noted that Spain had suspended hostilities on April 9 and it had been the Cuban rebels rejecting armistice. An armistice would need to be imposed and the Cuban insurgents disarmed. It was hardly the speech of a committed imperialist thundering for war.

Also important to appreciating American reluctance as an imperial power is that even with extensive reporting on the horrific treatment of Cubans by Spain, 266 Americans killed in sabotage against the USS *Maine,* substantial loss of trade and strong presidential leadership, the Congress, and therefore the public, had reservations. Congress did not approve the president's request outright; McKinley was only able to garner sufficient votes with an amendment precluding the American government establishing "permanent control" over Cuba by outright annexation or colonial control. The measure, titled the Teller Amendment, passed 42-35 in the Senate and 311-6 in the House of Representatives. The U.S. Congress, frenzied as it was about sabotage and Spanish perfidy, only supported war in Cuba to allow "control of the island to its people."[32]

Perfidious Albion(s)

The terms on which McKinley made the American case gave Spain opportunity to consolidate European monarchies against the American claim, but, hobbled by its own domestic upheavals, Spain failed to capitalize. The Spanish considered Cuba not a colony but an actual province of Spain. Americans were asserting a universal human right superior to the sovereignty and sanctity of the state. It was, in 1898, still a radical proposition that people had rights and loaned them in limited ways to governments for agreed purposes. If the notion gained standing that governments did not have inherent rights superior to those of their subjects, such a claim could be used against any monarchy. The German government saw the nature of the challenge, fulminating, "this notoriously disreputable Republic has the assurance to pose as a censor of the morals of European monarchies."[33]

Having barely concluded its domestic Indian Wars, America was in no position to make grandiose statements about governments' treatment of indigenous populations. European and American racism of the time prevented that argument being employed; where hypocrisy was alleged against American policy, it was in pointing out that the Monroe Doctrine had pledged not to interfere with existing European colonies.[34]

The British government was formally neutral; it had signed a pact with Germany and Italy committing itself not to assist any side in the conflict. Having an empire on which the sun never set, Britain had a principled interest in keeping both insurrectionists and outside powers from challenging colonial control; yet the British government privately assured the American government of its support. Britain saw the republican tint of McKinley's war message, but was less concerned—for three reasons. First, Britain rightly laid claim to the original assertion of citizen rights constraining government in the Magna Carta and championed itself since the Ministry of Henry John Temple, Third Viscount Palmerston as the natural ally of constitutional governments. Second, having passed through several iterations of expanding democratization, Britain had confidence in the resilience of its political system that the unlimited monarchies in Europe did not. Third, the government of Robert Arthur Talbot Gascoyne-Cecil, Third Marquess of Salisbury firmly believed that an internationally engaged United States would converge on British policies and be a valuable support, learning from experience that its republican principles were impractical when applied to other countries.[35] As the *London Times* put it, "Anglo-Saxon vigor will call out latent colonial abilities in the United States."[36]

Paramount among Britain's interests was the necessity of preventing war with either European continental alliance, the nexus of France and Russia or the Triple Alliance of Austria-Hungary, Germany, and Italy. Each contained a rising power with policies of colonial and commercial expansion. Splendid isolation had left Britain alone among the great powers of Europe, and Salisbury's aggressive new imperialism put Britain at increased risk of conflict with the continental alliances. With Germany's triumph of unification in 1871 and Kaiser Wilhelm II forcing Otto von Bismarck into retirement, consolidation of Britain's empire in India and conquests of Burma and Egypt, tension with Boers in the Transvaal, and Russian assertiveness in Asia and trade in that region of greater interest to British merchants, obligations elsewhere had taken precedence over the Caribbean. One possible solution to Britain's strategic dilemma would be to draw strength from the empire, pulling the confederation closer and giving it a commonly accepted basis for mutual support; another would be alliances with rising powers not yet aligned, such as Japan and the United States. Britain sensibly chose both.

As early as the 1870s Britain had concluded that America shared enough of Britain's international agenda to be a potential ally, that American power could be harnessed to British interests, both in the Caribbean and throughout the Pacific.[37] Writing in the *Atlantic Monthly*, James Bryce acknowledged the fundamental shift in British attitudes: "rather than being dreaded as a fountain of democratic propaganda, America is looked upon as the champion of popular government against the great military monarchies of continental Europe."[38]

The Salisbury government had actually proposed a formal alliance with America; it was rejected as contravention of George Washington's legacy of eschewing entangling alliances. Americans did not then see Britain as enough like America for alliance to seem a natural act. Informal opportunities abounded, though.

The objectives of the two countries were perfectly aligned to advocate an open door for trade outside the British imperial holdings. The *London Times* viewed America's annexation of the Philippines "with equanimity and indeed with satisfaction. We can only say that while we would welcome the Americans in the Philippines as kinfolks and allies united with us in the Far East by the most powerful bonds of common interest, we should regard very differently the acquisition of the archipelago by any other power."[39]

Britain also supported expansion of American international involvement in the belief that having such obligations would attenuate U.S. commitment to its domestic political ideology as a universal creed—that is, international responsibilities would force American policies to be less doctrinarily republican and more responsible, by which Britain meant more akin to the behavior of other states. America becoming a colonial power would solve Britain's problem of America's revolutionary ideals making it a force favoring novel interpretations of international practice such as it had propounded with the Monroe Doctrine, during the Oregon Boundary Dispute, and during the 1895 Venezuelan debt crisis. British policy came to encourage American internationalism both to underwrite with its independent resources Britain's policies and to defang American alternatives to the existing rules of international order.

The problem was getting Americans active. Britain had encouraged American commercial and political designs on the Hawaiian Islands, conceded the Caribbean to American prominence with the Venezuela decision in 1895, and taken without umbrage congressional rejection of the arbitration treaty. In 1896, Britain had corralled France and Germany into a joint request that Spain "accept the good offices of the United States over the Cuban rebellion." Spain refused, and Germany pulled away to support Spain. When war broke out, Britain kept neutral and—advantageously to America—kept France and Italy likewise unengaged.

Britain made greater progress on the civic front with America than with policy. An "era of good feelings" had blossomed between the two countries as a result of the goodwill generated during negotiations over the arbitration treaty. In 1897 Britain gave the United States the Mayflower register, an American delegation honored Queen Victoria's diamond jubilee with great fanfare, newspapers in Britain and America began routinely reprinting each others' articles and mirroring each others' coverage, and President McKinley began using the term "Anglo-America" in speeches. When the *Maine* was sunk, the *London Times* declared, "nowhere will the feeling be so general or profound as amongst their British and Irish kinsfolks at home and in the colonies."[40]

As war approached, activity in both the civic and policy realms intensified. Newspapers in both countries were rife with rumor the British fleet would protect American coasts.[41] Consultations were frequent and at high levels between the two governments in Washington; in London, Parliament was alive with questions about the extent of support to American forces.[42] After the joint European peace letter, the *London Times* printed an assurance the government had not acted in a manner hostile to America, and the House of Commons debated whether the government had offended the United States.[43] The *Spectator* of London confidently asserted that "if America were really attacked by a great Continental coalition, England would be at her side in twenty-four hours."[44] Americans unaccustomed to friendliness from the British press read their president's policy described as "firmness, caution and pacific circumspection," a reflection of the "sober and conscientious mass of the American people."[45] Praise in the British press was so fulsome of American soldiery that it prompted an envious Canadian reaction: "It seems to us that the English papers are getting altogether too sloppy in their Anglo-American-Alliance admiration of the prowess of Uncle Sam's troops."[46]

Perhaps the most important assurance British collusion provided America as it went to war with Spain was an affirmation of motive. Americans considered their war humanitarian; Britain did, too.[47] Amid opprobrium from other European countries, Britain's affirmation cemented in the public mind a sense of the two countries being alike and different from others. British poet laureate Alfred Austin captured the sentiment during the war in "A Voice from the West":

Tis a proud free people calling loud
To a people proud and free.

A Splendid Little War

For the Spanish-American War, the fight in the West (Cuba) gets most of the attention because the war began there, ease of access allowed extensive newspaper coverage, and the volunteer army units of the Rough Riders made such good press during the American invasion. But the Caribbean theater was less strategically important than the Pacific (the Philippines) in gauging a rising America. America did not need to open a Pacific theater of operations in order to relieve Spanish depredations in Cuba. Doing so was an opportunistic choice; what was undertaken as a war measure became a strategic redirection for the country.[48]

The choice made tactical sense, pressing Spain's overstretched naval forces and threatening the government with loss of possessions beyond Cuba unless American demands about Cuba were met. American war plans dating back to 1896 included a feint against Spanish forces in the Pacific just to ensure its fleet was tied down there.[49] But sailing time between the Atlantic and Pacific Oceans meant effectively that fleets in the two theaters were not fungible.

On April 25, 1898, President McKinley declared war on Spain, and Spanish control of Cuba was quickly overturned. Spanish control of Manila Bay fell even faster: the American navy under Commodore George Dewey defeated the Spanish fleet in a single engagement without losing a ship.[50] Defeating Spain was not the end of hostilities in the Philippines, however, because Germany moved to challenge American control. Kaiser Wilhelm II demanded a cession (a share of commercial activity and location from which to conduct trade), declaring that the Americans were no match for the combined German and Spanish effort. (The Kaiser was unaware that the Spanish effort already lay on the seabed of Manila Harbor). He, too, saw commonality between Britain and the United States, proclaiming that "the United States with Monroeism is nearly as much in the way of Powers desiring to expand as Great Britain.[51]

Dewey's fleet was not the peer of the German flotilla assembled in Manila Bay. The German squadron consisted of five men of war, two of which had greater displacement than any vessel in Dewey's command; they also had aboard fourteen hundred infantrymen.[52] German vessels began sounding the harbor, violated Dewey's blockade regulations, moved to resupply Spanish forces aground, and even sought a naval base at Subic Bay.[53] But American war efforts had received invaluable assistance by aligning with the Philippine independence movement: Dewey knew the harbor wasn't mined and knew the extent of German collusion with Spain aground because of Philippine intelligence.

American war efforts received even more important assistance from Great Britain. Britain was officially neutral, but practiced "a benevolent neutrality which left no question as to which belligerent she favored."[54] British consuls in Spanish territories accepted responsibility for American nationals, even feeding them in Cuba. In Cairo, Gibraltar, and Singapore, British diplomats facilitated American efforts and inhibited those of Spain. Britain provided the negotiating intermediary for a clandestine agreement between Spain and America on terms for the surrender of Manila.[55] Britain controlled the Pacific telegraph cable (out of Hong Kong) and permitted Dewey its use to communicate with Washington, allowed the American navy use of British facilities in Chinese anchorages, and looked the other way during American espionage activities conducted against Spain in Gibraltar.[56] British vessels cheerfully allowed themselves to be stopped and searched, their passengers questioned.

The commander of the British squadron dispatched to Manila even more overtly assisted the American war effort. Captain Chichester of the Royal Navy loaned Dewey landing craft, allowed him to buy fuel from Royal Navy coaling ships, and then let him buy the ships outright, enlisting British crews.[57] During land operations he reinforced American forces, bringing a gunboat to bear on Cebu. On several occasions during the confrontation in Manila, Chichester insisted to German commander Otto von Diederichs that he was acting under orders in support of the Americans, meaning his government would not disavow his actions.[58]

Chichester was pivotal in preventing conflict between the German and American forces in Manila. At the tensest moments between Dewey and Diederichs, Chichester found creative ways to reinforce American authority and raise the costs for German interference. Most notably, as Dewey prepared to fire on Manila during the ground campaign, the Germans, in an effort to prevent the Americans forcing surrender of the Spanish, refused to move out of bombardment range and trained their guns on American ships. The British squadron commander sailed between the German and American lines, thus ensuring that the Germans could not fire on the Americans without also committing an act of war against Britain. Dewey considered it material assistance in turning back the Germany challenge for Manila.[59] When American forces took Manila on August 9, Chichester fired a twenty-one-gun salute, flying an American flag on his mast.[60]

That Britain was acting in conjunction with America despite its pledge of neutrality was widely recognized both in the United States and Europe. The *New York Times* editorialized that "we are fighting England's battles in Cuba, as England is fighting our battles in the

East."[61] The French government seethed, "Great Britain is the hypocritical partner of the United States. Their alliance against Spain is a disgrace; but it is just as well to have them work together now, since together they will have to render an account to international justice."[62]

Imperialem Americana

Having decisively attained its war aims, why would America not allow Cubans to run Cuba? McKinley's war declaration established temporary American control of Cuba but also outlined the aspiration for transition to Cuban control: "When it shall appear hereafter that there is within the island a government capable of performing the duties and discharging the functions of a separate nation, and having, as a matter of fact, the proper forms and attributes of nationality, such government can be promptly and readily recognized and the relations and interests of the United States with such nation adjusted."[63]

This was the American expectation of its empire: affirmation of the desire of all peoples for self-governance, insistence that governments surrendered their legitimacy by harming their subjects, willingness to assist liberation movements within limited bounds that did not incur lasting obligations of foreign entanglements, acknowledgment that societies in transition from authoritarian rule to self-governance need to develop the attributes and functions of states, and acceptance that by intervening the United States had a responsibility to provide governance while indigenous governance developed.

McKinley's explication of U.S. values and responsibilities in America's engagement with the world is at great variance with the bombast of claims made by the United States in the previous sixty years. Gone was the stridency of Andrew Jackson and James Polk. Gone was the hypocrisy of superior claim made in expropriating British, Indian, and Mexican lands to consolidate U.S. domestic territory. McKinley's forthright public explanations and use of principles constituent to the American republic in the conduct of its international policies now felt more situated in the realm of the founding fathers than in the belligerency of Jacksonian America.

McKinley's statements were more than empty rhetoric; American actions were guided and constrained by those principles during the Spanish-American War. There is a sense of accountability—both to America's domestic political principles and to international opinion—in McKinley's policies not in evidence during the boisterousness of America's rise. America was becoming more liberal as it was becoming more powerful.

Yet the liberal internationalism of McKinley's policy is not the history of American involvement in Cuba, Guam, Hawaii, the Philippines, or Puerto Rico. Guam, Hawaii, and Puerto Rico were quickly annexed. The Philippines remained under American control until 1945. American influence in Cuba allowed commercial exploitation so pervasive and long-standing that it fostered support for a communist revolution. How can we explain McKinley's pivot from so restrained an origin to acquisition of colonies not only in the Caribbean but also the Pacific?

First, McKinley emphasized (as had Ulysses S. Grant before him during the Indian Wars) that he quickly came to consider independence "impracticable."[64] He had always doubted that the Cuban insurgency "possesses beyond dispute the attributes of statehood," believing "the real question is whether the community claiming recognition is or is not independent beyond peradventure." And he concluded the Cuban community was not. The evaluation bears considerable similarity to the British during the American Civil War withholding recognition of new states until de facto independence had been established.

Second, McKinley was concerned about European countries taking over the newly liberated territories; the United States feared Spain—or other European states—reclaiming it. Having broken Spain's control and experienced Germany's clawing for influence, American policy risked opening Cuba and the Philippines up for the colonial aspirations of Germany and Russia. McKinley justifiably did not want America to be in the position of doing the liberating only to see the countries quickly subjugated by another imperial power even more able than Spain to threaten American interests.

The ease of Dewey's success against the Spanish navy also tempted McKinley to expand the political and military aims of the war.[65] Only after receiving Dewey's report of the action in Manila Bay— with his assurance that the capital could be taken at any time if only he had soldiers to do so—did McKinley dispatch troops; the initial American plan had been narrowly to secure the port of Manila, not overturn Spanish governance on the islands. Restraint of the kind embodied in the Teller Amendment was thrown to the wind with euphoria at realizing the country's strength. America many have been reluctant to embark on imperial pursuits, but it did not release its grasp on Cuba, Guam, Hawaii, the Philippines, or Puerto Rico once it held them. The war effort succeeding so spectacularly reinforced the illiberal tendency in American foreign policy debate: what had been necessary to persuade the American public to go to war against Spain was no longer a constraint once America was victorious.

The other Pacific possession that came into play for America in 1898 was Hawaii. Annexation of the islands had been posited by the administration of President Benjamin Harrison in its closing days, with the president saying that "it is essential that none of the other great powers shall secure these islands. Such a possession would not consist with our safety and with the peace of the world." His successor, President Cleveland, withdrew the treaty from congressional consideration believing it did not have the support of the Hawaiian people. It did, however, have vehement support from the next elected American president; William McKinley openly advocated annexation of Hawaii, arguing that "we need Hawaii just as much and a good deal more than we did California. It is Manifest Destiny."[66]

Economic arguments were an important part of McKinley's advocacy of a Pacific perspective. Although he had come to power supporting protectionism for American industries (in the Congress, McKinley had crafted tariff legislation), as president he strongly supported an open-door policy. American industries had (as did the British, who also advocated open trade) substantial advantages in less-developed Asian markets; other Europeans with less of a jump on industrialization preferred closed markets with colonial preference.

The ease and speed with which McKinley's restraints were eschewed justifies skepticism about how deeply rooted they actually were in American political culture. McKinley's noble principles may have been in keeping with the American political creed, but they were by no means in keeping with American foreign policy practice, as every tribe and nationality whose territory America arrogated to itself in the making of its continental country could attest. Most of the American public gave little thought to the issues associated with America's role in the world, considering themselves little affected by them; those who did tended to be at the sharp edge of encounters with Indian tribes or foreign possessors of coveted land, and this gave a hard, practical edge to American foreign policy.

With Congress being a bellwether of public attitudes, passage of the Platt Amendment constituent to the treaty ending war with Spain illustrates the change in American attitudes before and after the war. As America went to war in 1898, the Teller Amendment embodied the limits Congress set in approving the action: Cuba was to be liberated, not annexed or administered in perpetuity by the United States. After the rout of Spanish forces, in 1901 Congress effectively repudiated Teller's constraints by legislating stringent terms for withdrawal of American forces from conquered Cuba, including the right for the United States to intervene unilaterally there, restrictions on Cuban foreign and commercial relations, and perpetual control of the prime naval base at Guantanamo.

The changes in McKinley's policies are even more difficult to justify regarding the Philippines. Cuba could be considered so physically close to the United States as to merit concern for the type of government on the island; indeed, that had been part of McKinley's argument for intervening there. There was no such case to be made for an archipelago lying seven thousand miles from America's shores (and that necessitated other possessions as coaling stations en route). That the case for continuing involvement in the Pacific was more challenging is reflected in the split within McKinley's cabinet on the issue. Its members were unanimous in support of forcing Spain to cede both Cuba and Puerto Rico, but they disagreed on the Philippines.[67] The Congress, too, debated Pacific possessions at length, considering whether moving out of the western hemisphere violated the Monroe Doctrine. Civil society organizations also mobilized, creating the Anti-Imperialist League to advocate against accession of territories.

Public attitudes never fully or comfortably embraced America as an imperial power. As Bradford Perkins concludes, "the whiff of imperialism in 1898 failed to intoxicate Americans for long."[68] Even with euphoria over America's success in battle, President McKinley struggled to get the Hawaiian treaty approved (and with it accession also of Guam and Wake Island). He undertook a determined public campaign to build support, giving speeches to between twenty and twenty-five thousand people a day on a ten-day barnstorm.[69] McKinley had also to circumvent the regular order of business with a joint resolution of Congress instead of gaining ratification by a two-thirds majority of the Senate.[70] One result of the Spanish-American War was that expansionism beyond the contiguous territory of the American continent became a major issue in American politics. In the presidential election of 1900, McKinley was opposed by William Jennings Bryan, and contesting McKinley's imperialism was a central element of Bryan's election platform.

Giving some ground to public wariness, McKinley established a commission to evaluate how to transition the Philippines to indigenous control. That commission determined that the Philippines must develop an American-style system of administration and public education before it would be fit for self-government. It concluded that "the Filipinos are wholly unprepared for independence . . . there being no Philippine nation, but only a collection of different peoples, the transition should not occur."[71] President McKinley agreed, offering the Philippines "the largest measure of local self-government consistent with peace and good order" but threatening to "send all the force necessary to suppress the insurrection if Filipino resistance continued."[72] The Philippine-American War would prove more costly to the United States than had the war against one of Europe's great powers.

So America—a country founded by people without public education, who developed their own unique political organs for governance, a country that had not only justified its war against Spain on the argument that the peoples under Spanish rule had a right to independence but also eagerly utilized the assistance of independence movements in Cuba and the Philippines in its war efforts—had now persuaded itself other countries could not be entrusted with those same liberties. America had become an empire. And Salisbury's bet had proven right that an America more engaged with the world would not uphold its domestic political creed.

E Duobus Unum

In the aftermath of America's victory in Manila, Britain and America amicably resolved their last outstanding boundary dispute (over the northern boundary of Canada), and Prime Minister Salisbury bolstered McKinley to win the argument over Hawaii's annexation. In the Hay-Pauncefote Treaty, President McKinley conceded to Britain that the United States would not fortify the Panama Canal. The Senate refused those terms, sending negotiators back to the bargaining table. What is significant is how unified the two governments were on cooperation, conceding each other so much.[73] The sense of sameness had taken root, and the two countries no longer required parsimoniousness toward each other's interests. As British foreign secretary Arthur Balfour wrote Alfred Thayer Mahan in late 1899, "It becomes more and more obvious—to me at least, as it is I think to you—that our interests, both in the narrow and in the wide use of that term, are identical. We have not only the same ideas of progress, freedom, civilization, religion, morality, but we have the same interests in peace."[74]

When Queen Victoria died in 1901, the House of Representatives adjourned and President McKinley had flags lowered to half-staff, a tribute never before offered a foreign head of state.[75] McKinley's assassination later that year occasioned an outpouring of grief in Britain that again united the societies. Both the British and American governments became effusive about their commonalities. Theodore Roosevelt told British ambassador Mortimer Durand there was "a great change of feeling in the last few years" in which "no one in America thinks of England as a possible enemy . . . Germany [is] the chosen foe of the Navy, and not just the Navy. Since the Spanish war, the feeling toward England is thoroughly friendly."[76] Secretary of War William Howard Taft privately told the British that "the time is at hand when you and we can speak to the nations with a common voice and a common policy on all external questions."[77]

Economic protectionism and political corruption, both phenomena the British government had long associated with democracy in America, drew efforts of American domestic reformers in both parties and were mainstream political issues from the mid-1880s forward, removing yet another restraint on affinity and close cooperation. American opinion makers begin to extoll "interdependence" between Britain and America, as well.[78] A centripetal element of the Anglo-American relationship developed in belief on the part of both countries that they were, in some fundamental way, like each other and unlike other powerful states: democratic, free-trading, naval powers that established and upheld international principles.

Cooperation with America moved into the center of British strategic objectives. Joseph Chamberlain, head of the British Colonial

Office, made the case for Anglo-American alliance effusively and publicly in 1898 "to establish and to maintain bonds of permanent amity with our kinsmen across the Atlantic":

> I do not know what arrangements may be possible with us, but this I know and feel, that the closer, the more cordial, the fuller, and the more definite these arrangements are, with the consent of both peoples, the better it will be for both and for the world. And I even go so far as to say that, terrible as war may be, even war itself would be cheaply purchased if in a great and noble cause the Stars and Stripes and the Union Jack should wave together over an Anglo-Saxon alliance.[79]

In debating whether to seek alliance with Germany in 1901 the secretary of state for foreign affairs, Henry Petty-Fitzmaurice, Fifth Marquess of Landsdowne, warned of the "risk of entangling ourselves in a policy which might be hostile to America. With our knowledge of the German Emperor's views in regard to the United States, this is to my mind a formidable obstacle." The only stipulation placed on cooperation by Britain with Germany was that it "not apply to questions on the American Continent, nor bind either High Contracting Party to join in hostilities against the United States of America."[80]

The idea of Anglo-American cooperation would become so central to British strategic planning that by 1904 Earl of Selborne, the first lord of the admiralty, listed friendship with the United States as "the principal aim" of British policy—more so than preservation of the empire—and considered "war with the United States of America as the greatest evil which could befall the British Empire."[81]

Perhaps the best summation of the quickening of relations between Great Britain and the United States after the Spanish-American War was given by the German ambassador to London, explaining to his government in Berlin that "England will stand far more from America than from any other Power, and even in purely diplomatic issues it is more difficult to make England take sides against America than to make any other Power do so."[82]

The sense of strategic commonality and affection was finally reciprocated by the United States at the turn of the twentieth century: Americans embraced Anglo-America for the first time. Whereas a rising America had defined itself in contravention to British mores and politics, a risen America considered Britain its only confidante and ally. There grew an affection, gratitude, and sense of similarity of domestic political culture driving the Anglo-American alliance,[83] a sense that they were like each other and unlike other states, a "moral union."[84] After the Spanish-American War, Ambassador to London John Hay would say, "there is a sanction like that of religion which binds us in partnership in the serious work of the world. . . . We are joint ministers in the same sacred mission of freedom and progress, charged with duties we cannot evade."[85]

A rising America clearly preferred Britain to any other great power, and even sympathized with Great Britain's troubles in the Boer War and rationalized its draconian war effort. America reinforced British policies on continental Europe. Hay negotiated the opening for an end to the Boer War, involving the United States to such an extent that the *Kansas City Times* thundered, "England has committed the crime of the century—and this Government has been an accessory."[86] Pacific policies were coordinated and even merged. Britain and America undertook joint diplomatic and military action to overturn German involvement in Samoa. Consanguinity between Britain and America had become manifest.

Some Americans suspected they were being manipulated; the *Advocate of Peace* warned that despite "a deep and growing attachment of the English people, of the nation as a whole, for our country, we recognize, and with the greatest pleasure," Americans should beware:

> What more natural under these circumstances than that these British leaders should hasten to take advantage of the situation created by the Spanish-American war to try and draw the United States into formal alliance with Great Britain. It is a move whose selfishness is but poorly concealed. The purpose of it on their part is to strengthen the power of their country and enable her to go on with her schemes regardless of the other powers. It does not grow out of any particularly love for this country.[87]

The view was one of a very slender minority, however. More mainstream were the views of the *Chicago Tribune,* which noted that "the two great branches of the Anglo-Saxon race are drawing nearer and nearer together for coöperation in peace, and, in logical sequence, in war as well," and the *New York Times,* asserting that "we as well as continental countries will certainly conclude that the understanding has reached a more definite stage than was believed."[88]

The growing together of Britain and America at the end of the nineteenth century was an extraordinary event, unique in the annals of hegemonic transition. Seeing the gathering strength of a rising rival, Great Britain chose to encourage and make possible that rival's continued success. Clear-eyed assessment of its own strategic position led Britain to enact policies that catapulted the United States into the first rank of great powers. Great Britain's strategy was only possible because of public attitudes and activist civil society fostering connection between the two countries. The combination of government policy and uncoordinated acts by civil society resulted by the turn of the twentieth century in an extraordinary collusion between a rising power and the hegemon.

The *Economist* would naturally vantage the business relationship, saying Great Britain and American were "almost forced into partnership" by their need for open markets. Still, it could see that for Great Britain and America, "business partnership is not exactly an alliance [but] the distance between them is not very wide."[89] At the height of British power, and in anticipation of much greater power on the part of America, there was a convergence of perspective between the two countries, recognized by the leaders making choices about government policy and by the citizens of both countries. Britain had seen an emerging deficit of relative power and responded by fostering a relationship that with the affectionate bonds of civil society made cumulative power possible.

9

European Power:
World War I

World War I

August 4, 1914 Britain declares war on Germany after violation of Belgian neutrality.

February 1915 Germany begins submarine warfare campaign to disrupt U.S. supplies to Entente countries.

May 1915 Germany sinks the passenger ship *Lusitania,* killing over a thousand civilians, including 128 Americans; Secretary of State William Jennings Bryan resigns, considering President Woodrow Wilson's response to Germany a violation of American neutrality.

August 1915 "Cruiser rules" reduce risk to neutral and passenger shipping.

December 1916 President Wilson proposes peace negotiations; Germany refuses.

January 1917 Germany resumes unrestricted submarine warfare; President Wilson calls for "peace without victory."

February 1917 German foreign minister Arthur Zimmerman acknowledges authenticity of telegram offering Mexico help from Germany in recovering territory lost to the United States in return for a Mexican declaration of war against the United States.

April 1917 America declares war on the Central Powers.

January 1918 President Wilson publishes his Fourteen Points, the U.S. aims and terms for peace.

Spring 1918 The German offensive.

Summer 1918 United States provides ten thousand soldiers per day to the war effort.

November 11, 1918 Armistice goes into effect.

January 1919–January 1920 Versailles Peace Conference.

March 1920 U.S. Senate votes 49–35 against participating in the League of Nations.

The jubilant sense of sameness, the enthusiastic support for each other's endeavors, and the recognition of kindred states so evident between Great Britain and the United States during the Spanish-American War was a remarkably fleeting moment. Britain had welcomed American power waxing stronger in the belief that the two nations' interests were converging, and that appeared to be true at the end of the nineteenth century. But barely had American might supplanted Britain's internationally before the new hegemon sought to rewrite the rules of Britain's world order. Britain's hegemony comprised political balance among European powers, acquisition of colonies for economic gain, preferential trading within its empire, open trade and investment outside it, and military enforcement of its economic policies. As a rising power America aspired to and enacted similar policies: the United States became a responsible stakeholder in the British order, playing by the rules and seeing its interests served.

If the Spanish-American War was the moment when established powers were confronted with the burgeoning power of a rising United States, World War I was the moment when they become reliant upon it. The war resulted in alliance between Britain and America but, paradoxically, also broke the sense of affectionate sameness between the two countries. Britain once again looked like a European power—because it was fighting there, and because of what it was fighting for.

The United States recoiled from the web of European alliances that pulled Britain into the war, considered Britain little different from the other squabbling, militaristic, double-dealing Europeans engaged in a paroxysm of pointless bloodletting. From a British perspective, the United States made a fortune on the war, decimated the economies even of its allies, contributed its military stingily and on terms that made for little utility, and demanded an outsize role in determining the terms of peace. Britain's expectations that it could continue to dominate the relationship proved unfounded. As with the Monroe Doctrine in 1823, the United States contributed little but took the lion's share of credit. And yet, for all those aggravations, the United States was essential for producing the outcome Britain had bled so much to attain.

America as a risen power not only used its might to economic advantage, and refused to use its power to sustain Britain's position in the international order, but envisioned a wholly different kind of international order. The United States had begun to see itself as the rule setter of the international order, and the order it envisioned was a universalization of American domestic political values. President Woodrow Wilson's belief that the American public would support continued engagement in the world provided that world was remade in America's image proved premature. It would, however, eventually become the basis for the Pax Americana, and World War I decimating all of the European combatants would be a main contributing factor to the U.S. ability to impose its will on the order.[1]

The Guns and Butter of August

Germany's challenge on the continent proved nearly sufficient to conquer Europe in its entirety—even the power of the British Empire thrown into the maw was sufficient only to stalemate. By the time the United States entered the war in 1917, Russia had ceased to fight, allowing Germany to concentrate its effort in the west, where the grisly attrition of trench warfare had been going on inconclusively for two years. Social pressures that exploded into the Bolshevik Revolution were worryingly reflected in Austria-Hungary, Italy, and even France. French soldiers mutinied after suffering 100,000 casualties in a week during the Nivelle Offensive; in Britain the Marquess of Lansdowne published a letter calling for negotiations with Germany; and even the Royal Navy's admiral John Jellicoe believed the war could not go on much longer.[2]

Amid this maelstrom raging in Europe, the United States sailed unconcerned. President Wilson spoke for the nation when he described the war as "one with which we have nothing to do, whose causes cannot touch us."[3] The Congress was so chary of being sucked down the Charybdis that had already pulled in all of Europe that legislation forbade any infraction of strict neutrality, initially even refusing loans to belligerents, and in 1916 passed legislation opposing passports for travel on conveyance of or to belligerent countries as the means of preventing U.S. casualties in the ongoing maritime combat. President Wilson seemed often to make no distinction between the Central and Allied powers. Running for reelection in 1916, he'd had to promise he would continue to keep the United States out of the war. A Wilson loyalist described the U.S. foreign policy goal as "to win the largest possible freedom of trade with all belligerents for American citizens, within the bounds of neutrality."[4]

In February 1915, Germany declared the British Isles a war zone and shipping within their waters subject to attack. In May it torpedoed the passenger ship *Lusitania,* killing over a thousand civilians, including 128 Americans. Although President Wilson made clear the United States intended to remain neutral, asserting "America is too proud to fight," his letter to the German government calling for "strict accountability for any infringement of those [neutral state] rights" precipitated the resignation of Secretary of State William Jennings Bryan, who considered it to be taking the Allied side of the European argument.[5] By August another passenger ship had been sunk, and the German government agreed to restrict its campaign, to allow the crew to abandon, to search for contraband before sinking, and to cease to target civilian shipping.[6] These "cruiser rules" greatly limited the effectiveness of the submarines and made them vulnerable to Allied merchant ships with concealed weaponry, but they also kept the United States committed to remaining out of the war.[7]

As early as February 1916, fearing a separate U.S. peace with Germany, the British government drew the United States into a serious exchange about American involvement in the war, producing a joint paper that would have the United States propose a peace conference at a time suggested by Britain and France. If Germany refused to participate or proved unreasonable in negotiations, the United States would enter the war. In reviewing the paper, President Wilson inserted "probably" into the formulation. The main elements of the peace were moderate: restoration of Belgium, transfer of Alsace and Lorraine to France, an outlet to the sea for Russia, and compensation for Germany's loss of territory through concessions outside Europe.[8]

The predominant lines of American policy, though, were sustaining export markets, building military strength (the 1916 Naval Law aspired to a "navy second to none"—a clear reference to overtaking Britain), and calls for "a new and more wholesome diplomacy."[9] Wilson's December 1916 peace proposal, coming in rapid succession after a similar German one, incensed the British government by paralleling British and German war aims and fomenting neutral sentiment within Britain.[10] Prime Minister David Lloyd George—newly installed with a mandate to break the war's stalemate and worried that Britain's negotiating position was weak because Germany was occupying Allied territory, having success with its submarine campaign, and Allied unity tenuous—fulminated against Wilson, claiming that "he has not given the least thought to the effect of his action upon European affairs."[11]

Britain wanted "guarantees for a permanent peace before stopping the war," and they believed Wilson wanted peace "quite irrespective of terms."[12] Wilson understood that American and British war aims were in conflict. Assessing the prospects for his negotiations proposal, Wilson said, "England and France have not the same views with regard to peace that we have by any means. . . . When the war is over we can force them to our way of thinking because by that time they will, among other things, be financially in our hands."[13]

In fact, they already were. So concerned was the British cabinet about American commitment to peace overtures that it initiated a government-wide evaluation of effects should the United States try and force British compliance.[14] The conclusion was that by cutting funding and munitions, "if [Wilson] desired to put a stop to the war, and was prepared to pay the price for doing so, such an achievement is in his power."[15] The United States had reached such a magnitude of power that it could now impose its will on Great Britain. In order to forestall conflict with the United States, the British coordinated a palliative Allied response (while intimidating neutral states away from supporting Wilson's peace initiative); Germany assisted by rejecting the proposal outright.

While Secretary of State Robert Lansing attempted to assure the British that "the President's preferences were with the democracies," their suspicions of wandering U.S. commitment were justified.[16] In the preceding two years, President Wilson had threatened war to sustain trade.[17] Yet he'd failed to secure legislative approval of an armed ship bill that he'd initiated to demonstrate national unity, and had to undertake the arming without congressional authorization.[18] Wilson was assiduous in pursuing a general peace because, having threatened Germany over the submarine campaign, and with a Congress staunchly opposed to involvement, he was caught in the vise of "war or ignominious surrender."[19]

Germany's announcement in January 1917 that it would resume unrestricted submarine warfare was the proximate cause for American involvement. That it should precipitate America joining the war against such a backdrop of public opposition is surprising. German submarine warfare had only taken 236 American lives by April 1917, all but fourteen of those on vessels that had been flying belligerent flags.[20] Even after breaking diplomatic relations with Germany, the president described himself as "eager to remain neutral."[21]

Wilson didn't believe Americans would support war over submarines, "but that if it came to a 'really big' issue, such as peace, the people of America would support him in using armed force against Germany, if she refused terms that the President considered just."[22] So he cast America's involvement as essential to creating a different kind of international order that was "not a balance of power but a community of power."[23] Wilson used his second inaugural to press the case, commenting that "tragical events . . . have made us citizens of the world. Our own fortunes as a nation are involved, whether we would have it so or not." He went even further on April 2, arguing as he called the Congress early into session for the war vote that "civilization itself seeming to be in the balance."

Economics helped Wilson's case for war, too. Until 1917, America's main interest in the war was as an export market. Neutrality was initially associated with maximizing those exports, but as the war progressed, strict adherence to neutrality policy became costly and "politicians simply responded in a predictable way to overwhelming societal pressure to protect American trade."[24] Eleven percent of U.S. gross domestic product was directly attributable to trade. Before the war, 63 percent of American exports went to countries that would be Entente allies; during the war, that proportion grew to 80 percent.[25] As Benjamin Fordham argues, "the U.S. economy would certainly have recovered from the loss of a substantial part of this trade, but the political fortunes of the politicians who permitted it to happen might not have."[26] Moreover, those politicians were concentrated in states Woodrow Wilson had needed to carry in his 1916 reelection bid, so he was beholden to their views.

Finally, agitation surrounding the February 1916 release of the Arthur Zimmerman telegram, in which Germany offered Mexico assistance in regaining the territory it had lost to the United States, aided Wilson's case. Mexico, weighing Porfirio Diaz's lament, assessed the prospects as unpropitious.[27] Germany's was a creative, even elegant gambit to threaten opening a front the United States had been unsuccessful at policing during Wilson's administration. While designed to remind Americans of the advantages of remaining out of Europe's war, though, the prospect of Germany instigating trouble on America's borders stiffened anti-German feeling.[28]

The President's war bill passed the Senate by a vote of 82–6, and the House by 373–50.

Reinforcements

Both sides of the stalemated conflict were reaching the point of exhaustion when the United States joined the Great War.[29] Having pivoted from a western front strategy to attacking the Central Powers on their periphery—and that proving no more tractable for producing military victory—the British government was deeply pessimistic not only about the war but also that it would "sink to the status of a second-class power."[30]

Coming to power in December 1916, Prime Minister Lloyd George attempted to revivify British prospects, establishing an Imperial War Cabinet with representation by British dominions, forcing greater cohesion of Allied military efforts under French general Ferdinand Foch, pulling forward a more daring set of British general officers, probing for military opportunities on the eastern front with military incursions in Persia and Russia, fomenting agitation within the Austro-Hungarian and Ottoman Empires, reaching agreement with France on respective colonial prospects in the Middle East, and easing manpower shortages by relying more heavily on colonial (especially Indian) troops.[31] Creative as these longer-term moves were, they were moves of desperation, illustrating just how close Britain was to reaching the point of exhaustion when the United States joined the war.[32]

The German submarine campaign was claiming one in four British merchant ships by the spring of 1917, Britain's finances were sufficient for only three weeks of purchases in the United States, and on more than one occasion it came within hours of defaulting on its loans.[33] Social cohesion was under pressure in Britain from conscription, rationing, class divisions, and the ruthless arithmetic of attrition on the battlefields.

Germany undertook the decision to return to unrestricted warfare, believing that America and Britain were already allied and that the United States would soon join the war.[34] Britain had maintained a naval blockade of the continent since 1914; the blockade had infringed on American commerce, but was calibrated carefully to fall just shy of the threshold to provoke American support for Germany. Britain also craftily supplanted German buyers of American cotton and copper, hired a prominent American banker to purchase its credit, spent extravagantly on munitions in America; by the time the United States entered the war, 40 percent of British military spending went to the United States, and Britain had sixteen hundred Ministry of Munitions staff working in the United States to coordinate supplies.[35]

Indeed, British economic statesmanship during the war was of an extraordinarily high order in pulling America into tacit support for the British war effort. Even as it declared war, the United States had done no planning for it before April 1917.[36] Britain thus anticipated it could continue to dominate the relationship, guiding American government departments and folding American war efforts into its own.[37]

What Britain wanted was for the United States to force neutral shipping into Allied use, commandeer interned German ships, contribute immediately a half million soldiers to fill out British units, have mobilizing U.S. military forces use British gun patterns to speed arming, and to grant a credit flow of $185 million dollars per month, with the United States providing financing to Britain so that it could sustain the value of the pound sterling and preserve its international stature by extending credit to others.[38]

What Britain got was very much less. The British were "down on our knees to the Americans," entreating for credit, munitions, supplies, and soldiers.[39] The American army was, by admission of its own chief of staff, Payton C. March, "a very small force . . . of no practical military value as far as the fighting in France was concerned."[40] Britain and France urgently needed manpower and wanted to sow inexperienced and untrained Americans into their existing units.[41] The United States adamantly refused, insisting on the early appearance of a U.S. division to show its flag, and a smaller force of 120,000 per month, with an additional 150,000 if Britain could provide transport. The U.S. force would be "associated" rather than "amalgamated" into the Allied command, training to its own doctrine and commanding its own sector of the western front.[42]

The arrogance of American negotiators staggered British leaders weary from the hard lessons of war.[43] When the British and French negotiators warned they might be defeated before the United States mounted an effective force, General John J. Pershing, the American commander, expressed confidence that the American Expeditionary Force would be able to win the war by itself.[44] Tasker Bliss, the former army chief of staff assigned to the Allied Supreme War Council, brushed off British and French urgency for forces, claiming that "the time has come for the English and the French to stand fast and wait until our reinforcements can reach them in such a way as to give the final, shattering blow."[45]

On March 21, 1918, Germany launched a spring offensive, seeking to end the war before U.S. troops could arrive in force (350,000 American troops had arrived in Europe when the German offensive began).[46] Untrained, and heavily reliant on Allied shipping and supplies, U.S. forces were "a very heavy burden for a failing Entente to bear."[47] The urgency of the moment engendered some compromise from the American military leaders given full rein by President Wilson to determine the terms of U.S. involvement. Pershing relented and allowed fighting under British and French command. Because of the inadequate state of U.S. forces' proficiency, they "served mostly as replacements for Allied divisions in quiet sectors."[48]

The United States still wanted to strike a shattering blow, believing American forces were up to the task. But they were not. U.S. forces under Pershing's command went into battle with a nine-to-one advantage over second-line German troops yet barely scraped out a victory—and with heavy casualties. The British under Douglas Haig succeeded against Germany's best. While much praise has been lavished on American soldiers for turning the tide of the war, it was the fierceness of experienced Allied soldiers that won the toughest fights.

Because while the Americans lacked in the kinetic power, they had an abundance of potential: the army would burgeon from twenty-seven thousand to over two million in less than two years. By the summer of 1918, the United States was providing ten thousand soldiers per day to the Allied war effort.[49] What America contributed to the Allied war effort was less actuality than potential—but that potential turned the course of the war, precipitating the German offensive and, when it failed and German forces were pushed back to the 1918 starting line, the German peace offers of September 1917.

While the American narrative of the war is of "tireless battle with the extremism of Allied war aims," in the war's closing months, the United States actually sought to prolong it.[50] When the November 11, 1918, armistice went into effect, General Pershing objected to any terms short of unconditional surrender and ordered soldiers to continue fighting after the armistice was signed.[51] Nor was Pershing acting out of step with his political leadership; the American president was strikingly stoic about the 53,402 American combat deaths.[52] As Allen Lynch concludes, "Wilson was determined to conduct the war in such a way as to leave the United States with the maximum freedom of action at the Peace Conference."[53] For all his hesitance to join the war, Wilson proved willing to pay a very high price for the United States to be a great power and set the rules of international order. From the perspective of Wilson's aims, the war may have ended too soon, before America's full power was brought to bear.[54]

The United States was not the only power that saw opportunity in the war. Japan had been allied to Great Britain since 1902.[55] In the first week of the war in Europe, Japan offered to join the Entente if it would be allowed to take Germany's Pacific territories.[56] Japan declared war on both Germany and Austria-Hungary in August 1914, sweeping the Pacific clear of German colonial forces and taking possession of Tsingtao Province in China and the Caroline, Mariana, and Marshall Islands by November 1914.

Japan not only advanced its own territorial aspirations by joining the Entente but also crucially assisted Britain's own efforts by putting down a mutiny of Indian troops in Singapore, engaging in antisubmarine warfare against Germany, and dispatching ships to Cape Town and Malta to provide much-needed naval escorts for troop ships from Britain's dominions. So significant was Japan's contribution that it earned a seat at the table in Europe's most important diplomatic conclave since the Congress of Vienna a hundred years earlier.

Versailles

Woodrow Wilson banged up against the limits of European willingness to accept a more expansive role during postwar peace negotiations. David Stevenson characterizes Allied obduracy at Versailles as comparable to the difficulty of winning the war against Germany.[57]

Wilson had been clear, and public, about American aims both before and while America was at war. In January 1918 he published his Fourteen Points, a program seeking a "peaceful liberal capitalist world order under international law, safe both from traditional imperialism and revolutionary socialism, within whose stable liberal confines a missionary America could find moral and economic preeminence."[58] The points delineated solutions to eight specific territorial issues contested in the war, as well as advocating for free trade, free seas, open politics, impartial adjustment of colonial claims, disarmament, and a "general association of nations." Wilson termed it "a just and stable peace such as can be secured only by removing the chief provocations to war."[59] Victor Mametey more critically concludes that "the president's proposals were not a program but a creed."[60]

The peace negotiated at Versailles diverged sharply from the "peace without victory" Wilson had earlier propounded. As Marc Trachtenberg argues, there developed a "punitive undercurrent" as Germany came to be seen as the moral transgressor.[61] By the time of the Versailles conference, Wilson "was not willing to change anything in the Treaty because it was severe; that he wanted this to be a historic lesson, so that people might know that they could not do anything of the sort the Germans attempted without suffering the severest kind of punishment."[62]

That crucial shift created a common starting point for British and American policy. Lloyd George was similarly inclined, as minutes from discussions in his cabinet make clear:

> Germany had committed a great crime and it was necessary to make it impossible that anyone should be tempted to repeat that offence. At the first moment when we were in a position to put the lash on Germany's back she said, 'I give up.' The question arose whether we ought not to continue lashing her as she had lashed France. Mr. Chamberlain said that vengeance was too expensive these days. The Prime Minister said it was not vengeance but justice."[63]

French prime minister Georges Clemenceau considered justice not so readily defined.[64] More practically, the main issue France wanted addressed was the problem of German power, not national redemption. On that issue—as on several other of the worst contradictions that bedeviled the postwar peace—British and American policy aligned. Both governments avoided an enormous number of strategic questions: the totality of Germany's borders and their implications; establishment of a new balance of power or—more pointedly—how to prevent Germany from dominating Europe; that stripping Germany of its colonies would concentrate its power in Europe; the economic dependence of surrounding states on Germany; the weakness and mutual hostility of newly created sovereign states and of German minority communities within them; how to enforce the treaty in the east; and the implications of needing Germany as a "barrier to the contagion" for Bolshevism.[65]

Lloyd George's major statement of principles, the Fontainebleau Memorandum, which was hailed as a moderating force in the negotiations, was of a piece with that confused jumble of outstanding issues, because the accomodationist peace it advocated would result in German domination of Europe—precisely the outcome the war had been fought to prevent.[66]

In addition to that long list of important elements unconsidered, the treaties contained contradictory elements, such as article 10—whose territorial guarantee would require toothsome enforcement—alongside disarmament provisions. As a result, the treaties relied on Germany accepting a heavy burden of responsibility and complying voluntarily because many of the provisions were unenforceable.[67] Versailles could only work if Germany accepted its terms, was rendered too weak for effective resistance, or was enforced by victors, yet the treaties achieved none of these goals.[68]

Both the United States and Britain advanced the most impractical and destructive of these, such as the territorial "guarantee" (in which Britain was only implicated after America had committed), the severity of reparations, and war crimes trials.[69] Even on the touchiest issue of principle between Britain and the United States, self-determination, America gave ground. It allowed Britain to perpetuate its own possessions and to acquire the choicest of Germany's, and it accepted the Sykes-Picot distribution of the Middle East between Britain and France. The widest fundamental gaps at the Versailles negotiations turned out not to be between the United States and European powers but between the combined attitude of the United States and Britain from that of France and the other European powers.

Wilson proved surprisingly ineffectual at Versailles given his adroit manipulation of British vulnerability before and during the war. He did not use America's economic leverage to insist on concessions on other elements of treaty. Perhaps it represented in-experience or the effects of his failing health; or maybe the economic motives characterizing American policy prior to the war reasserted their dominance in U.S. policy.

Despite all these yawning gaps, Wilson proclaimed "the great game, now forever discredited, of the balance of power."[70] Force would be reserved for enforcing law and justice; henceforth the dis-putes among nations would be the subject of mediation rather than clandestine diplomacy or war. The League of Nations would estab-lish universal principles and practices for independent nations to resolve disputes.

Internationally, as domestically, Wilson's moralistic inflexibility contributed to his difficulties. As I. M. Destler concludes, Wilson's treaty went down to defeat because he would not make the conces-sions necessary for ratification.[71] Americans would recoil from European intrigue, returning to their historical norm of remaining isolated from the world's political machinations. The effect of American power would leave a lasting imprint on Europe, how-ever, because "what American society displayed repeatedly was its capacity to create, produce, and distribute desirable visions of pro-gress on an unrivalled, industrial scale."[72]

Over There

For the four years prior to becoming a combatant in World War I, the United States was formally neutral; in practice, it favored the Allies—and particularly Britain. The British and American govern-ments reached a tacit agreement on blockade enforcement that left

American cargoes only lightly interfered with, and the Wilson administration never did press Britain to respect freedom of the seas, as was insisted on with Germany.[73] While only an "associated" and not an "allied" power, and ostensibly fighting for "peace without victory," America threw its might behind Britain's strategy and ensured Britain achieved its aims, giving Britain more leeway than it did other powers.

The Great War shifted attention from concessions in China and Russo-Japanese rivalry back to Europe as the net of alliance systems pulled into direct conflict the powers that had been contending with America in the Pacific. Devastation wrought by European powers on each other leveled down the competition for hegemony: with the end of World War I, America was paramount.[74] Even if America's power was still largely potential, it had become the banker and provisioner of European powers. There was no obvious reason at the time, though, why European states—and particularly Britain—could not quickly regain their footing and again contest for hegemony.[75]

As American power grew, so did the nation's ambition. But that ambition was constrained by a public deeply distrustful of traditional great power politics. For the United States to assert itself internationally, it would need to be seen by its own public as an effective advocate for peace, the architect of a new kind of international order.[76] Whereas a weak United States had to settle for considering itself different from and more virtuous than others, a strong United States inexperienced in international politics sought to transform them. American policy became evangelical for self-determination and arms limitation as means to avoid the recurrence of war.

America's performance orchestrating the Great War's cessation was even grander than the Russo-Japanese peace for which Theodore Roosevelt was awarded a Nobel Prize, involving as it did an all-star supporting cast and filming on location in Versailles. In negotiating the peace of Versailles, the United States moved to center stage in European—and therefore world—politics. Woodrow Wilson basked in the international glow, playing up America as a new kind of great power, one unfettered to the base gamesmanship that had brought Europe to ruin, one seeking a peace for the ages based on principles applying equally to all states.[77] Wilson saw the opportunity to contrast America as a different kind of great power, one that established among nations those truths Americans held to be self-evident in their domestic political creed. It was an open refutation of the British international order, with its established concepts of protecting national and international sovereignty, imperial preference for trade, and markets forced open by military might.[78]

Wilson's sweeping claims for the settlement were wildly naive: revolutionizing international law "by putting morals in it," and fundamentally reshaping behavior by states such that "the very things that have always been sought in imperialistic wars are henceforth foregone by every ambitious nation in the world." These were, however, the selling points for Americans; craven as businesses might be (sugar growers in Hawaii in 1893 come to mind as a particularly egregious example), and ruthless as the practice of imperial consolidation might be, Americans still had to be cajoled and negotiated into supporting international involvement on the part of their government.[79]

Woodrow Wilson was not an adroit enough politician in 1919 to overcome concerns about the League of Nations supplanting Congress's constitutional power to declare war and the isolationist sentiment still deeply rooted in American public attitudes; he had been reelected in 1916 on the slogan "he kept us out of war." Warren

Harding was elected to the presidency in 1920 campaigning for a return to "normalcy," a major component of which was disentanglement from international, and especially European, involvement.

Another problem with Wilson's aspirations for the United States as beneficent arbiter of the international order was a strong public sentiment that American actions favored Britain too much. While Wilson argued that the Treaty of Versailles had "the purpose to see that every government dealt with in this great settlement is put in the hands of the people and taken out of the hands of coteries and of sovereigns, who had no right to rule over the people," he clearly did not intend that to apply to the British Isles. The treaty broke up the Austro-Hungarian Empire, but left Britain's colonial possessions untouched.

German and Irish Americans both mobilized in opposition to the European settlement, especially after Britain's suppression of the 1916 Easter Rising in Ireland. Wilson came surprisingly close to accusing both German and Irish Americans of treason, saying,

> There is an organized propaganda against the League of Nations and against the treaty proceeding from exactly the same sources that the organized propaganda proceeded from which threatened this country here and there with disloyalty, and I want to say—I cannot say too often—any man who carries a hyphen about with him carries a dagger that he is ready to plunge into the vitals of this Republic whenever he gets ready. If I can catch any man with a hyphen in this great contest I will know that I have got an enemy of the Republic. My fellow citizens, it is only certain bodies of foreign sympathies, certain bodies of sympathy with foreign nations that are organized against this great document which the American representatives have brought back from Paris.[80]

It was a shocking indictment of his fellow Americans, especially egregious in light of Wilson's own Anglophile policies. He claimed to object to partiality in American foreign policy, yet he practiced it himself.

That immigrant communities would have strong allegiances to their places of origin was not new in American politics—indeed, it is what Henry John Temple, Third Viscount Palmerston feared of American democracy in the 1860s. Wilson's agitation against German and Irish Americans was an attempt to mark as un-American opposition to his foreign policy. He was unsuccessful; the public was not persuaded that the two immigrant groups were uniquely invidious. They simply practiced effectively the sympathies many other immigrant Americans felt in reaction to events in or directed toward their countries of origin. Wilson failed to organize the countervailing forces and groups; his foreign policy can be seen as both the high water mark of American internationalist ambitions and of American activism on Britain's agenda as America became the hegemon of the international order.

If Wilson was outplayed, he did succeed in tapping into a widespread public desire for an end to the grasping power politics that visited upon the combatants' societies a seemingly senseless devastation.[81] America had always been a moralizer in international politics, despite the moral disfigurement of its own domestic practices of slavery and Indian extermination, and even when its international practice was indistinguishable from other great powers. Europe's carnage called into question its emulation, and America began striking virtuous poses as an advocate of negotiated peace and economic interdependence.[82]

America had often exemplified the aspirations of people yearning to be free; with its entry into World War I and its conduct of the postwar peace negotiations, it put the best elements of its domestic political ideology on a pedestal not only as the most virtuous organization of relations between a people and their government but also as the form of government least likely to be predatory internationally. As Adam Tooze concludes, "The Great War may have begun in the eyes of many participants as a clash of empires, a classic great power war, but it ended as something far more morally and politically charged—a crusading victory for a coalition that proclaimed itself the champion of a new world order."[83] It only ended that way because of American involvement.

10

Imposing Power:
The Washington Naval Treaties

> ### The Washington Naval Treaties
>
> *November 1921* The United States convenes the Washington Naval Conference to forestall an arms race among countries with security interests in the Pacific.
>
> *February 1922* Treaties decide the limiting of naval armaments by type and tonnage in national distributions of five (United States); five (Britain); three (Japan); one (France) and one (Italy).

Wariness of international involvement characteristic of an earlier, weaker America reasserted itself as an enduring national trait in the aftermath of World War I.[1] By 1920 the ghastly pointlessness of the war, the advance of democracy in other countries, and the concentration by Great Britain on European power and colonial connection made the English Channel once again seem narrow and the Atlantic Ocean wide. Affection underlying the "special relationship" endured (as in some quarters did the newfound racial commonality of Anglo-Saxonism), but belief was transitory by governments of the United States and Great Britain that their interests were fundamentally the same and their power cumulative.[2] As Adam Tooze concludes, "Britain's governments in the 1920s again and again found themselves confronting the painful fact that the United States was a power unlike any other. It had emerged, quite suddenly, as a novel kind of 'super-state', exercising a veto over the financial and security concerns of the other major states of the world."[3]

At the Versailles negotiations in 1919, the United States attempted to bring forth a new kind of international order, one in which it offered its continuing involvement for revision to existing rules. In this, President Woodrow Wilson was unsuccessful, both at home and abroad: the American public recoiled from the commitments and the "'great' powers in Europe" were not willing to accept American leadership.[4] At Washington in 1921, the United States began to achieve a changing of the rules with a set of treaties to voluntarily restrain the means of war, achieved by diplomacy conducted in public. This marks the moment at which Britain ceded primacy to the United States.[5]

In 1921 the United States convened a disarmament negotiation among the naval powers of the Pacific. At the Washington Naval Conference, France, Great Britain, Italy, Japan, and the United States agreed to discontinue their capital ship programs and build no more for ten years; to reduce their fleets of battleships and carriers to agreed ratios; and not to fortify their holdings in the Pacific.[6] These measures were in conjunction with other treaties that grappled with the political and economic issues driving geopolitical competition in East Asia: Japan withdrew from Shantung and Siberia, China was opened to trade on an equal basis, and the Anglo-Japanese alliance was replaced by a four-power consultative treaty.

The treaties were a triumph for America. President Warren G. Harding recognized flagging support for the aggressive 1916 ship-building program and bartered it away, gaining equality with the world's dominant maritime power, contained Japan's rise, and reduced the threat of Anglo-Japanese cooperation. Harding's administration believed the Washington Treaties would prevent war, cost less, and have more public appeal than continued naval building programs.[7] The president drew worldwide acclaim for his opening statement claiming that "our hundred millions want less of armament and none of war."[8]

The United States viewed the fleet ratios capping its navy and Great Britain's at parity as a means for Britain to limit the challenge to its supremacy of the seas; Britain viewed the limit as pejorative, given the three-ocean requirement of its empire. Great Britain was, however, wholly ineffective in convincing the Harding government that the Royal Navy ought to have its superior requirements acknowledged. Even worse from the British perspective, "this conference worked because the US threatened to enter into an arms race with Britain and bankrupt her if Britain did not agree."[9]

The United States also forced an end to the Anglo-Japanese defense alliance on which Britain relied to balance its exclusion from European alliances, manage its trading interests in China, and protect the approaches to the jewel in the crown of its empire.[10] A risen America was willing to impose its power on Great Britain to achieve the broader goal of shaping the international order.

The most striking element of the Washington Naval Treaties, though, is that their fundamental purpose was to prevent Anglo-American competition.[11] Britain was still the world's paramount naval force; in tonnage and number of ships, the Royal Navy equaled the rest of the world combined.[12] But America and Japan were rising fast; postwar Britain was unable to match their naval spending and conscious of its evaporating hegemony. For all the political, economic, and cultural similarities celebrated in the Great Rapprochement between Britain and the United States, by 1922 it was American power—not Japanese—that most concerned the British government. Winston Churchill cautioned that the United States would "have a good chance of becoming the strongest Naval Power in the world and thus obtaining the complete mastery of the Pacific."[13] Britain had enabled America's rise; as America pulled abreast, both countries ceased to believe the interests of the two countries were indivisible. Britain's colonial policies and alliance with Japan made suspect any claims of special relationship with the United States. A contending America was again viewed as competitor, untrustworthy and dangerously naive for all its strength. If the British did not regret their policy of enabling America's rise, they unquestionably saw the error of reliance on an imperial America behaving in the same manner as imperial Britain did.

Threat Assessment

Even as Britain and America seemed to the rest of the world to be a cumulative force, competition between them reemerged, and not just in ideas about the organizing principles of the international system. Traditional great power contentions over trade and maritime control crept back into their evaluations of each other as early 1917, with Prime Minister David Lloyd George and President Woodrow Wilson's special envoy at Versailles worrying that Anglo-American military competition could become as invidious as that between Britain and Germany leading up to World War I.[14]

One reason for this had been Britain's 1902 alliance with Japan. Britain's policy of splendid isolation, practiced by governments across especially the latter half of the nineteenth century, was perhaps less a strategic choice than putting a brave face on the lack of alternatives: it was excluded from international alliances as much as it chose to spurn them. The same calculus that had led the prime minister, Robert Arthur Talbot Gascoyne-Cecil, Third Marquess of Salisbury, to change policy and embrace America during the 1895 Venezuela debt crisis led the British government to actively seek collusion unsuccessfully with Germany and Russia; Britain found a willing ally only in a modernizing and militarizing Japan. And while the treaty was explicitly limited to Asia, it galled Washington that Britain's need to support Japan during the Russo-Japanese War prevented constructive engagement in Theodore Roosevelt's peace process, and that Britain continued its allegiance to Japan even after the collapse of German and Russian prospects (the ostensible motivation for the alliance).[15] Even though the United States rejected matrimony with Great Britain, it still expected monogamy. The Anglo-Japanese defense alliance called into question just how special the American alignment was for Britain.

In the early years of World War I, American strategists anticipated that whichever European collective won the war would surge out of it to be a serious threat to American global interests; only late in the war was it apparent that none of the Europeans would emerge victorious. During the time of American neutrality, its navy constituted about 11 percent of global power projection, one-third of Britain's punch and slightly less than Germany's. While European great powers were busy destroying each other, the United States continued the military buildup Mahan had theorized and McKinley had launched.

The General Board, established to determine military requirements, concluded in 1912 that the necessity of protecting the Panama canal, Pacific bases, and trade ought to result in an American navy of greater size than the next two contenders—a wholesale importation of Britain's "two power" naval force sizing standard. The 1916 Naval Act planned to build that American navy within a decade, at a cost of $500 million, a Mahanian dream come true. Within the first three years, the act appropriated funds for construction of ten battleships, six battle cruisers, ten scout cruisers, and fifty destroyers.

The explicit purpose of the 1916 naval program was to bring Britain's naval supremacy to an end. In the Great War, Britain had imposed a naval blockade over U.S. objections, curtailing American commerce in continental Europe and spurring the German submarine warfare that ultimately brought the United States into a war it ardently wished to forgo. The 1916 naval program was adopted to ensure Britain would not in future have that option.[16]

The British government initially thought restraint in its shipbuilding program would dissuade the Americans from continuing with the 1916 program after the end of the war; it did not. At Versailles, Prime Minister Lloyd George tried to bundle the League of Nations that President Wilson so wanted with a naval limitation agreement that maintained British dominance of the seas; Wilson refused.[17] Lloyd George gamely made another attempt in 1919, and it was likewise rejected.

Wilson made his argument to Americans for support of the League of Nations as the only alternative to "building a navy second to none." In consequence, the public anticipated an arms buildup when the Senate rejected the League.[18] That the United States was determined to either constrain the naval competition or win it is clear from Wilson successor Harding's description of the American approach to the Washington negotiations: "We'll talk sweetly and patiently to them at first; but if they don't agree then we'll say 'God damn you, if it's a race, then the United States is going to go to it.'"[19]

Public support for the approach proved shallow, however. When Harding brought forward spending bills continuing the 1916 naval program, the Navy Bill was only approved in the Senate with an amendment advocating a 50 percent reduction in shipbuilding by the United States, Britain, and Japan as an alternative the president should pursue.[20] The Congress preferred restraint by the major naval powers to a competition among them.

Even with spending reductions on the horizon, the United States had already achieved a powerful navy; by 1920, the Office of Naval Operations estimated that American capital ships already built or authorized by Congress were "sufficient to assure the United States of superiority in battle forces over Britain and Japan for some years."[21] The Anglo-Japanese alliance was a central concern for the General Board, which "conceived that the alliance could only be directed against the United States."[22] The American navy began developing war plans to handle a "red-orange contingency"—a war against both Britain and Japan.

If Wilson lost the peace of Versailles through an inability to persuade his country to participate in it, Britain may be said to have won it, achieving acceptance of all the private agreements between the Allies about colonial mandates, attribution to Germany as the sole cause of the war, and severe reparations.[23] As Eric Goldstein summarizes, "The Paris peace had established the framework of a post-war order which was generally congenial to Britain; Germany had been reduced to a manageable size for European equilibrium, France had been prevented from achieving western European hegemony, the League of Nations enshrined British principles without undue British commitments, and the richest colonial spoils had passed to Britain through the facility of League mandates."[24]

The principal postwar British concern was "how to protect Britain's position as the center of a world economic system."[25] The weight of debt on Britain coming out of the war argued for speedy resumption of revenue-producing activity, and the least damaged markets were in Asia. Britain's comparative advantages were numerous relative to other European powers: Germany was hobbled, and Russia was consumed with its revolution and in tatters from defeat by Japan and losses in the Great War. An early mover advantage was in view for Britain if ways could be found to limit American and Japanese power.

The United States played an outsize role in that evaluation, as during the war it had reversed the flow of capital that Britain had seeded into America's westward expansion. Britain was deeply in debt to the United States, had lost non-European market share to American businesses, was experiencing domestic unrest with the return to the labor force of its soldiery, and felt its economic constraints. The British ambassador in Washington wrote bitterly that "they look for the opportunity to treat us as a vassal state so long as the debt remains unpaid."[26]

Prime Minister Lloyd George insisted "friendly co-operation with the United States is for us a cardinal principle, dictated by what seems to us the proper nature of things, dictated by instinct quite as much as by reason and common sense." The Foreign Office supported that view, but wistfully noted that "if we were able to count with certainty upon the active cooperation of the United States, the need for an alliance with Japan would not be apparent."[27] Yet Foreign Minister George Curzon admitted that "official relations with the American Government almost ceased to exist, and for ten months we practically did no business with America at all."[28] Winston Churchill believed Britain was about to "drift into direct naval rivalry with the United States."[29]

Foreign policy, as always, bedeviled the British government; it had never truly felt the strength of its dominance in the years it was the hegemon of the world order, and it felt its postwar weakness keenly. On the Continent, revolutions toppled monarchial governments in Austria-Hungary, Germany, and Russia. Germany was tightly constrained by the Versailles agreement, but France—a preoccupation nearly as worrisome as Germany—was sowing resentment in Germany with the "most vengeful policies towards a defeated enemy since Tamerlane at Aleppo and Damascus."[30]

Maritime power remained Britain's comparative advantage among European states and the connective tissue of its empire; both the United States and Japan were chomping at the bit to overtake Britain and thereby demonstrate their arrival in the sea lanes of power. The Japanese challenge was dealt with by alliance that accepted Japanese land acquisitions in East Asia in return for that nation's cooperation against Russia and Germany. Having failed to contain the American challenge by negotiated limits, Britain's alternative was to enter overtly into strategic competition with the United States, the creditor of its extensive wartime debt and supposed inseparable friend, and cinch tighter its "unsympathetic alliance" with Japan.[31]

In the run-up to negotiations in Washington, internal British government criticism of the United States became pronounced. An assessment prepared for the British delegation cautioned that, "in point of fact, their conduct is often erratic, inconsistent and bears the stamp of political inexperience."[32] Britain's dominions were likewise leery of American policies, considering the United States an improbable ally, less predictable than Japan, and not to be relied upon for security.[33] Canada's representative was the most suspicious of American motives in calling the conference, viewing it as a means to get past public opposition and construct the largest navy in the world, allowing the United States to be "a law unto itself."[34]

Negotiations

The British government tried in vain to preface the Washington conference with a bilateral set of Anglo-American negotiations; "the main object of the conversation would be to induce the United States of America to make a concession and to abandon her intention to build a great Navy."[35] The American government did not provide Britain that opportunity—neither the concession nor even the meeting—and kept its proposals secret until the conference opened.

Once the American proposals for fleet limits were presented at the conference, the scope of British government derision expanded further: As Foreign Office Chief of the Far Eastern Division, Victor Wellesley, noted, "The extraordinary nebulosity and ignorance displayed in these tentative proposals suggest such a complete lack of grasp of the situation on the part of the United States Government that nothing short of a regular course of education seems to offer the slightest chance of the matter being put on anything like a rational basis."[36] In fact, the Americans had carefully thought through the "naval holiday": the "stop now" proposals would have ended construction in all classes of capital ships. The negotiations produced treaties that limited tonnage, armaments, ship types and expansion of facilities. In particular, battleships, cruisers, and aircraft carriers were each subject to numerical limits; submarines and destroyers were limited by magnitude to ten tons' displacement. The ratios of ships assigned nations were explicit:

Country	Ships	Displacement (tons)
United States	5	525,000
Great Britain	5	525,000
Japan	3	315,000
France	1.67	175,000
Italy	1.67	175,000

Britain argued for a larger apportionment, 150 percent of the American allotment of cruisers and destroyers, because its imperial responsibilities dictated a three-ocean navy, whereas America operated only in the Atlantic and Pacific oceans and Japan in the Pacific alone. The United States countered that Britain was allied with Japan (and France) and thus already had the benefit of an overall numerical superiority as well as reinforcement in its third ocean of operations. Secretary of State Charles Evans Hughes cautioned that the Japanese connection was turning American public attitudes against Britain.[37]

Britain also sought abolition of submarines as a class, their utility having been devastatingly demonstrated by the Germans in the war, but it was not successful in this. Great Britain achieved no meaningful alteration to any of the American proposals; in fact, Britain alone among the powers represented at the conference failed to preserve its central objective. As a measure of relative influence, Japan and France attained the two major changes to the treaties.

The French went into negotiations with the perspective that "the pretended disarmament of the accords of Washington is not a disarmament of peace, but a disarmament of war. All the powers that participated have argued with the idea of being able, if the occasion arises, to make war in the best conditions and cheaper."[38] Demonstrating once again the French flair for grand conceptualization, the government of Aristide Briand outlined its objectives for the conference as concluding a Franco-American security arrangement, positioning itself to mediate between Britain and America or, at a minimum, reviving the Versailles proposal for an Anglo-American guarantee for France against Germany.[39] None of those prospects were attainable.

Illustrative of just how powerful America had become, and how much the Anglo-American rapprochement had faded, the French designed their negotiating position to preserve a fleet "sufficient to tip the balance in war between the United States and Great Britain."[40] It insisted to that end that "auxiliary ships"—light cruisers and submarines—be excluded from limitation. Despite concerns by Briand that "the rupture of the conference . . . will put us opposite the English and American war debts," the French government held fast.[41] A position taken in order to maximize potential influence with the United States so alienated America that Secretary Hughes considered excluding the French midway through the negotiation.[42] France's successful protection of auxiliary ships would accelerate development of the "treaty cruiser" compliant with the treaties' limits on ten thousand tons and gunned at less than 8" caliber, redirecting naval competition in the interwar years.[43]

The Japanese government attained the other significant diversion from American intentions for the Washington Naval Treaties. Japan gained an important concession with article 19, which prevented fortification of Pacific bases. Both the United States and Britain wanted defenses for their far-flung Pacific possessions; Japan ensured their vulnerability in striking distance of its home operating bases. To attain that and to constrain the American naval building program, the Japanese government accepted a limit only 60 percent of the British and American ceilings, withdrew from Shantung and Siberia, and sacrificed the Anglo-Japanese defense treaty.[44]

The American proposals were accepted in principal on the second day of the conference; the treaties were completed in less than four months,[45] and the Harding administration was thrilled. Secretary of State Hughes proclaimed, "this treaty ends, absolutely ends, the race in competitive armament."[46] President Harding delivered the treaties to Congress in person; Senator Henry Cabot Lodge masterfully navigated the ratification process to prevent a repetition of the League of Nations' fate.[47]

That the treaties were not all the administration claimed was recognized at the time. Even American commentators noted that "without minimizing the achievements of the conference, it is well to recall that the problems of land armaments, submarines, naval vessels under 10,000 tons and aircraft remain."[48] The British government concluded it was unilaterally disadvantaged, fretting that "it would be a most serious matter if as a result of the Washington Conference Great Britain were the only power to be disarmed," and the Air Staff estimated that, consistent with the treaty limits, France could drop thirty-one tons per day of bombs on London.[49] Britain's first sea lord, Admiral David Beatty, considered the agreement as surrendering supremacy of the sea to America and threatened to resign "rather than go down to posterity as the First Sea Lord in office at the time such a shameful decision" was made.[50] Yet Britain did adopt the treaties, in a tangible acceptance of the new rules America was establishing as its power became dominant.

Denouement

The Washington Naval Treaties didn't actually prevent competition in armaments; they just redirected it away from battleships, rewarding conversion of existing ships and spurring development of new concepts and technologies.[51] The treaties had no verification provisions, and as the Pacific arms race they sought to prevent gathered momentum in the late 1920s, cheating became rampant. The United States and Japan proved the most innovative adapters in skirting the treaty's terms. America rebuilt nine of the fifteen ships originally slated for destruction and improved existing ship classes with antiaircraft and antitorpedo defenses. Both Japan and America pressed forward with submarine development and utilization of ship-borne aircraft, catapulting forward into carrier-based fleets.

Japan was perhaps the treaty's main beneficiary, gaining as it did the status of inclusion in a major international undertaking, recognition of its control in Manchuria and Mongolia, and some ability to constrain the growing American fleet presence in East Asia. Article 19 of the treaty left unprotected British and American Pacific bases; Japan would use this provision to great advantage in the next war.

If Britain could be said to have won the peace after World War I, it could also be said to have lost the postwar disarmament race. The treaties have been described by an eminent British historian as "one of the major catastrophes of English history" for conceding Britain's maritime supremacy, limiting the classes of war ships predominant in the Royal Navy and determinative of its operations, and allowing the United States to sever the Anglo-Japanese alliance.[52]

As Britain had the world's most powerful navy, the restraints in the Washington Naval Treaties did have a disproportionate effect on Britain's power. Fleet reductions in the treaties were greatest for Britain, which had to scrap twenty extant capital ships. Hulls already laid for *Nelson*- and *Rodney*-class ships had to be redesigned for smaller displacements to remain within Britain's apportionment (these would come to be referred to as "cherry tree classes" because they were chopped down by Washington). In constraining dread-naught ships, the Washington Naval Treaties checked Britain's strongest suit. And while creative accounting by America found ways to rebuild most of its restricted ships, Britain's postwar financial straits meant that it only rebuilt four of fifteen. Still, to the extent the treaties were deleterious to the British Navy, it is largely because the British Admiralty was slower to innovate than navies of the other treaty powers.

If the Washington Naval Treaties diverted competition from the arena of British dominance, why did the United Kingdom agree to the deal? Principally because the British government believed they would lose the competition in Asia as it was shaping up. Britain's central interest was protecting their dominions of Australia and New Zealand, and imperial possessions of Hong Kong and Singa-pore. While the British fleet was nearly three times the size of the American one at the start of World War I, the United States had achieved rough naval parity by the end of the war. The American economy had three times the gross domestic product of Britain in 1922 (and six times that of Japan). Britain had not yet recovered from the financial expenditure of World War I, and confidence was de-clining that it could regain its footing on anything like the ground it had stood before the war. So Britain probably couldn't afford to carry out the government's shipbuilding program, whereas Amer-ica clearly could.[53] And, in keeping with the narrative of British in-dustrial decline, British government civilians and opinion shapers worried the dreadnaught race had "caused" World War I, which gave further impetus to disarmament rather than buildup of military capacity.

The British government failed to achieve many of the preferential deals it argued for, but the treaties were not the disaster so often claimed. It was a reasonable bet, and the outcome probably did produce a balance of power more conducive to Britain's interests than a shipbuilding program would have.[54] The treaties averted a massive expense at a time Britain could ill afford it; clamped down on Japanese and American shipbuilding programs; constrained to parity or below the development of maritime power in both America and Japan for a decade; preserved positive diplomatic relationships with all the treaty powers for a decade; ensured bases throughout the Pacific would not be fortified against them; and gained formal approval of its open-door trading policy.[55] Even within the constraints of the treaties, Britain built six aircraft carriers between 1920 and World War II. It was a huge success to contain an American maritime challenge "far more dangerous to Britain than that which suffused German foreign policy before 1914."[56]

Although the United States had to decommission two *Lexington*-class cruisers, it converted them to aircraft carriers (often cited as evidence America had the shift to carriers planned). Yet at the time the Washington Naval Treaties were being negotiated, the Department of the Navy had a low opinion of naval aviation, considered the conversion only "slightly preferred to scrapping." The American navy remained under the carrier limit until 1933, and only built with real intent when New Deal funding became available and Japan withdrew from the treaties the following year.

It proves bad luck that Britain had built five treaty-compliant ships just before Japan unraveled the treaty and others leapt forward, but it does not prove the treaties were themselves disastrous for Britain. The outsize destructive effect many British military historians attribute to the Washington Naval Treaties is perhaps less a function of the agreements themselves than the adamancy with which the British Admiralty remained committed to the battleship rather than shifting the navy's fulcrum to the submarine or aircraft carrier, and the misfortune that removable armor proved less revolutionary than carrier-based aircraft.[57] By Britain persevering in the belief that battleships would be required to win critical engagements (holding faster to the ideas of Alfred Thayer Mahan than did Americans), with submarines and airpower operationally limited to attrition roles, the other treaty states did overtake British naval supremacy.

The End of Anglo-Saxony

The Washington Naval Treaties conclusively proved that America had not only supplanted Britain as the most powerful country in the international order but also that Britain's strategy of harnessing American might to British interests quickly faltered. Britain's calculations in becoming party to the treaties only make sense if Britain believed the United States was likely to be an antagonist to its interests. What Britain was doing in signing on to the treaties was preventing an arms race with America. The special relationship so fulsomely expressed by Theodore Roosevelt and William Howard Taft in 1904 would not have necessitated this outcome. But, in fact, Britain was more confident of cooperation with Japan in Asia than it was of cooperation with the United States. That is the change evidenced by the Washington Naval Treaties. If Britain really believed in the special relationship, it could leave American naval power unconstrained—in fact, it should desire American power to be unlimited.

But Britain did not have that confidence in 1923. A major reason why it did not was the emerging universalism in American foreign policy. In 1923 America looked like one among many international players Britain had to manage their interests with a weather eye toward. Britain's acute problem in providing ground forces to defend its imperial possessions was not allayed by the special relationship with the United States; its need for other allies, and the nature of those allies, frayed the sense of unique sameness between Britain and America. When America was a rising power, Britain looked like the only country in the international order that shared America's values; as a risen power, America saw the potential to create an entire international order that shared its values. Britain had become only one among many.

The next iteration of naval negotiations would founder in 1927 on a "sharp divergence of view between the United States and Great Britain."[58] Baron Robert Vansittart, former head of the Foreign Office America Department and subsequent diplomatic advisor to the prime minister, captured the shift in British attitudes in 1927:

> A war with America would indeed be the most futile and damnable of all, but it is not "unthinkable," and we shall the more surely avoid it by cutting that word from our vocabulary. If it is childish—and it is—to suppose that two nations must forever be enemies, it is also childish to stake one's whole existence on the gamble that two must forever be friends (especially when they never have been really).[59]

The Washington Naval Treaties show the British-American collusion coming apart: the fundamental truth is that Britain would not have signed the treaties if it had not needed to constrain American power. There would have been no need to prevent an arms race between the naval powers operating in East Asia if Great Britain and

America had remained in the state of grace wherein Britain considered American military power additive to its own.

The United States also saw Britain differently from how it had during the Spanish-American War heyday. At Versailles in 1919, the United States had given Britain its choice terms and Germany's best colonies. At Washington in 1922, the United States made no special provision for the demands of Britain's colonial holdings, further hemming in British power by forcing an end to the Anglo-Japanese defense alliance. Britain had become just another European power for a hegemonic America to deal with. The vaunted Anglo-Saxon communion essential to Britain's strategy proved unattainable because the United States envisioned a different international order than did Britain, and used its growing power to try and change the rules of order.

11

Sharp Relief: World War II

World War II

1940 The Destroyers for Bases Agreement transfers fifty American cruisers to Britain in return for ninety-nine-year leases on British bases in the western hemisphere.

January 1941 Harry Hopkins mission to London to determine whether Britain could hold out against Nazi Germany.

January 1941 Franklin Delano Roosevelt directs the Joint Chiefs of Staff to plan on the basis of a Europe-first war effort.

March 1941 The Lend-Lease program extends $50 billion in U.S. assistance to thirty countries fighting Nazi Germany.

July 1941 Hopkins mission to Moscow to determine whether the Soviet Union could hold out against Nazi Germany.

August 1941 Atlantic Charter commits the United States and Great Britain to "the right of all peoples to choose the government under which they will live" and other principles for the war effort. Joint military planning commences.

February–July 1942 The United States repeatedly threatens to shift the war effort to the Pacific unless Britain commits to a cross-channel attack.

1942–1943 General Douglas MacArthur and Admiral Ernest King refuse offers of British forces out of concern the United States will be associated with restoration of Britain's colonies.

November 1943 Franklin Delano Roosevelt and Joseph Stalin discuss ideas for Indian independence at the Yalta Conference.

1944 Winston Churchill's plan for postwar British-U.S. integration: merged military and diplomatic staffs, joint citizenship.

The relationship between Great Britain and United States during the Second World War was unique in the American experience. No country before or since has had such intimate involvement in American governmental decisions as Britain had, such fulsome knowledge and participation in the programs and strategies by which America engages with the world. Nor had Britain previously given itself over to a relationship that violated Henry John Temple, Third Viscount Palmerston's axiom of there being no permanent friends, only permanent interests. In facing the enormity of threats looming on both the Pacific and European fronts, Britain and America cooperated to an extraordinary degree, merging intelligence, weapons programs, military planning, command, and operations; developing a common strategy and resource prioritization; and developing a vision for a postwar international order.[1] Indeed, the very idea of a special relationship is the product of World War II collaboration.[2]

This deep and abiding cooperation between Britain and America serves to camouflage the awkward adjustment of Britain from status of rule setter to subject in an American-dominated international order. Britain actively cultivated the notion of a special relationship in order to maximize potential influence over a country that understood its superiority of strength.[3] By the time Britain was at war in 1939, the differential between the two countries was enormous and would be revealed still more fulsomely over the course of the war. Even in the depths of its Great Depression, American gross domestic product was almost three times that of Britain; debts outstanding from Britain to the United States were in excess of $11 billion and still unremitted after 1932.[4] Relative to the United States, Britain never recovered its stature after World War I.

Also over the course of the war would be revealed the rules of order the United States would establish as its power became the defining element of the postwar international order. If the 1922 Washington Naval Treaties show a rising America beginning to set terms for interaction between states, the terms of British-American interaction in the lead up to and conduct of the war reveal the extent to which America would impose not just its power but also its ideology on those terms.

That ideology clashed most directly with British interests on the question of colonialism. American opposition would increase with time to both the commercial advantages and political subjugation Britain's practice entailed. It is not enough to say in rebuttal that the United States, too, was an imperial power in the interwar years, because America had recoiled from being an empire soon after becoming one. President Woodrow Wilson had begun the process of normalization with American colonies in 1916, transitioning Puerto

Ricans into American citizenship and getting the Congress (controlled by his party) to pass legislation promising Philippine independence. He also shifted the basis of relations toward cooperative involvement with states in the western hemisphere and encouraged their democratization—policies that were sustained by succeeding American governments. The United States stopped marshaling military forces to back up its economic policies.

America suspected throughout wartime cooperation that British choices were designed to deliver U.S. power for the preservation of Britain's empire. Britain's relationship with Japan, the terms of the Lend-Lease program, decisions about where to attack Germany, planning for the postwar order, and Britain sending troops to the Pacific after V-E Day were all affected by disagreement between Britain and the United States over Britain's empire.[5] In those disputes, America explicitly tied its assistance to an end of British imperial policies, both political and economic. It also threatened American support for insurrection in British dominions if Britain did not comply. For all its warmth, the special relationship did not extend to sustaining the sole remaining basis for outsize British power in the international order.

In fact, many in the British government believed America used its expansive power to force Britain into a weaker standing.[6] That view from London probably gives Britain too much credit, however, assuming as it does that American efforts were directed uniquely at Britain. In fact, the United States was looking past Britain as it attempted to shape an international order in which American domestic political structures and practices could be universalized and in that way the international order made peaceful. If a diminished Britain were a consequence of setting new rules to make the order governable on American terms, that was a price—even in the closest political affinity the United States had ever experienced with another country—that America was willing to pay.

The British-American special relationship served a crucial and abiding purpose for American hegemony, however: it taught the United States the importance of setting rules to legitimate its power. During World War II, Britain limbered America up for multilateralism, which would become the means by which postwar America established and cost-effectively sustained its dominance of the international order.

An Anglo-Japanese Special Relationship

Wilson's proposals at Versailles, the Washington Naval Treaties, and the Kellogg-Briand Pact (the 1928 treaty that renounced war as an instrument of policy) had done much to create a sense of the United States as both naive and ambitious. As Frank Kendall concludes, "No nation was less prepared psychologically for the maneuvering and bargaining that had traditionally constituted international diplomacy and war avoidance."[7]

The British keenly felt the pinch of their constraints in the 1930s. The government was constantly troubled by the gap between defense requirements for sustaining its empire and available resources. Friction with the United States over war debt was constant; in 1934, Congress passed the Johnson Act, denying credit to countries that had not repaid their World War I loans; David Reynolds notes that "the 1930s as a whole were a decade of Anglo-American suspicion and estrangement."[8] Britain had demanding problems to manage, and the United States was little help.

In April 1934, the government of Japan announced its Amau Doctrine, declaring (in tones unmistakably similar to some elements of America's Monroe Doctrine) itself arbiter of China's sovereignty and determiner of the rules of trade in Asia. British prime minister Neville Chamberlain considered Japan's domination of Manchuria a regional issue (rather than one infringing on Britain's interests) and sought an agreement with Japan, believing that country "willing to pay a price" for good relations.[9] He proposed ending the numerical limitations imposed in the Washington Naval Treaties; Japan countered with a nonaggression pact that Chamberlain took seriously enough to put before his cabinet for consideration.[10]

Franklin Delano Roosevelt's reaction to the prospect of Britain once again allied with Japan was the threat that if Britain continued to "play with Japan," the United States would commence agitating in the British dominions "in a definite effort to make [them] understand clearly that their future security is linked with us in the United States."[11] The threat of American ability to work effectively in Britain's restive dominions that the administration of Abraham Lincoln had hinted at during the American Civil War was overtly proffered in 1934. America's political culture was no longer unique in 1934—World War I had finally destroyed both restrictions on democratic participation and many of the class prohibitions on social mobility in Britain—but the empire continued to be vulnerable to such threats.

Chamberlain was sufficiently alarmed by the American reaction that he reconsidered the bilateral agreement, instead convening another multilateral naval conference in London. Japan refused to sign up to the arms limits in London. The United States, however, made an extraordinary proposal to the British. The U.S. "neutralization plan" for the Pacific would have abrogated the Washington Treaties' restriction on fortifications, provided American funding for British fortifications in Hong Kong and Singapore, committed the

United States to bilateral naval parity, and even exchange ships' officers between the British and American fleets.[12] This astonishingly good deal was rejected by the British government, its Foreign Office considering it "a little too naïve and simplistic," and Chamberlain disdaining American "meddling in the affairs of Europe."[13]

The Lend-Lease Program

By 1940, the British government was pleading for American meddling in the affairs of Europe; Prime Minister Winston Churchill wrote to Roosevelt, "I trust you realize, Mr. President, that the voice and force of the United States may count for nothing if they are withheld too long."[14] Congress had passed the Fourth Neutrality Act, allowing cash sale of weapons to belligerents—a big step in principle, but one that had little meaning in practice.[15] Roosevelt used that authority to negotiate the Destroyers for Bases Agreement, trading fifty old U.S. cruisers to the British in return for ninety-nine-year leases on British air and naval bases from Newfoundland to the Caribbean, and the promise that if Britain surrendered to Germany, its fleet would be sent abroad.[16] The deal adroitly circumvented the America military's objections to sending war materials that might be needed by U.S. forces to Britain, set conditions for Britain's potential armistice negotiations with Germany, gained for the United States stronger defense positions in the western hemisphere, and thereby assured congressional and public support.[17]

Public opposition remained formidable to greater involvement from the United States in order to save Britain from the fate that had consumed Austria, Belgium, Czechoslovakia, Denmark, France, Luxembourg, the Netherlands, Norway, and Poland. The current was still strong enough in 1940 that Roosevelt had to insist throughout the presidential campaign that "your boys are not going to be sent into any foreign wars."[18]

Other countries continuing to send their boys to war was essential to Roosevelt keeping that promise—especially Great Britain and the Soviet Union, the two European powers still standing against Nazi Germany. In January 1941, Roosevelt sent confidant Harry Hopkins to London to assess Britain's ability to hold out. Hopkins's mission was a welcome encouragement in Britain, especially his message that "the President is determined that we shall win the war together. . . . Make no mistake about it. He has sent me here to tell you that at all costs and by all means he will carry you through, no matter what happens to him—there is nothing that he will not do so far as he has human power."[19] The Churchill government in 1941 and exponents of the Anglo-American relationship since have played up the importance of the Hopkins mission and the personal nature of connection to the American president, but the use of envoys and opaque lines of authority that keep contributors feeling uniquely important but Roosevelt's options open was characteristic of his political style and may not signify especial importance. The mission did, however, provide Roosevelt confidence that Britain would hold out, and merited American support.

Lend-Lease legislation in March 1941 permitted extension of assistance "to any country whose defense the President deems vital to the defense of the US," which ended up being thirty countries at a cost of over $50 billion. The program was not only an "unequivocal declaration of economic warfare," but hinted at direct American military involvement, since the U.S. Navy was authorized to escort convoys delivering the equipment.[20] Repayment for the equipment was deferred, and not explicitly required in U.S. dollars; what was explicit was the trade of support in the war for agreement to participation in a liberalized postwar international economic order—that is, the American order.

That the United States didn't press Britain over Hong Kong or imperial preference in setting Lend-Lease parameters suggests it wanted to sustain British strength in the course of the war, but set different rules for after the war had been won.[21]

The Roosevelt administration was anxious to extend participation in the Lend-Lease program to the Soviet Union in order to forestall its capitulation to Germany. As he had before extending assistance to Britain, Roosevelt sent Henry Hopkins to Moscow to determine whether the Soviet Union had the grit to continue fighting Nazi Germany.[22] Asked by Hopkins (as he had Churchill in London) what the United States could do to assist the Soviet war effort, Joseph Stalin requested an announcement from Roosevelt that the United States would join the war against Adolf Hitler—that is, the Soviet Union was angling for the same outcome Britain wanted. But whereas Britain would campaign throughout the war to harness American power under British military leadership, Stalin asked Hopkins to "tell the President that he would welcome American troops on any part of the Russian front" under American command.[23]

Churchill shrewdly tried to insinuate Britain into the U.S.-Soviet relationship, cabling Stalin in advance of the Hopkins mission to position Britain as an intermediary and guarantor of U.S. involvement. Hopkins delivered a rather different outcome: he proposed to Stalin a trilateral U.S.–British–Soviet Union conference on "strategic interests" to align their war efforts.[24] The bilateral special relationship Britain wanted among the English-speaking peoples looked of greater interest to the United States as a more general conclave of anti-Nazi states.

America offered the Soviet Union $1 billion in assistance, giving it precedence over aid to Britain and more favorable terms.[25] British economic planners suspected easier terms were on offer not because of the relative poverty of China and the Soviet Union but because, unlike Great Britain, they were not American economic rivals.[26] Even with Britain's hold on Suez faltering, imperiling also Britain's control over India, America had competing priorities.

Britain's priority, as stated by Churchill, was "to get the Americans into the war."[27] When Roosevelt and Churchill met in August 1941, Churchill anticipated an American declaration of war, or "some further forward step." He did not get it; instead Roosevelt intended a morale fillip in the form of the Atlantic Charter, committing the free countries to principles for a postwar world toward which they were fighting. Among those principles was "the right of all peoples to choose the government under which they will live," something obviously at variance with British colonial practice. Roosevelt wanted British commitment to engage in no secret treaties (as they had at Versailles), to repay Lend-Lease debt (since they had ceased payment in 1932 on World War I debt), and an end to imperial preference in trading arrangements. The charter's aims, in fact, read like a banner waving the domestic arrangements of Franklin Roosevelt's American ideology: rejection of territory acquired by force, trade liberalization, establishment of international labor standards, restoration to power of indigenous governments in occupied countries, and self-determination.

When challenged about getting so little and giving so much, Prime Minister Churchill pronounced it "imprudent" to object, an abject statement about American leverage in the negotiations. What Churchill got from the Atlantic Charter was also hugely significant: the apparent alignment of American power with the British war effort. Churchill perhaps overstated the extent of that alignment, reporting to his cabinet that "Roosevelt said he would wage war but not declare it," escorting convoys and shooting on sight any Axis interference to force an incident that precipitated America joining the war.[28] No such order was apparently ever issued by Roosevelt,[29] but intensive military cooperation got underway. A "transatlantic essay contest" of military option plans assigning U.S. land, sea, and air forces commenced in the British and American military.[30]

The "Europe First" Strategy

In 1939 Roosevelt had hoped to limit American military involvement in the European theater to air and naval assets.[31] The vast Pacific had become "an American ocean," and would require primacy of effort.[32] Not only was the Pacific the strategic priority, but expectations were low that Europe was recoverable; blitzkrieg was securing victory for Germany before the resource mobilization that was Allied strength could be brought to bear.[33] Army Chief of Staff George Marshall expected Britain to surrender; in April 1940 Roosevelt directed Treasury Secretary Hans Morgenthau to commence planning for Britain's defeat.[34]

But Japan's alliance with Germany and Italy in 1940 evidently convinced Roosevelt that the war efforts across both theaters would become integral.[35] It was in that context that greater American involvement in the European theater became the priority effort in Anglo-American military planning. Roosevelt's direction in January 1941 was for the his Joint Chiefs of Staff to plan on the basis of a defensive war in the Pacific, a "very conservative approach" to protecting the western hemisphere and the main effort in the European theater.[36] The Europe First approach was reinforced also by the politics of the Soviets' demand for a cross-channel invasion if they were to continue fighting on the Eastern front.

The Joint Chiefs of Staff did not ever seem to have become reconciled to the "Europe first" approach.[37] American forces were making advances in the Pacific, the British were unwilling to commit to a date for the cross-channel invasion, the Soviet Union was faltering in the face of the German onslaught, and the Joint Chiefs wanted the economy of scale of ending the dispersion of U.S. forces. In February 1942 Eisenhower wrote Marshall that if the British would not commit to a cross-channel attack, "we must turn our backs upon the Eastern Atlantic and go, full out, as quickly as possible, against Japan."[38] Secretary of War Henry L. Stimson and General George Marshall both recorded issuing the same threat to their British counterparts in July 1942 about shifting American effort to the Pacific.[39] Marshall wrote to President Roosevelt that his object was "again to force the British into acceptance of a concentrated effort against Germany, and if this proves impossible, to turn immediately to the Pacific with strong forces for a decision against Japan."[40]

In consultation, Roosevelt's paramount concern about shifting effort to the Pacific was that it would make the Soviet predicament worse.[41] The president asked to see the Joint Chiefs' plans for a "Pacific first" strategy; when Marshall admitted they had not developed one, Roosevelt determined to continue with the "Europe first" approach. The President also "suggested that the record 'should be altered so that it would not appear in later years that we had proposed what amounted to abandonment of the British,'" which is exactly what had been under serious consideration by the United States.[42]

After the president's direction, the Joint Chiefs began seriously developing Pacific alternatives. When Admiral William D. Leahy, the president's chief of staff, objected that the work contradicted Roosevelt's instruction, General Marshall and Admiral Ernest King, the chief of naval operations, assured him that American forces were now numerous enough to secure Great Britain "and thus mollify the President." And that seems to have satisfied Leahy's concern.[43] By November 1942, the American military had concluded "the entire question of Germany vs Japan first is 'largely academic.'"[44]

But then the Soviet Union persevered at Stalingrad, relieving concern that it could not sustain its war effort, and the British were once again equivocating on a cross-channel invasion.[45] Great Britain called the Cairo Conference to reconsider the agreed cross-channel invasion, but Churchill's legitimate concerns about the plans for Operation Overlord did not dissuade the United States or Soviet Union from their insistence that the invasion go forward.[46] As late as July 1943, Secretary Stimson told European commander Dwight Eisenhower that the American public favored swinging to the Pacific once the Mediterranean had been cleared, thus suggesting the option was still under consideration.[47]

Empire

If the combined strategy was tenuous, there was one thing the American government was absolutely clear about: no American forces would be committed to help Britain hold or regain its empire.[48] Americans suspected Britain was "conducting its war effort mainly in the interest of the empire," pulling operations toward the Mediterranean for advantage in Egypt instead of taking Germany on in France.[49] Even if that were uncharitable, it is uncontestable that the fight in the Pacific was, for Britain, largely about preservation of its empire.

The contrast between Britain as a vast empire and the United States as the dominant military and economic force in the relationship increasingly rankled British officials as the war progressed. In 1942 the British embassy in Washington could report with some surprise that "even outside the Isolationist ranks the view gained powerful support that the war should be largely American led and American managed."[50] By 1944 Anthony Eden was bitterly complaining that Americans had "'a much exaggerated conception' of the military contribution they were making in the war. They lie freely about this . . . and we are too polite to put them right, or it may be difficult to do so without giving information to the enemy."[51] In 1945, John Balfour, the British Charge d'Affairs in Washington, discouragingly reported that Britain was "expected to take her place as junior partner in an orbit of power predominantly under American aegis."[52]

As the war wound down, both Admiral King and General MacArthur refused the offer of British forces for their campaigns in the Pacific.[53] Churchill pressed the issue of troops at the Quebec Conference of 1943, fearing the United States would liberate British colonies and not return them to British rule.[54] American disaffection for Britain's empire was so far advanced that Roosevelt at the 1943 Tehran Conference was privately discussing with Stalin the manner of India's independence. Roosevelt remarkably told Stalin that he felt that "the best solution would be reform from the bottom, somewhat on the Soviet line."[55]

America's changed policies toward Latin America might have provided a stronger example than Soviet revolution for unwinding Britain's empire. Latin America had long been intruded upon by the United States while it was a rising power, but as an established power America became more liberal in its policies toward states in the western hemisphere. The same threat of hostile European powers colonizing fragile states in Latin America that provoked the Monroe Doctrine in 1823 emerged again during World War II. Instead of the gunboat diplomacy that characterized American policy from the 1890s through 1914, Roosevelt orchestrated hemispheric solidarity with a steady drumbeat of diplomatic engagement: at Montevideo in 1933, countries of the Americas agreed that "no state has the right to intervene in the internal or external affairs of another"; at Buenos Aires in 1936, they agreed that "whenever peace of the Americas are threatened, the 21 countries will consult together with the thought of cooperating to preserve the peace of the Continent"; at Havana in 1940 they agreed (in a precursor to the language that would later resound in the North Atlantic Treaty) that "any attempt on the part of a non-American State against the integrity or inviolability of the territory, the sovereignty, or the political independence of an American State shall be considered as an act of aggression against the States which sign this declaration."[56]

The United States not only mastered the art of positive engagement with its southern neighbors but also acted in ways that brought the western hemisphere into participating in American policies.[57] The Havana declaration essentially multilateralized the Monroe Doctrine into a collective policy of self-defense, giving all the countries in the hemisphere responsibility for preserving each other's independence from interference on the part of non-American states. As part of the deal, the United States made available to other countries in the region the air and naval bases it had acquired as part of the Destroyers for Bases Agreement with Britain. So much had relations changed between the United States and other countries of the western hemisphere because of this good neighbor policy that after Pearl Harbor was attacked, all of the countries of the hemisphere save Argentina and Chile broke diplomatic relations with the Axis powers.

The British government considered preservation of the empire an essential component of the realm and crucial to aiding the nation's postwar economic health. The Foreign Office and Ministry of Economic Warfare saw Roosevelt's concept for a liberal free-trade international economic order as a thinly veiled scheme to "produce an American economic dictatorship."[58] Suspicion never abated that American interest in decolonization was a stalking horse for destroying Britain's economic model of imperial tariff preferences.[59]

Churchill instructed postwar planners to take no actions that would get in the way of closer British-U.S. integration, but his program for much more intensive integration after the war—he envisioned merged military and foreign office staffs, even joint citizenship—foundered on the issue of colonialism. There was no path to attaining both objectives—of empire and of intertwining with the United States. In explaining the lack of enthusiasm Americans had for the British empire, a study commissioned by Churchill's office selected the fig leaf that 25 percent of Americans were descended from the German or Irish and were therefore "anti-British."[60] How that had not prevented the strong wartime attachment was not explained.

Whether to continue the alliance became an uncomfortable question for the United States in the war's aftermath. Ideology, which had pulled Britain and America into a sense of sameness in the 1870s and 1880s as America became an empire and Britain became democratic, now divided it. David Reynolds concludes, "British liberal values were democratized in America and turned back as a critique of British politics in the nineteenth century. Gladstone's synthesis of liberalism in foreign policy was Americanized by Wilson and applied by him and his Democratic successors as a critique of British imperialism in the twentieth century."[61]

American energies were quickly diverted to and consumed with determining conquered Germany and Japan's role in the postwar order. General Dwight D. Eisenhower had promised Germans, "We come as conquerors, but not as oppressors."[62] MacArthur was likewise engaged in building a stable, prosperous democracy in Japan. As the dominant Western power, the United States was determined to prevent a Carthaginian peace like that which the European victors had imposed on Germany after World War I. American power would be put to different purposes, establishing a new kind of peace that fostered recovery of conquered powers provided they accepted the rules America established: democratic governance, free markets, and adherence to what was coming to be considered the American order. America gave Britain a prominent role in the postwar European order, but one no more prominent than that of France.

If the relationship was not all the British hoped for, it nonetheless remained one of distinction, succinctly summed up in General Marshall's instructions to General Joseph Stilwell during the war to get along with Great Britain because, in spite of everything, "the British are our most reliable allies."[63]

12

Lessons from a Peaceful Transition

LOOKING ACROSS A hundred years of America growing stronger and more assertive in the international order, the most striking element is how highly contingent a peaceful outcome was in the transition from British to American hegemony. This peacefulness hinged on a unique sense of political sameness, both domestically and in international practice, for the crucial years of America surpassing Britain that allowed the hegemon to diminish the importance of relative power between them. The sense of sameness dissipated soon after the transition, and America set sail on radically changing the international order to more closely reflect its domestic political compact.

To the extent that the British to American transition is illustrative for future changes, it cautions deep skepticism—both that the transition can occur peacefully and that, even if it should occur peacefully, the international order that results will operate on terms the United States has set in its hegemony. This is especially true if the subsequent hegemon emerges not from within the American order but from the much more probable direction of China.

In stark terms, the lessons of the British to American case for future hegemonic transitions are four: (1) the prospects for a peaceful hegemonic transition are small even in the most conducive circumstances; (2) differences in political culture and structure of government make an American to Chinese hegemonic transition much less likely to be peaceful; (3) America is making the same strategic choice with China that Great Britain did with a rising America, that it can be induced to comply with extant rules; and (4) America ought to expect that a hegemonic China will rewrite the rules to reflect its domestic political culture, just as America itself did.

Lessons

The Crossing of Courses

That Great Britain failed to maintain its dominance in the international order is a simple fact; the United States grew richer, stronger, and more assertive. As a result, America demanded and received the ability to reset the rules by which states operated internationally. Since the establishment of the state system, and even before, hegemonic transitions have occurred by force. A rising power tests its mettle against the dominant power, succeeding or failing by force of arms. That was not the character of the transition from British to American dominance; it was uniquely peaceful. Why it was uniquely peaceful has been the subject of this book.

Theories about state behavior necessarily look to explain the preponderance of the data. As the only peaceful transition, the Anglo-American hegemonic transition is an outlier, so it is not surprising that prevailing theories provide imperfect explanations for its history. Yet it is an extremely important case, as the only transition achieved without cataclysmic violence. Understanding why it occurred without violence is essential to determining whether future hegemonic transitions can occur peacefully, and what the nature of the international order will be once such transitions have occurred.

A realpolitik explanation for what transpired between Great Britain and the United States from 1823 to 1922 would be that a rising power began probing the established hegemon, backed off when it met resistance, and advanced when the hegemon was distracted or otherwise unwilling to counter the challenge. Building on a reputation for twisting the lion's tail, an upstart America cannily took credit for what Britain would need to do to prevent European colonization of the western hemisphere in 1823, was slapped down while attempting a steal of the Oregon Territory in 1853, managed to threaten just enough trouble for Britain in 1861–1863 to tip the scales against recognition of the Confederacy, burnished its strength winning the Indian Wars, and consolidated a continental economic platform. Ultimately the economic and military strength of the rising power were so compelling that, confronted with war during the 1895 Venezuelan debt crises, Great Britain instead conceded. Cooperation over Venezuela and during the Spanish-American War would illustrate a waning power buying goodwill with a new hegemon—that is, jumping on the bandwagon. Being more concerned with a rising Germany than a fading Britain, the United States joined in the Great War on the Allied side and brokered a peace, both at Versailles and in the Washington Naval Treaties, that locked in its own superiority.

All seems sensible enough in that telling. But the realpolitik story line cannot adequately account for several elements of the history, the most important elements in producing a peaceful transition: why Britain at the height of its powers offered cooperation to its rising rival in 1823; why Britain declined to press its advantage over Oregon in 1845; why Britain resisted an inexpensive opportunity to deal a devastating blow before 1863 during the American Civil War; why the two countries developed such a vibrant sense of sameness during their introspective decades, unique for both countries from any other international relations; why Britain encouraged American expansion into the Pacific and enabled American success in the Spanish-American War; why the United States grew more liberal as it grew more powerful; and why America in the time of its hegemony used its power to try and create a different kind of international order.

Many elements of British strategy accounted for by realpolitik as a waning power accommodating a waxing power seem instead to be characteristics of British foreign policy across the whole of its dominance of the international order; to use Silicon Valley terminology, they are features, not bugs. Great Britain was a peculiar kind of hegemon. It never seemed to feel its own strength, perhaps because the strategy it employed across 150 years always required partnerships to succeed. Balancing conflicting interests and quarrelsome partners for temporary gain was Great Britain's genius. In contrast to America during its hegemony, Britain seemed always intensely conscious of its vulnerabilities rather than exalting in its strengths. How else to explain Great Britain, ascendant in 1823, seeking out common cause with an America barely able to protect its own coastline in order to prevent further European colonization in the western hemisphere?

Great Britain had a genius for piecing together mosaics of marginal contributors for tactical advantage. Governments from those of Earl of Liverpool to David Lloyd George were always temporizing, finding narrow bases for ephemeral collusion to specific purpose with a fluid collection of partners. It was a cost-efficient geostrategy that succeeded spectacularly until the international order calcified into standing alliances. And when that more rigid international order emerged at the end of the nineteenth century, Britain had laid the trace lines for more stable cooperation with two of the three emergent great powers, Japan and the United States.

It is unfair to British statesmen to conclude, as Paul Kennedy does, that they always accommodated their challengers.[1] They did not, at least, always accommodate the United States, pushing back on both American territorial demands for Oregon and the revisionist legal claims for superiority in law of democratic governments. President James Polk probably lost more in the 1845 confrontation over Oregon than he would have gained by playing a longer hand and letting the tide of American settlers make the case for the boundary location of British Columbia. The government of Henry John Temple, Third Viscount Palmerston was sorely tempted twice before 1863 to recognize the Confederate States during the American Civil War, considering it in Britain's interests to do so. The British inclination even in 1895 was to put America in its subordinate place and deride its claims for a sphere of influence in the Americas. British governments defined their interests expansively and threatened force effectively to constrain American challenges. Confrontation was a routine part of British-American interaction for much of the nineteenth century.

The theory that democracy produced a peaceful transition is only partly borne out in the Anglo-American transition. The difference in form of government between Great Britain and America did increase the likelihood of hegemonic confrontation between the two countries. British statesmen were appalled at the type of government on display in America. In part this was a reflection of class privilege in Britain, but leaders' aversion to democracy was more than just prejudice. Speaking the same language, the British had a front row seat for the demagoguery, recklessness, and corruption of electoral politics on display in America after the decorum of the founding fathers gave way to Jacksonian America. They were not inaccurate in anticipating that democracy would produce a bellicose state unwilling to accept the established practices of great powers. A rising America was an illiberal America in very many respects. Yet even democratic British leaders did not predict that a risen America would choose to reconstruct the international order in profoundly liberal ways.

British leaders before 1867 feared how American influence could permeate their national boundary, a concern uniquely posed by America. The American experiment echoed through British debates on electoral reform; it was the only model of functioning democracy and therefore the basis for comparison of what Britain wanted and did not want in its own democratization. Before the electoral reforms, British governments worried about infection of American attitudes in the British body politic. They had a rich appreciation for the appeal of American ideals: George Canning championed James Monroe's announcement in 1823 because it associated Britain with America's international appeal. Robert Peel declined to push British advantage over James Polk's 1845 exposure in Oregon when British reformers took up America's case. In 1863 Palmerston was cautious not to expose his government to pressure for greater democratization by aligning with a Southern cause unpopular with those least represented in British politics. The process of British democratization eventually brought the political cultures of the two countries together and gave them a sense of distinction from other states, all of which were differently constituted. Before electoral reform in Britain, though, the democratic divide was cause for deep distrust between Britain and America.

Democratization was not the only threat America posed to British policy, however. Choices about America had a unique resonance because of immigration. British leaders had no trepidation about domestic repercussions of policy toward other countries; with America, British leaders had to calculate the way anti-American policies would affect attitudes in Ireland, Scotland, and even within England. No other country could play a positive role in mobilizing public sentiment, reaching into domestic politics to affect foreign policy. Palmerston saw the dimensions of that challenge in 1863 and pulled back from recognizing the Confederacy. The foreign policy gain wasn't worth the domestic policy cost of greater difficulty controlling Ireland and Scotland. Franklin Delano Roosevelt threatened revolt in Britain's colonies if Britain made a separate peace with Japan in 1936. America's ability to reach into other countries' domestic policies, and the comparative difficulty of other countries being able to effect a more kaleidoscopic American body politic, provided a significant bargaining advantage in American foreign policy.

Democracy and immigration affected foreign policy in one other important way for Great Britain: Americans mobilizing against their own government's policies considered too beneficial to Britain. American nationality initially defined itself in contrast to Britain, creating a natural antipathy. But even as that generalized effect abated, the specific effect of American immigrant constituencies grew to penalize British foreign policy because of British domestic policy. Robert Arthur Talbot Gascoyne-Cecil, Third Marquess of Salisbury got stung in Senate consideration of the arbitration treaty by the scorpion tail of Irish American resentment of Britain's insensitivity during the Great Irish Famine. President Woodrow Wilson's fury at "hyphenated Americans" denying the League of

Nations shows the Irish American retribution for Irish partition and German American resentment of ascribing all war guilt and severe reparations to Germany.

Another significant advantage afforded a rising America was recourse to the public. Due to the American political system's frequent elections being tied more tightly to public attitudes, presidents could reinforce their authority in foreign policy by appealing to public sentiment. James Monroe, James Polk, Abraham Lincoln, and Grover Cleveland all played this card to great effect during foreign policy negotiations with Britain, capitalizing on the caricature of the masses as easily whipped into an uncontrollable frenzy. Woodrow Wilson and Theodore Roosevelt were acknowledged to be swimming against strong currents of public opposition. Canning understood Monroe was grandstanding with his 1823 proclamation and declined to even acknowledge it. Peel struck a deal over Oregon before America's victory in Mexico out of concern that the public would then push Polk to greater intransigence. Palmerston gave Lincoln leeway during the *Trent* affair, considering him hemmed in by public opinion. Salisbury changed tack on Venezuela after the roar of public support for Cleveland's unexpectedly aggressive assertion of the Monroe Doctrine in 1895. Democracy was thus a structural advantage for a rising America as it engaged the established great power. That would not have been the case if Britain were not democratizing; an authoritarian state would have had greater latitude in ignoring public attitudes.

But theories that domestic politics are determinative of foreign policy also falter as explanation for British and American behavior in the transition. Britain did become more accommodating toward America once both were democracies, and public sentiment did trend strongly in America's favor. But Salisbury did not make the strategic shift in response to public attitudes in 1895; if they were all important, the Salisbury government would not have initially taken a strong stand on Venezuela. Salisbury made the shift because the Venezuelan crisis brought into focus a strategic problem Britain needed to solve: it was overextended and looking for power to underwrite British objectives. Public sentimentality about America enabled a choice, but it did not dictate that choice.

America is the even more difficult case to make for domestic politics driving foreign policy. As loud and combative as the American public was, and careful as American presidents had to be in marshaling opinion to support of their policies, opinion factors much more in campaigning than governing. Public attitudes did not factor at all in President Monroe's declaration. President Polk did not allow public enthusiasm for "Fifty-four forty or fight" to prevent compromise with Britain over the Oregon boundary. President Lincoln did not allow public outrage over the *Trent* affair drive a damaging choice during the Civil War. President Cleveland did not allow a restive public to force his hand on the annexation of Hawaii nor in Venezuela. President William McKinley was not stampeded to war with Spain with the sinking of the USS *Maine*. President Theodore Roosevelt only expanded the Monroe Doctrine in 1902 responding to the Arbitration Court's decision, not public or business interests. Public attitudes did press on President Warren G. Harding in 1921 to find some means less destructive and costly than war for the United States to engage in the world, but perhaps that shows that hegemony gives American presidents the latitude—the margin for error—to indulge public attitudes.

America's vaunted morality, such a prominent part of its own description of itself, proved limber between 1823 and 1923; it never impinged on the destruction of Indian tribes and their way of life. In fact, an alternate morality in the form of Manifest Destiny was developed to rationalize westward expansion. The morality of colonialism was, to America's credit, a major political issue from the 1870s onward as America began expanding its political control beyond territory inhabited by Americans. But the issue was more abstract, as it did not affect Americans directly. As with the influence of public attitudes, America's morality in foreign policy correlates with the increase in its power. Like public opinion, indulging morality in foreign policy may be a luxury of hegemony.

Something important changed in interactions between Great Britain and America in 1895—or, more accurately, the 1895 Venezuelan debt crises revealed changes that had been long accruing. Ernest May, who considers domestic politics and morality the driving forces of American foreign policy across this time frame, even concedes that "Cleveland and Olney startled England and the United States into one another's arms."[2] The 1870s had been introspective years for both Great Britain and the United States, with Britain adapting to the changes wrought by expansion of the voting franchise and America consolidating its hold over a continental expanse. The result of this was an America that in many important respects had become an empire and a Britain that had become a democracy. The result of the changes was to make the currency of power less important in the British-American relationship than it was in other state relationships.

Both of these changes were essential in the peaceful transition of hegemony. Great Britain would not have trusted that America out in the world would act as Britain did had America not eschewed its republican morality with the conquest of its Indian Wars. America would not have considered Britain its natural ally if Britain had not democratized. The transformations of both societies occurring simultaneously is an historical anomaly—serendipitous, but anomalous. If America had not come to act like a traditional great power rather than continuing to propound its ideology in foreign policy, Great Britain might well have countered rather than encouraged America's role in the world. If Great Britain had not become a related government, the United States might well have forced foreign policy concessions from Britain as it did from other countries.

The sense of sameness that pervades Anglo-American relations in the late nineteenth century allowed the British and American governments to view each other's power in less threatening terms. Their shifting national perceptions, their ideas of each other and the international order, are hugely important in making the hegemonic transition peaceful. Britain did not lose the will to enforce its international order—something sorrowfully evident by the three million British casualties in World War I. What explains Great Britain not contesting America's challenge to the established international order is instead that Britain and the United States came to perceive each other's power in uniquely unthreatening terms. This perspective was the basis for peaceful resolution to the 1895 Venezuelan debt crisis, British endorsement of Hawaii's annexation in 1898, assistance to American arms during the Spanish-American War, encouragement for Cuba and the Philippines as American colonies, America's 1902 willingness to enforce commercial contracts in the western hemisphere, America's lenient attitude toward Britain's World War I blockade and even its choice to join the allied war effort on land in 1917. During the crucial passage of dominance from Great Britain to the United States, the two countries viewed their interests as indistinguishable, their military power as cumulative. They enabled and justified each other's foreign policy choices, a collusion championed in Rudyard Kipling's *White Man's Burden*.

The glittering moment of Anglo-American sameness was remarkably short-lived. The Great War undoubtedly had much to do with America recoiling from a traditional great power role. America risking so little and demanding so much in the aftermath of the war would remind Britain of tiresome pre-rapprochement American grandstanding. America emerged from World War I as the international order's strongest country by far. Neither its economy nor its military suffered losses of the kind or magnitude of Europe's great powers, and its potential far outstripped its performance. The "war to end all wars" left America standing tallest among contenders for dominance of the international order. What America chose to do with that power is what drove an end to the special intertwining of British and American interests.

First at Versailles, and then even more adamantly in the Washington Naval Treaties, a hegemonic United States attempted to build an international order of great power restraint. Limiting the means of war would remove the causes of war, prejudice governments toward domestic preoccupations, and allow mutually enriching economic competition. America mistook international politics to be a macrocosm of its domestic politics.

America's transformation—or perhaps reversion is more accurate, since many of the notions pervade American thinking about international relations before 1890—alarmed the British government. Lord Salisbury, Joseph Chamberlain, and Arthur Balfour had built British strategy on a foundation of American might underwriting British interests; those interests were diverging from America's. The ultimate achievement of that British strategy, American soldiers providing the winning margin of a European land war in reinforcement of Britain, would be the *anagnorisis* for America to bring about a very different international order.[3]

After World War I, republican messianism returned to American foreign policy, and a hegemonic America became ambitious to change the rules of order. As it had prohibited European colonization of the nascent nations of the western hemisphere in 1823, proclaimed a superior right in law for representative governments in 1845, and renounced the right of states that abused their citizens in 1898, America would advance its republican principles. The reality of a hegemonic America was even more sweepingly ambitious than the Canadian representative of Britain's empire had warned in 1921: America was not satisfied being a law unto itself; it would bend the international order to make its law universal practice.

The world America wanted was one in which Britain was not uniquely advantaged or influential over America, because the rest of the world made itself like America and Britain. And the United States moved quickly to try and establish that world. The schism was apparent in the 1916 American naval program that would overtake Britain's navy, deplored by the British and American negotiators at Versailles, and made manifest in American proposals at the 1921 Washington Naval Conference. The resulting treaties established parity between the British and American navies and thus were importantly symbolic of America overtaking Britain as hegemon.

Implementation of the treaties would further showcase the innovative dynamism of America and Britain's other rising rival, Japan. It would take nineteen years of further Japanese dynamism to push Britain and the United States back into collusion, and the result of that war would redouble American belief that a state's domestic political culture was determinative of its behavior in the international order. This cast Britain's imperial policies after World War II in sharp and negative relief, making impossible the sustainment of

Britain's unique intertwining with the United States that had occurred during the war.

It is easy to imagine different Anglo-American relationships that might have resulted if the special relationship did not cohere at the historical moment that it did. There are so many particularities to both countries and in the timing and manner of their collusion in the late nineteenth and early twentieth centuries as America thrust outward and Britain became concerned about the burdens of its foreign policies. Could the cultural similarities have trumped British concern about a genuinely republican foreign policy? If America had seemed likely to advance self-determination in ways that threatened Britain's empire, or succeeded in fostering political change in countries with important economic resources, Britain might well have used its military might to prevent an expansion of American power. Instead of assisting American efforts in the Spanish-American War, Britain might have thrown its weight behind the Spanish crown, to positive effect for its relationships with continental European powers.

When Britain flirted with recognizing the Confederacy, the American minister to St. Petersburg, Cassius Marcellus Clay, publicly questioned, "Is England so secure in the future against home revolt or foreign ambition as to venture, now in our need, to plant the seeds of revenge in all our future?"[4] Might America have reached more aggressively in to British domestic politics, becoming an agent provocateur instead of a model for reform? That could have reignited a contest over Canada, which an America steaming out of its Civil War might have taken from British control (and thus perhaps wading into a quicksand of Canadian insurgency). A Fenian Army might have mobilized for Ireland itself, with overt American support (beyond throwing money into Irish flags during St Patrick's

Day parades) goading Britain's sore. Or the American government could have agitated Britain's workingmen and urban poor, threatening Britain with the revolution its elites so feared. American republicanism was probably too deeply in bone and anti-British sentiment too sturdy a factor in American politics in the nineteenth century to have given the British much confidence of turning the American people against their government.

But the transition from British to American hegemony reads more like a romance than a realpolitik primer. There is American yearning for the stature accorded by British attention; the courtship of convenience; marriage proposals offered several times by Britain and always formally spurned by America, even as it tried to retain the affectionate favors Britain was performing; development of tender regard for each other's peculiarities; a relationship maturing into sober appreciation of common interests and mutually beneficial patterns; anxiety from both as fissures emerged over what future each wanted; the heartbreak of separation; and experience with others reuniting them in gratitude.

Britain remains unique in its ability to understand and negotiate the corridors of American power, and more successful than any other state in harnessing American strength to advantage of its interests. It had the structural benefit of being the first mover, along with continuing advantages accruing from linguistic and cultural similarities. But these can be easily overstated. Britain's connection with America is less organic than cultivated, as the resurgence of a special relationship in the run up to and during World War II demonstrates. British governments often feel they have too little influence with American governments; all others wish they had what Britain has. It was, and is, in Britain's interest to capitalize on American power, and Britain is smart enough to do so shrewdly and with a light enough touch that Americans hardly ever notice. It is difficult to imagine America replicating that feat with any potentially rising powers.

The Same River Twice?

A hundred years after the moment when America shook off Britain and strode forward to reshape the international order in its image come other claimants for global dominance, growing in strength and testing alternatives to the American equation for dominance of the international order. China, in particular, merits examination because of the momentousness of its great leap forward since the economic reforms of 1978. Its dynamism has lifted hundreds of millions of people out of poverty, with an economic growth rate of 9.8 percent between 1978 and 2005.[5] After a century of humiliation, its success has fostered a swaggering nationalism. It is the world's second largest economy, and even if it fails to maintain its galloping growth rate it may well surpass the United States.

The Chinese government has a fundamentally different model of the relationship between the state and its people than does America: it is counting on prosperity preventing demands for political representation, a reversal of the dynamic that America asserts as the natural order of politics. It has an increasingly combative military being primed with high-tech weaponry. And it envisions a manifestly different regional order in Asia than does the United States.

John Maynard Keynes famously quipped that "practical men, who believe themselves to be quite exempt from any intellectual influence, are usually the slaves of some defunct economist." Many of the practical men and women running American policy toward a rising China are unwittingly enslaved to the ideas of living political scientist Francis Fukuyama. Policy makers often deride Fukuyama's

The End of History and the Last Man as though he were proclaiming that events would cease to occur, rather than ruminating on Hegel's critique of traditional liberalism and advocacy of a state with limited powers based on social consent.[6] Yet those same policy makers have also consistently across more than forty years supported an approach to the world based on the Fukuyaman belief that sustained success is impossible for states that are undemocratic and that there can be no successful challenger to the Western model of market economies and representative governance. It is the lesson the West took from World War II and the collapse of the Soviet bloc. It is enshrined in Robert Zoellick's solemn invocation for China to become a "responsible stakeholder" in the international order. It is the rationalization for American businesses to invest in and shift manufacturing to China.

What America means by "responsible stakeholder" is, of course, a China that accepts as given the rules of the international order America has established. America supports a powerful and prosperous China because it is wagering there cannot be a powerful and prosperous China unless it becomes democratic, that a democratic China will dovetail into the same interests as America, that sharing those interests it will share the burden of upholding them, and that in upholding those interests China will conduct itself as America conducts itself. It is the strategic calculation Salisbury's government made in 1895 about the United States.

Salisbury's reorientation of British policy was essential to a peaceful transition of hegemony between Great Britain and the United States. So, too, may a Fukuyaman orientation of American policy prove essential to a peaceful transition of hegemony between America and China should it occur. If prevention of war is the metric, Salisbury's policy is the right choice. But it merits recollecting that

Salisbury's gamble ultimately proved wrong: the United States did not fully share Britain's interests and did not uphold the rules Britain had established. A hegemonic America established its own rules, based on its domestic ideology.

G. John Ikenberry has emphasized the importance of liberality in the American-led order.[7] The rules are considered by participants—not just the dominant power—to be fair and fairly applied. This culture invests other powers in helping uphold the order and utilizes legitimacy to drive down the cost to the United States of sustaining the order. The American-led order thus has a great capacity to accommodate fluctuations of strength—which is to say that rising powers need not change the rules in order to become dominant in the existing order.

But China clearly does want to change the rules—even as it benefits from them. China has afforded the United States glimpses at least as numerous as nineteenth-century America did for Britain that the country's reflexes are different from those of the reigning hegemon. It does not embrace the philosophy that people have inherent rights and loan them in limited ways to government. It centralizes power beyond the constraint of laws or institutions. It does not hold the wielders of power accountable to the public by either election or journalism. It enforces a bias in favor of national corporations, both overtly through access to Chinese markets and opaquely through theft of intellectual property. It appears to view the international order as a tribute system, with weak states forced into compliance and strong states lulled into accepting small changes by threat of consequences out of all proportion to the infraction. It would thereby destroy the alliance system that is the basis for American presence in the region and provision of defense for the weak states on China's periphery. While China's is currently a regional strategy, there is little reason to believe it would not also constitute a global strategy if the nation is in the position to assert one. This suggests that China will pose a normative challenge as well as a power challenge to the American-led order.[8]

Salisbury, Chamberlain, and Balfour at least had the strong bases of common political culture and public affection between the two countries when they placed their bet on a rising America aligning so closely with Great Britain that both nations' power could be harnessed for Britain's interests. The United States is making the same bet on much shakier grounds with China.

To be sure, America has hedged its bets with China. It maintains alliance relationships that support America's military reach and intensify when China behaves threateningly. It is attempting a major trade pact that will set the rules for Asia's economies. It is purportedly "rebalancing" its attention to Asia. Its military forces are reengaged on the challenge of a great power war and the defense spending for adequate preparation. Few defense specialists believe China's military could defeat America's, but the Pentagon watches with anxiety at China's ability to develop asymmetric capabilities that might render moot America's military advantages.

Few defense specialists in 1895 would have agreed that America's military could defeat Britain's, and yet Salisbury fundamentally changed the course of British strategy to cede American objectives rather than persist in the rules of order Britain had set and previously enforced. Might not America cede China even more rather than fight a war that could collapse American power in the Pacific?

Another element of the challenge is that military power is a derivative index; it relies in large measure on a country's economic base. America's consolation thus far with China's meteoric rise is that China's economy is merely a cheap manufacturing base that has yet to prove it can navigate the middle-income trap, whereas America's wealth is driven by innovation. This, too, is Fukuyama's long shadow: belief that only free societies can foster the intellectual creativity to sustain dynamism. It is a complacency that Germany's rise in the prewar years ought to have shattered. Freedom is not the only motivator for innovation. Authoritarian capitalism in China is proving itself as creative and unrestrained as its American counterpart.

Prosperity is the main allure of the authoritarian model, especially when capitalism's champions lag.[9] Nationalism, too, is a powerful force. Moreover, the outsize disputatiousness and risk tolerance of Americans may itself be a national characteristic rather than a universal human attribute. Most Europeans choose forms of governance and economy less tumultuous than those of Americans; public acceptance of retrograde motion in democratizing societies is often a function of exhaustion with the enervation of political and economic change. The people of China could well choose a government less free but more predictable than America's—and prosper in the choice.

America naturally believes such a system is unsustainable. Not only would China have to impose it by force on free societies, but it is susceptible to corrosion from within. This is often mentioned in conjunction with the fact that nearly 150,000 Chinese students study at American universities each year. In Fukuyaman terms, education offers a path to China becoming part of the American order. American policy encourages the practice in the belief that while Chinese may not return home hoping their teenage daughters behave as American teenagers do, they surely want a government they can hold accountable. And if a government is accountable, then it will become liberal. But if the Chinese dream proves magnetic, America will have educated the political, economic, and military leaders that occasion its demise.

American government during the country's rise to prominence was not liberal. The government became liberal in conjunction with prosperity and power, and it could be argued that America's liberality was practiced to a greater extent in its foreign policy than in remaining true to its creed at home. The Fukuyaman mind-set takes as causality the increased liberalism of America; it may have simply been correlation.

The Lockean liberal ethos is so fully embedded in American hegemony, though, that it is difficult to imagine the United States refusing admission to Chinese students. Indeed, liberalism may so far pervade American political culture that courts would deny government the ability to proscribe university admissions on national security grounds. While conservatives bemoan the preoccupations of liberal societies, they are the defining element of the American brand and the seemingly inescapable basis for American foreign policy in the time of its hegemony. The American order will succeed or fail along Fukuyaman lines: either the United States will prove right that free people and free markets are the sole basis for sustainable prosperity and political power, and China will either fail to continue rising or become indistinguishable from other states in the American order, or China will prove resistant to the attractions of liberalism and overtake America as hegemon.

If the Chinese model sustains itself, then a dominant China is likely to recast the rules in ways that extrapolate to the international order its domestic political ideology, just as America did. Hegemony with Chinese characteristics would be a very different international order from the one America has fostered in its hegemony. It would encourage and support other authoritarian governments politically, financially, and socially. It would penalize states for interfering in the internal practices of repressive governments. It would offer privileged access to state-associated commercial concerns. It would prevent market forces levying penalties that make markets efficient and reliable allocators of capital. China lacks an ideology likely to appeal to America in the seductive way America's ideology appealed within Britain and beyond. Without such an ideology, any hegemonic transition will require imposition by force.

NOTES

ACKNOWLEDGMENTS

INDEX

Notes

Book epigraph: Henry Adams, *The Education of Henry Adams* (New York: Modern Library, 1931), 363.

1. OPENING SALVO

1. Robert Gilpin, *War and Change in World Politics* (New York: Cambridge University Press, 1981), 145.

2. The Belfer Center's Thucydides Trap Project identifies sixteen cases of hegemonic transition, four of which it identifies as peaceful. But two of the cases involve regional power relationships substantially affected by security guarantees of the international hegemon (the Soviet Union and Japan in the 1970s and 1980s, and Germany's post–World War II ascension over Britain and France), and one other of the cases posits a transition that did not occur (the Soviet Union challenging the United States, from 1940 to the 1980s). Belfer Center, "Thucydides Trap Case File: Sixteen Cases of Rise vs. Rule," September 23, 2013, http://belfercenter.ksg .harvard.edu/publication/24928/thucydides_trap_case_file.html ?webSyncID=c843ca08-96a0-980e-5293-06c0d2bb5ec6&session-GUID=c76e7ab1-0232-b4bd-5970-bb3d10650503.

3. Moral compromises in application of that ideology, both at home and abroad, are an important countervailing story in American history that I attempt to weave through in telling of hegemonic

transition. They were, however, not much acknowledged by the American government as it made the defining choices about America's role in the world.

4. Kevin Phillips, *The Cousins' Wars: Religion, Politics, and the Triumph of Anglo-America* (New York: Basic Books, 1999).

5. Paul Crook, "Whiggery and America: Accommodating the Radical Threat," in *Radicalism and Revolution in Britain, 1775–1848,* ed. Michael T. Davis (New York: St. Martin's Press, 2000), 191–206.

6. E. D. Steele, *Palmerston and Liberalism, 1855–1865* (Cambridge: Cambridge University Press, 1991).

7. I differ somewhat from Aaron Friedberg's view that Britain was slow to recognize the erosion of its eminence; Friedberg's tighter time frame doesn't capture some of Britain's earlier debate and overtures for American cooperation, such as the 1818 mutual sovereignty over Oregon or the 1823 proposal for joint authority in the western hemisphere. Aaron Friedberg, *The Weary Titan: Britain and the Experience of Relative Decline, 1895–1905* (Princeton, NJ: Princeton University Press, 1988).

8. Ernest R. May, *Imperial Democracy: The Emergence of America as a Great Power* (Chicago: Imprint Publications, 1991).

9. David Healy, *U.S. Expansionism: The Imperialist Urge in the 1890s* (Madison: University of Wisconsin Press, 1970).

10. Charles S. Campbell, *From Revolution to Rapprochement* (New York: John Wiley & Sons, 1974), 203.

11. I do not mean to suggest that American support for self-determination caused the breakup of the British Empire, but it fostered a norm of self-government that legitimated challenges to empires, including its own. The unfulfilled promise of Europe's mid-nineteenth-century revolutions, failures of governance by authoritarians of several stripes, indigenous opposition, imperial overstretch, and interstate wars were the motivating forces for the end of great power empires; see, for example, Paul Kennedy, *The*

Rise and Fall of the Great Powers (New York: Vintage Books, 1989). The result of self-determination, however, was an international order in which the United States and Britain were not the only democracies and therefore not only alike each other.

12. Carl Benn and Daniel Marston, *Liberty or Death: Wars That Forged a Nation* (Oxford: Osprey Publishing, 2006), 193–270; Kate Caffrey, *The Twilight's Last Gleaming: Britain vs. America 1812–1815* (New York: Stein & Day Publishing, 1977); Alfred LeRoy Burt, *The United States, Great Britain and British North America: From the Revolution to the Establishment of Peace after the War of 1812* (New York: Russell & Russell, 1961 [c1940]), 305–310; Warren Goodman, "The Origins of the War of 1812: A Survey of Changing Interpretations," *Mississippi Valley Historical Review* 28, no. 2 (September 1941): 171–186.

13. George C. Herring, *From Colony to Superpower: U.S. Foreign Relations since 1776* (New York: Oxford University Press, 2008).

14. Dexter Perkins, *A History of the Monroe Doctrine* (Boston: Little, Brown, 1955).

15. John Quincy Adams, *Memoirs,* ed. Charles Francis Adams, vol. 6 (Philadelphia: J. B. Lippincott & Co. 1875), 195.

16. Aristotle, *Poetics,* ed. and trans. Stephen Halliwell, Loeb Classical Library 199 (Cambridge, MA: Harvard University Press, 1995), 62–67.

17. Edmund Morris, "'A Matter of Extreme Urgency': Theodore Roosevelt, Wilhelm II, and the Venezuela Crisis of 1902," *Naval War College Review* 55, no. 2 (2002): 73–85.

18. Evan Thomas, *The War Lovers: Roosevelt, Lodge, Hearst, and the Rush to Empire, 1898* (New York: Little, Brown, 2010), 5–7.

19. Herring, *From Colony to Superpower,* chap. 8; Edward P. Crapol, "Coming to Terms with Empire: The Historiography of Late-Nineteenth-Century American Foreign Relations," *Diplomatic History* 16 (1992): 573–597; Hugh DeSantis, "The Imperialist Impulse and American Innocence, 1865–1900," in *American Foreign*

Relations: A Historiographical Review, ed. Gerald K. Haines and J. Samuel Walker (Westport, CT: Greenwood Press, 1981), 65–90.

20. Sterling Kernek, "The British Government's Reactions to President Wilson's 'Peace' Note of December 1916," *Historical Journal* 13, no. 4 (1970): 727; see also Lord Robert Cecil, "NOTE on the German Offer of Peace," December 15, 1916, FO 800/197, p. 22, The National Archives of the UK (TNA): Public Record Office (PRO), London; Sir Eric Drummond, "Memo: President Wilson's Peace Note," December, 31, 1916, FO 800/197, pp. 158–161, TNA:PRO, London.

21. Adam Tooze, *The Deluge: The Great War, America and the Remaking of the Global Order, 1916–1931* (New York: Penguin, 2015), 8.

22. Eric Goldstein notes that "the founding fathers of the United States had initially only desired greater influence in London, and in 1921 at Washington this was achieved, when London deferred to its former colony, which had now firmly seized the initiative." Eric Goldstein, "The Evolution of British Diplomatic Strategy for the Washington Conference," in *The Washington Conference, 1921–22: Naval Rivalry, East Asian Stability and the Road to Pearl Harbor,* ed. Erik Goldstein and John Maurer (Essex, UK: Frank Cass, 1994), 28.

23. Franklin Delano Roosevelt, quoted in Richard A. Harrison, "A Neutralization Plan for the Pacific: Roosevelt and Anglo-American Cooperation, 1934–1937," *Pacific Historical Review* 57, no. 1 (1988): 57.

24. Memorandum, Chief of Staff to President, "Latest British Proposals Relative to Bolero and Gymnast," July 10, 1942, cited in Mark A. Stoler, "The 'Pacific-First' Alternative in American World War II Strategy," *International History Review* 2, no. 3 (1980): 440.

25. Correlli Barnett, *The Collapse of British Power* (New York: Morrow, 1972), 98.

26. Churchill's quote is from his 1943 Harvard University speech; the American position is represented by former President Herbert

Hoover. Both are quoted in "Significant Statements Concerning Anglo-American Cooperation," *World Affairs* 106, no. 4 (1943): 267, 268.

27. John Colville, *Fringes of Power: Downing Street Diaries, 1939–1955,* diary entry for February 24, 1945 (New York: W. W. Norton & Co., 1985), 564.

28. William M. Franklin and William Gerber, eds., Foreign Relations of the United States, Diplomatic Papers, *The Conferences at Cairo and Tehran, 1943* (Washington, DC: GPO, 1961), 486.

29. Sebastian Rosato contests the notion that democratic countries externalize their norms, but he looks principally at wars of empire and does not count wars averted, which the Anglo-American rapprochement largely consists of; and, as he acknowledges, the significant exception of transatlantic cases. Sebastian Rosato, "The Flawed Logic of Democratic Peace Theory," *American Political Science Review* 97, no. 4 (2003): 585.

30. John Rawls argues that neither the United States nor Britain were reliably liberal before the twentieth century; others, including British governments in the nineteenth century, made the distinction between democratic governments, which they acknowledged America to be, and liberal governments, which they rightly denied America was and considered itself to be. John Rawls, *The Law of Peoples* (Cambridge, MA: Harvard University Press, 2002), 53–54; see also Steele, *Palmerston and Liberalism,* 295.

31. Although he marks its inception after World War II, Rosato makes a strong case that what is termed democratic peace is actually an imperial peace based on American power. Rosato, "The Flawed Logic of Democratic Peace Theory," 599.

32. William J. Dixon, "Democracy and the Peaceful Settlement of International Conflict," *American Political Science Review* 88, no. 1 (1994): 14–32; Bruce Russett, "The Democratic Peace," *International Security* 19 (1995): 164–184.

2. IN THEORY AND IN PRACTICE

1. Geoffrey Blainey, *The Causes of War,* 3rd ed. (New York: Free Press, 1988), 293.

2. Robert Gilpin, *War and Change in International Politics* (New York: Cambridge University Press, 1981), 7.

3. Kenneth N. Waltz, *Man, the State, and War: A Theoretical Analysis* (New York: Columbia University Press), 14.

4. Joseph S. Nye Jr., "Limits of American Power," *Political Science Quarterly* 117, no. 4 (2002): 545.

5. Jack Snyder, "Imperial Temptations," *National Interest* 71 (2003): 29–40.

6. Gilpin, *War and Change in World Politics,* 34.

7. Robert O. Keohane, *After Hegemony: Cooperation and Discord in the World Political Economy* (Princeton, NJ: Princeton University Press, 2005), 9, 16.

8. Ian Clark, "Bringing Hegemony Back In: The United States and International Order," *International Affairs* 85, no. 1 (2009): 23.

9. Gilpin, *War and Change in World Politics,* 145.

10. Patrick O'Brien and G. A. Pigman, "Free Trade, British Hegemony and the International Economic Order in the Nineteenth Century," *Review of International Studies* 18, no. 2 (1992): 112.

11. Robert Cox, *Production, Power, and World Order: Social Forces in the Making of History* (New York: Columbia University Press, 1987), 399–400.

12. Richard Ned Lebow and Robert Kelly, "Thucydides and Hegemony: Athens and the United States," *Review of International Studies* 27, no. 4 (2001): 595.

13. Michael Doyle argues that hegemony requires making subjects out of the subjugated, as Rome did. Michael Doye, *Empires* (Ithaca, NY: Cornell University Press, 1986), 37–45.

14. Lebow and Kelly, "Thucydides and Hegemony," 593.

15. Clark, "Bringing Hegemony Back In," 24.

16. Arthur Stein, "The Hegemon's Dilemma: Great Britain, the United States, and the International Economic Order," *International Organization* 38, no. 2 (1984): 358.

17. Geir Lundestad, "Empire by Invitation? The United States and Western Europe, 1945–1952," *Journal of Peace Research* 23, no. 3 (1986): 263–277.

18. Daniel Deudney and G. John Ikenberry, "The Nature and Sources of Liberal International Order," *Review of International Studies* 25, no. 2 (1999): 180, 179.

19. Martha Finnemore, *National Interests in International Society* (Ithaca, NY: Cornell University Press, 1996), 2.

20. The exceptions are wealthy states such as Qatar, Singapore, and Switzerland that lack the scale of resources to become dominant powers.

21. The determinism inherent in neorealism is most easily refuted by soldiers and military historians because of their rich appreciation for the contingencies of outcome in warfare. Sir Robert Thompson's seminal "Regular Armies and Insurgency," in *Regular Armies and Insurgency,* ed. Ronald Haycock (London: Croom Helm, 1979), for example, emphasizes, "one of the very difficult things for a regular army to understand is that an undefeated army can lose a war" (9).

22. Alexander Wendt, *Social Theory of International Politics* (Cambridge: Cambridge University Press, 1999), 1–4.

23. Alexander Wendt, "Anarchy Is What States Make of It: The Social Construction of Power Politics," *International Organization* 46, no. 2 (1992): 410.

24. Wendt, *Social Theory of International Politics,* 193.

25. Martin Griffiths, Terry O'Callaghan, and Steven C. Roach, *International Relations: The Key Concepts,* 2nd ed. (London: Routledge, 2008), 52.

26. Wendt, "Anarchy," 395.

27. Wendt, *Social Theory of International Politics,* 1.

28. Wendt, "Anarchy," 397.

29. John Baylis, Steve Smith, and Patricia Owens, *The Globalization of World Politics: An Introduction to International Relations,* 5th ed. (Oxford: Oxford University Press, 2011), 237.

30. Srdjan Vucetic, *The Anglosphere: A Genealogy of a Racialized Identity in International Relations* (Stanford, CA: Stanford University Press, 2011), argues for a solely race-based explanation for the sense of sameness, noting that "it was the cooperation based on race and racism that paved the way for the Anglo-American 'special relationship'" (47). Such a monocausal explanation fails to capture how much the end of slavery and the Union (exsanguinated to achieve abolition) changed attitudes in Britain, something evidenced by prominent Britons from Charles Dickens to Lord Halifax. For an account of these wide-ranging influences, see Kathleen Burk, *Old World, New World: Great Britain and America from the Beginning* (New York: Grove Press, 2007). Vucetic's account also excludes the extent to which British statesmen cultivated the special relationship on the basis of democratic values to distinguish Britain from other potential American allies. Bradford Perkins, the popularizer of the term "Great Rapprochement," dates its inception to 1865, making abolition a central element. Daniel Walker Howe, *What Hath God Wrought: The Transformation of America, 1815–1848* (Oxford: Oxford University Press, 2007) also shows how travel writers, religious figures, and suffragettes fostered more positive attitudes in both Britain and the United States. Anglo-Saxonism did not emerge as a transatlantic idea until the 1880s; by focusing on Anglo-Saxonism rather than the broader cultural convergence, Vucetic misses other vital contributors to the sense of sameness.

31. Adam Tooze, *The Deluge: The Great War, America and the Remaking of the Global Order, 1916–1931* (New York: Penguin, 2015), 21.

32. Wendt, "Anarchy," 391.

33. Seymour Martin Lipset, *The First New Nation* (New York: Basic Books, 1963); Seymour Martin Lipset, *American Exceptionalism: A*

Double-Edged Sword (New York: W. W. Norton, 1996); Donald E. Pease, *The New American Exceptionalism* (Minneapolis: University of Minnesota Press, 2009); Gordon Wood, Introduction to *The Idea of America: Reflections on the Birth of the United States* (New York: Penguin Press, 2011), 1–22; Elisabeth Glaser and Hermann Wellenreuther, eds., *Bridging the Atlantic: The Question of American Exceptionalism in Perspective* (Cambridge: Cambridge University Press, 2002); Robert W. Tucker and David C. Hendrickson, *Empire of Liberty: The Statecraft of Thomas Jefferson* (New York: Oxford University Press, 1990); Richard W. Etulain, *Does the Frontier Experience Make America Exceptional?* (Boston: Bedford / St. Martin's, 1999); Godfrey Hodgson, *The Myth of American Exceptionalism* (New Haven, CT: Yale University Press, 2009).

34. Akira Iriye, *The Cambridge History of American Foreign Relations,* vol. 3, *The Globalizing of America, 1913–1945* (Cambridge: Cambridge University Press, 1993), 33.

35. Walt Whitman, *Song of Myself,* part 51.

36. William A. Williams, *The Tragedy of American Diplomacy* (Cleveland: World Pub. Co., 1959); Elizabeth Cobbs Hoffman, *American Umpire* (Cambridge, MA: Harvard University Press, 2013); Niall Ferguson, *Empire: The Rise and Demise of the British World Order and the Lessons for Global Power* (New York: Basic Books, 2004); Niall Ferguson, *Colossus: The Rise and Fall of the American Empire* (New York: Penguin Books, 2005); Alfred W. McCoy and Francisco A. Scarano, *Colonial Crucible: Empire in the Making of the Modern American State* (Madison: University of Wisconsin Press, 2009).

37. *Hegemon* is not just the American word for empire, as Niall Ferguson mischievously suggests in *Colossus.* He asserts that the United States is culturally uncomfortable with the term *empire* but its behavior parallels Britain's when Britain was an empire. *Empire* connotes physical control over territory and political control over the domestic structure and choices of a nation or nations deemed separate. Dominions such as Canada and

Australia are constituent parts of the mother country; possessions such as India and Hong Kong are not, and so termed
imperial holdings. Ferguson, *Colossus,* 287. Julian Go argues that
both the self-definition and the actions of Britain and the
United States are indistinguishable at comparable points in
their imperial trajectories. Although Go's study parallels
nineteenth-century Britain and twentieth-century America, it
raises the possibility that Britain and the United States may
have felt similar to each other and different from others as the
nineteenth century drew to a close because the domestic forces
that would produce similar imperial experiences were already
shaping their bodies politic. Julian Go, *Patterns of Empire: The
British and American Empires, 1688 to the Present* (New York:
Cambridge University Press, 2011), 39, 44–49.

38. Adam Watson, *The Evolution of International Society* (London:
Routledge, 1992), 15–16.

39. Stephen Chilton, "Defining Political Culture," *Western Political
Quarterly* 41, no. 3 (1988): 419–445. David Calleo is a notable
exception in weighing American diffidence; see David P. Calleo,
"Reflections on American Hegemony in the Post-War Era," in *Two
Hegemonies: Britain 1846–1914 and the United States 1941–2001,* ed.
Patrick Karl O'Brien and Armand Clesse (Aldershot, England:
Ashgate, 2002), Niall Ferguson emphasizes the importance of
hegemonic will in his review of *Two Hegemonies;* see Ferguson,
"Hegemony or Empire?"

40. Orhan Pamuk, *Other Colors: Essays and a Story,* trans. Maureen
Freely (New York: Vintage International, 2008).

41. O'Brien and Clesse, eds., *Two Hegemonies.*

42. It should also be noted that *Two Hegemonies* is a volume of conference papers, with several of the contributions appearing as light
reflections, along the order of after-dinner speeches, from
towering thinkers.

43. Charles A. Kupchan, *How Enemies Become Friends: The Sources of Stable Peace* (Princeton, NJ: Princeton University Press, 2010), 73.

44. *The Weary Titan: Britain and the Experience of Relative Decline, 1895–1905* (Princeton, NJ: Princeton University Press, 1988). One of *The Weary Titan*'s real delights is incidentally revealing the role of misleading indicators on which the British government relied because they simply lacked more meaningful data (80–81).

45. Ibid., 97–99; for predictions of expanded welfare, see Eric Hobsbawm, *Industry and Empire* (New York: New York Press, 1999), 327.

46. For example, in 1899 Director of Naval Intelligence Reginald Custance determined that not only the United States but also Argentina and Chile were superior in naval power to Britain. Friedberg, *The Weary Titan,* 167. Another telling insight is the British assessment from 1861, during the American Civil War, that Canada was indefensible. See Kenneth Bourne, "British Preparations for War with the North, 1861–1862," *English Historical Review* 76, no. 301 (1961): 600.

47. Friedberg, *The Weary Titan,* 255, 221.

48. And Friedberg does in several places acknowledge that important elements of trends he cites predate his time frame. Most relevant for the functioning of his argument, he acknowledges that British sea power had been declining for fifteen years, that Britain worried as early as 1830 about a Franco-Russian alliance fusing their navies (a concern that increased after the Crimean War), and that in 1892 the directors of military and naval intelligence were already concluding that "Great Britain unsupported cannot prevent the coup-de-main." Friedberg, *The Weary Titan,* 138, 145, 155.

49. Ephraim Douglass Adams even considers the British to have made a fundamental decision not to oppose American power as early as 1850. See Ephraim Douglass Adams, *Great Britain and the American Civil War,* vol. 1 (Project Gutenberg, 2004), 31.

50. Lloyd C. Gardner, Walter F. LaFeber, and Thomas J. McCormick, *Creation of the American Empire: U.S. Diplomatic History* (Chicago: Rand McNally, 1973), 186.

51. Howe, *What Hath God Wrought.*

52. Kevin Phillips, *The Cousins' Wars: Religion, Politics, and the Triumph of Anglo-America* (New York: Basic Books, 1999), 503.

53. Walter Russell Mead, *God and Gold: Britain, America, and the Making of the Modern World* (New York: Knopf, 2007). Mead gives short shrift to the influences of Dutch culture—in particular, religious tolerance—that Russell Shorto persuasively argues affected British colonists in the New World. See Russell Shorto, *The Island at the Center of the World: The Epic Story of Dutch Manhattan and the Forgotten Colony That Shaped America* (New York: Vintage, 2005).

3. THEFT ON THE HIGH SEAS: MONROE'S DOCTRINE

1. J. H. Clapham, "The Economic Condition of Europe after the Napoleonic War," *Scientific Monthly* 11, no. 4 (1920): 323.

2. Linda Colley, *Britons: Forging the Nation, 1707–1837* (New Haven, CT: Yale University Press, 2005), 1–9.

3. Roger Knight, *Britain against Napoleon: The Organisation of Victory, 1793–1815* (New York: Allen Lane, 2013).

4. George Canning, quoted in Dexter Perkins, *A History of the Monroe Doctrine* (Boston: Little, Brown, 1955), 61. It is interesting that Canning seemed to believe in 1825 that threat had been averted.

5. The secretary of the navy's 1822 annual report recorded nine ships operating in the West Indies: the thirty-six-gun frigate *Congress*, the twenty-four-gun corvette *John Adams*, an eighteen-gun sloop of war, one brig and four schooners carrying twelve guns each, and a gunboat listing a single gun. The other six ships of the fleet were dispersed in the Pacific, the Mediterranean, and off the coast of Africa. The secretary of war's 1823 annual report to the president recounted strict accountability for all funds, and successful attack by the Ricaree Indians on the Army's forces. See Smith

Thompson, "Conditions of the Navy, and Its Operations," in *Documents, Legislative and Executive, of the Congress of the United States: Naval Affairs,* vol. 1 (Washington, DC: Gales and Seaton, 1834), 804; and J. C. Calhoun, "Condition of the Military Establishment and the Fortifications, and the Returns of the Militia," in *Documents, Legislative and Executive, of the Congress of the United States: Military Affairs,* vol. 2 (Washington, DC: Gales and Seaton, 1834), 554. These documents can be found at the Library of Congress database American State Papers, 1789–1838, https://memory.loc.gov/ammem/amlaw/lwsplink.html.

6. James Monroe, "Seventh Annual Message" (speech, Washington, DC, December 2, 1823), in *Compilation of the Messages and Papers of the Presidents,* ed. James D. Richardson, vol. 2 (Project Gutenberg, 2004), 287.

7. Daniel Walker Howe, *What Hath God Wrought: The Transformation of America, 1815–1848* (Oxford: Oxford University Press, 2007), 115.

8. Perkins, *A History of the Monroe Doctrine,* chap. 2.

9. Gale McGee argues that Canning deserves little credit for his 1823 overture because of these earlier inquiries, but he fails to distinguish the difference between an instruction to determine whether common attitudes exist and an official government proposal to act jointly. Moreover, Monroe and Adams were interested narrowly in the issue of recognizing the independence of former Spanish colonies, not in threatening military action to preserve that independence. It also probably merits noting that Adams's recounting of the event on which McGee's account relies was provided after the Monroe Doctrine had been announced and Canning was claiming credit for Britain as the first government to support Latin American independence. See Gale W. McGee, "The Monroe Doctrine—A Stopgap Measure," *Mississippi Valley Historical Review* 38 (1951): 233–235.

10. George Washington and Thomas Jefferson would probably not have put such emphasis on avoiding permanent alliances and

foreign entanglements unless there were strong forces pulling the American government in that direction.

11. Stanislaus M. Hamilton, ed., *The Writings of James Monroe,* 1:134, cited in Perkins, *A History of the Monroe Doctrine,* 9. The present account leans heavily on Perkins; not only are his works the most detailed and trenchant on the Monroe Doctrine, but his *History of the Monroe Doctrine* has added poignancy for its asides, having been written in 1941 when the doctrine was being cited by opponents of America entering World War II.

12. Thomas Jefferson, *Works,* 8:145, cited in Perkins, *A History of the Monroe Doctrine,* 19.

13. George C. Herring, *From Colony to Superpower: U.S. Foreign Relations since 1776* (New York: Oxford University Press, 2008), 152.

14. John Quincy Adams, *Memoirs,* ed. Charles Francis Adams, vol. 6 (Philadelphia: J. B. Lippincott & Co. 1875), 163; see also Samuel Flagg Bemis, *John Quincy Adams and the Foundations of American Foreign Policy* (New York: Knopf, 1949), 368.

15. President Jefferson's 1803 purchase of the Louisiana Territory from France doubled the size of America's political boundaries to incorporate land that would eventually comprise fifteen American states. It extended the writ of the federal government to the Rocky Mountains in the West, and from the Gulf of Mexico to British Canada, unhindering navigation on the entire expanse of the Mississippi River. Congressional approval nearly faltered in part over extending citizenship to "foreigners," by which was meant free blacks and citizens of France and Spain living in the Louisiana Territories, whose fidelity to the U.S. government was suspect by dint of "having no experience of democracy." The House of Representatives only approved the Louisiana Purchase by two votes. Walter Nugent, *Habits of Empire: A History of American Expansion* (New York: Vintage Books, 2008), 65–66.

16. Perkins, *A History of the Monroe Doctrine,* 29.

17. Herring, *From Colony to Superpower,* 153.

18. Perkins, *A History of the Monroe Doctrine,* 50, unequivocally concludes that "not one of the Continental powers cherished any designs of reconquest in the New World in November or December 1823."

19. James Monroe to Thomas Jefferson, October 17, 1823, in Stanislaus M. Hamilton, ed., *The Writings of James Monroe,* vol. 6 (New York: G. P. Putnam's Sons, 1902), 323–325.

20. John Quincy Adams, *Memoirs,* vol. 6 (Philadelphia: Lippincott, 1897), 185. In light of both Monroe and Adams's testimonies, it is difficult to give credence to Ernest May's conclusion that neither Monroe nor Adams considered European intervention in the hemisphere likely—Adams, surely, but not Monroe. Ernest R. May, *The Making of the Monroe Doctrine* (Cambridge, MA: Harvard University Press, 1992), 130–131.

21. Adams, *Memoirs,* 6:152. Leonard Lawson concludes on slender evidence that Britain had a necessity of good relations with the United States for Britain's security. Leonard Axel Lawson, *The Relation of British Policy to the Declaration of the Monroe Doctrine* (New York: Columbia University, 1922), 109.

22. Richard Rush, *Memoranda of a Residence at the Court of London Comprising Incidents Official and Personal from 1819–1825: Including Negotiations on the Oregon Question, and Other Unsettled Questions between the United States and Great Britain* (Philadelphia: Lea & Blanchard, 1845), 445.

23. Ibid., 449.

24. George Canning, quoted in Lawson, *The Relation of British Policy,* 123. This statement is not, however, recounted by Rush in his memoir.

25. Rush, *Memoranda of a Residence at the Court of London,* 400–401.

26. Ibid., 432.

27. Ibid., 432–435.

28. Ibid., 412–413. Canning's note is reprinted in T. B. Edgington, *The Monroe Doctrine* (Boston: Little, Brown, 1905), 7–9.

29. Augustus Granville Stapleton, *The Political Life of the Right Honourable George Canning: From His Acceptance of the Seals of the Foreign Department, in September 1822, to the Period of His Death, in August 1827: Together with a Short Review of Foreign Affairs Subsequently to That Event,* vol. 2 (London: Longman, Rees, Orme, Brown and Green, 1831), 22.

30. Perkins, *A History of the Monroe Doctrine,* 38.

31. John Quincy Adams, *Memoirs,* 6:177. Given subsequent American interventions in Latin America, that would have been a very shrewd move by Canning, at a minimum driving up the reputational costs to the United States for its interventions.

32. Canning did not explain his silence on the subject until November, and news of it did not reach Washington until the following February, three months after Monroe's message to the Congress. McGee, "The Monroe Doctrine," 238.

33. Rush, *Memoranda of a Residence at the Court of London,* 451.

34. Henry Addington to George Canning, December 1, 1823, quoted in McGee, "The Monroe Doctrine," 238.

35. U.S. Department of State, "The Monroe Doctrine (1823)," http://web.archive.org/web/20120108131055/http://eca.state.gov/education/engteaching/pubs/AmLnC/br50.htm; May, *The Making of the Monroe Doctrine,* 191.

36. Thomas Jefferson, *The Writings of Thomas Jefferson,* ed. Paul Leicester Ford, vol. 10 (New York: G. P. Putnam's Sons, 1899), 277–278.

37. James Madison to James Monroe, October 30, 1823, in Hamilton, ed., *The Writings of James Monroe,* 6:394, quoted in Perkins, *A History of the Monroe Doctrine,* 46.

38. It was Adams's singularity in opposition among the Monroe cabinet that leads Ernest May to suspect a domestic politics motive—that of Adams positioning himself for the coming presidential election. This was also the conjecture of the French ambassador in Washington. May's argument cannot be proven, since Adams gives no such testimony in his diary or correspon-

dence, nor do others in their direct accounts of him; moreover, May does not disprove the alternative explanations based on Adams's stalwart support for manifest destiny and justifiable concern about Britain's latitude to change its position absent a public commitment to independence of Latin American countries from Spain. See May, *The Making of the Monroe Doctrine,* 182–186; for the French Ambassador's view, see Perkins, *A History of the Monroe Doctrine,* 57.

39. Lawson, *The Relation of British Policy,* 121.

40. Adams, *Memoirs,* 6:195. Monroe may have taken the sweep of the declaration from Madison's recommendation for common action with Britain in support of Greece, as well as in the western hemisphere. See McGee, "The Monroe Doctrine," 289.

41. Adams, quoted in Donald Sheehan, *The Making of American History,* Book I: *The Emergence of a Nation* (New York: Holt, Rinehard and Wniston, 1954), 270–271.

42. Monroe, "Seventh Annual Message," 287.

43. John Quincy Adams, quoted in McGee, "The Monroe Doctrine," 242. McGee does not ascribe duplicity to Adams in giving this false account; he instead concludes the decision was yet in the making and that Monroe's famous declaration was a stopgap measure until the Canning-Rush negotiations were concluded. The ringing republicanism of Monroe's declaration makes that conclusion difficult to sustain.

44. Perkins, *A History of the Monroe Doctrine,* 56.

45. Ibid., 27, 57.

46. Tsar Alexander to Baron Tuyll, quoted in Perkins, *A History of the Monroe Doctrine,* 57.

47. Dexter Perkins, *The Monroe Doctrine 1823–1826* (Cambridge, MA: Harvard University Press, 1927), 228–235.

48. W. C. Ford, "John Quincy Adams and the Monroe Doctrine," pt. 2, *American Historical Review* 8 (1902): 47, quoted in Perkins, *A History of the Monroe Doctrine,* 48.

49. Ford, "John Quincy Adams and the Monroe Doctrine," 38, quoted in Perkins, *A History of the Monroe Doctrine,* 48.

50. George Canning, quoted in Perkins, *A History of the Monroe Doctrine,* 32.

51. George Canning, quoted in George Dangerfield, *The Era of Good Feelings* (New York: Harcourt, Brace and Company, 1952), 306.

52. Lawson, *The Relation of British Policy,* 111.

53. Perkins, *The Monroe Doctrine 1823–26,* 258.

54. Perkins, *A History of the Monroe Doctrine,* 62.

55. This conclusion is borne out in H. W. V. Temperly, "The Later American Policy of George Canning," *American Historical Review* 11, no. 4 (1906): 779–797.

56. John Quincy Adams, quoted in Perkins, *A History of the Monroe Doctrine,* 190.

57. Paul Kennedy, *The Rise and Fall of the Great Powers* (London: Unwin Hyman, 1988), 178.

58. Ibid., 178.

59. Henry Kissinger writes that "under the umbrella of the Monroe Doctrine, America could pursue policies which were not all that different from the dreams of any European king—expanding its commerce and influence, annexing territory—in short, turning itself into a great power." But this conflates the policy of the Monroe declaration with the much later and more expansive interpretation undertaken during the Venezuelan debt crises. See Henry Kissinger, *Diplomacy* (New York: Simon and Schuster, 1994), 36.

60. Adams, *Memoirs,* 6:203.

4. PARALLEL LATITUDES: OREGON'S BOUNDARIES

1. George C. Herring *From Colony to Superpower: U.S. Foreign Relations Since 1776* (New York: Oxford University Press, 2008), 147.

2. Britain took the Falkland Islands in 1833, and was involved in Central America from its holding in Guyana. When the United States entered into a treaty with the government of New Grenada,

the United States expressed its hope that both Britain and France would also. Dexter Perkins, *A History of the Monroe Doctrine* (Boston: Little, Brown, 1963), 93.

3. Richard Rush, *Memoranda of a Residence at the Court of London, Comprising Incidents Official and Personal from 1819–1825: Including Negotiations on the Oregon Question, and Other Unsettled Questions between the United States and Great Britain* (Pennsylvania: Lea and Blanchard, 1845), 629.

4. Britain and the United States held a shared sovereignty in Oregon. In 1824, negotiators agreed to postpone any decision for ten years, and then in 1827 agreed to postpone decision indefinitely. Also included in 1827 was a stipulation that either side could renounce joint administration with one year's notice.

5. For a laudatory evaluation of Polk's foreign policy, see Henry Nau, *Conservative Internationalism: Armed Diplomacy under Jefferson, Polk, Truman, and Reagan* (Princeton, NJ: Princeton University Press, 2013); for one more critical, see David Pletcher, *The Diplomacy of Annexation: Texas, Oregon, and the Mexican War* (Columbia: University of Missouri Press, 1973); Perkins, *A History of the Monroe Doctrine* (Boston: Little, Brown, 1955), 85, concludes of Oregon that "it was no diplomatic triumph."

6. Wellington's defense of the establishment in 1830 is characteristic of the British attitude: "He was fully convinced that the country possessed, at the present moment, a legislature which answered all the good purposes of legislation,—and this to a greater degree than any legislature ever had answered, in any country whatever." "Chapter XIX The Period of Reform, 1815–1852" in *Readings in English History Drawn from the Original Sources: Intended to Illustrate a Short History of England,* ed. Edward Potts Cheyney (Boston: Ginn and Company, 1922), 680. See also Paul Crook, "Whiggery and America: Accommodating the Radical Threat," in *Radicalism and Revolution in Britain, 1775–1848,* ed. Michael T. Davis (New York: St. Martin's Press, 2000), 198.

7. Evelyn Ashley, *The Life and Correspondence of Henry John Temple, Viscount Palmerston,* vol. 2 (London: Bentley, 1879), 412.

8. *London Times,* quoted in Pletcher, *The Diplomacy of Annexation,* 238.

9. Andrew Jackson, quoted in Robert Remini, "The Election of 1832," in *History of American Presidential Elections,* ed. Arthur Schlesinger and Fred Israel, vol. 1 (New York: Chelsea House, 1971), 509.

10. Even so ardent a fan of America as Alexis de Tocqueville described Jackson as "a man of violent temper and very moderate talents." Alexis de Tocqueville, *Democracy in America* I, ed. Phillips Bradley, trans. Henry Reeve and Francis Bowen (Ann Arbor: University of Michigan, 2005), 289.

11. Daniel Walker Howe, *What Hath God Wrought: The Transformation of America, 1815–1848* (Oxford: Oxford University Press, 2007), 328–366. See also G. D. Lillibridge, *Beacon of Freedom: The Impact of American Democracy upon Great Britain, 1830–1870* (Philadelphia: University of Pennsylvania Press, 1955), 37–41.

12. For a superb account of John Quincy Adams's presidency, see Charles N. Edel, *Nation Builder: John Quincy Adams and the Grand Strategy of the Republic* (Cambridge, MA: Harvard University Press, 2014).

13. Peter Rousseau, "Jacksonian Monetary Policy, Specie Flows, and the Panic of 1837," *Journal of Economic History* 62 (2002): 457.

14. For Jackson's continuing influence, see Walter Russell Mead, *Special Providence: American Foreign Policy and How It Changed the World* (New York: Knopf, 2011).

15. George Washington, quoted in Joseph Ellis, *His Excellency George Washington* (New York: Knopf, 2004), 212.

16. Around six hundred treaties were negotiated between the U.S. government and Native American tribes, resulting in the transfer of two square miles per hour from 1784 to 1911. Arthur Spirling, "US Treaty-Making with American Indians: Institutional Change and Relative Power, 1784-1911," *American Journal of Political Science* 56, no. 1 (2012): 84–97.

17. Jack Sosin, *Whitehall and the Wilderness: The Middle West in British Colonial Policy, 1760–1775* (Lincoln: University of Nebraska Press, 1971).

18. The American to the British Commissioners, September 26, 1814, *House Documents, Otherwise Publ. as Executive Documents: 13th Congress, 2d Session—49th Congress, 1st Session* (Washington: Government Printing Office, 1972), 43. See also H. Niles, ed., *Niles Weekly Register,* vol. 7 (Baltimore: Franklin Press, bound 1913), 233.

19. *House Documents, Otherwise Publ. as Executive Documents: 13th Congress, 2d Session—49th Congress, 1st Session* (Washington, DC: U.S. Government Printing Office, 1972), 44. In 1815, Americans still had the self-awareness to acknowledge the unfairness of their actions toward Indian tribes: "if this be a spirit of aggrandizement, the undersigned are prepared to admit, in that sense, its existence." Niles, *Niles Weekly Register,* vol. 7 (Baltimore: Franklin Press, bound 1913), 233. That awareness was heightened by the inclusion among the negotiators of Albert Gallatin, former treasury secretary and a noted expert on tribal cultures. Also among the negotiators was John Quincy Adams.

20. For President Madison's narrowing of terms from victory, as represented in attaining relief from the stated purposes of going to war, to accepting only cessation of hostilities as sufficient condition for ending the war, see Henry Adams, *History of the United States of America during the Administration of James Madison,* vol. 2, 1192; and Charles M. Gates, "The West in American Diplomacy, 1812–1815," *Mississippi Valley Historical Review* 26, no. 4 (1940): 499–510.

21. For a sense of the rarity of such an ensuring arrangement, see Stephen Krasner, *Sovereignty: Organized Hypocrisy* (Princeton, NJ: Princeton University Press, 1999).

22. John O'Sullivan, quoted in Thomas R. Hietala, *Manifest Design: American Exceptionalism and Empire* (Ithaca, NY: Cornell University Press, 1985), 255.

23. For an example of the argument about "the natural flow of events," See John O'Sullivan, "Annexation," *United States Magazine and Democratic Review* 17, no. 1 (1845): 5–10.

24. This was a popular slogan, not formally part of the 1845 presidential campaign.

25. John O'Sullivan, "Manifest Destiny" (editorial), *New York Morning News,* December 27, 1845.

26. Editorial, *Illinois State Register,* May 15, 1846.

27. Frederick Merk, *Manifest Destiny and Mission in American History* (Cambridge, MA: Harvard University Press, 1963), 215.

28. Robert C. Winthrop, "Speech of Mr. Winthrop, of Massachusetts, on the Oregon Question. Delivered in the House of Representatives of the United States, Jan. 3, 1846," https://archive.org/details /speechofmrwinthro1wint.

29. John Ward, *Andrew Jackson: Symbol for an Age* (New York: Oxford University Press, 1955), 136–137.

30. James K. Polk, "Inaugural Address of James Knox Polk, March 4, 1845," http://avalon.law.yale.edu/19th_century/polk.asp.

31. James Knox Polk, *The Diary of a President* (New York: Capricorn, 1968), 3–4.

32. Ulysses S. Grant, *Personal Memoirs of U. S. Grant* (Cleveland: World Pub. Co., 1952), 22–24.

33. Center for the Study of the Pacific Northwest, "British and American Activities in the Pacific Northwest, 1818–1848," http://www.washington.edu/uwired/outreach/cspn/Website /Classroom%20Materials/Pacific%20Northwest%20History /Lessons/Lesson%208/8.html.

34. A Convention to Regulate the Commerce Between the Territories of the United States and His Britannick Majesty, http://tcc.export .gov/Trade_Agreements/All_Trade_Agreements/exp_005413.asp.

35. For an explanation that ties British policies to the complicated party politics of government formation during consideration of repealing the Corn Laws, see Frederick Merk, "British Party

Politics and the Oregon Treaty," *American Historical Review* 37, no. 4 (July 1932): 653–677.

36. A detailed summary of the negotiation is provided by former American ambassador to London Edward Everett in his letter to Lord Russell, December 28, 1855, Edward Everett Papers, Massachusetts Historical Society, Reel 31, Vol. 105.

37. Merk, "British Party Politics and the Oregon Treaty," 654.

38. Even the indefatigable American negotiator Albert Gallatin could not make progress: the Webster-Ashburton Treaty of 1842, which found resolution for so many irritants going back to as far as Revolutionary War—even compensation for slave repatriation—had to exclude Oregon. Merk attributes the failure to resolve the Oregon dispute before 1845 almost entirely to the resistance of Lord Palmerston framing any concession from the 1824 position as dishonorable. See Merk, "British Party Politics and the Oregon Treaty," 654–657.

39. Crook, "Whiggery and America," 209.

40. Bertha Ann Reuter, *Anglo-American Relations during the Spanish-American War* (New York: The Macmillan Company, 1924), 2.

41. James Spedding, quoted in Crook, "Whiggery and America," 197.

42. John M. Owen, *Liberal Peace, Liberal War: American Politics and International Security* (Ithaca, NY: Cornell University Press, 1997), 104.

43. Henry John Temple, Third Viscount Palmerston, quoted in Crook, "Whiggery and America," 197.

44. For a terrific analysis of democracy in Victorian British literature, see Iain McCalman, "Controlling the Riots: Dickens, Barnaby Rudge and Romantic Revolution," in *Radicalism and Revolution in Britain, 1775–1848,* ed. Michael T. Davis (New York: St. Martin's Press, 2000); the quotation herein is from 218.

45. As a measure of aristocratic intransigence, Sir Francis Burdette's bill for universal suffrage, equalizing electoral districts, and confidential voting in the House of Commons garnered only a single other supporter. Thomas Erskine May, *The Constitutional*

History of England, vol. 1 (London; New York: Longmans, Green, 1912), 352-359, 406-407.

46. Revolutions in France had a greater hold on the fears of Britain's aristocracy, but less appeal to its middle and lower classes because of the frequency and violence associated with them from 1789 through Napoleon's dramatic revision of the social compact, the overthrow of the restored Bourbon monarchy in the July Revolution of 1830, and subsequent repression.

47. Bruce Morrison argues genuine fear of revolution in Britain was the primary cause of elite compromise. Bruce Morrison, "Channeling the 'Restless Spirit of Innovation': Elite Concessions and Institutional Change in the British Reform Act of 1832," *World Politics* 63, no. 2 (2011): 678-710. See also Lillibridge, *Beacon of Freedom,* 3.

48. Showing the salience of responding to public concern about political representation, Charles Grey, Second Earl Grey's first announcement as prime minister was commitment to continued parliamentary reform. May, *The Constitutional History of England,* 1:421-423.

49. The bank campaign was consequential, resulting in withdrawal of a quarter of the reserves in the first days of May 1832 after reform had been stymied. See David Gross, *99 Tactics of Successful Tax Resistance Campaigns* (San Luis Obispo: Picket Line Press, 2014), 176.

50. Crook, "Whiggery and America," 195.

51. David F. Krein, "The Great Landowners in the House of Commons, 1833-85," *Parliamentary History* 32, no. 3 (2013): 460-476; May, *The Constitutional History of England,* 1:316-317.

52. Eric J. Evans, *The Forging of the Modern State: Early Industrial Britain, 1783–1870,* 2nd ed. (Addison Wesley 1996), 229. Evans does not make the American comparison, but merely notes that the 1832 Reform Bill was the crucial acknowledgment of democratic legitimacy.

53. Bear F. Braumoeller, *The Great Powers and the International System: Systemic Theory in Empirical Perspectiveys* (New York: Cambridge University Press, 2012), 124; Paul Ziegler, *Palmerston* (New York: Houndmills, 2003), 131.

54. Editorial, *London Times,* December 27, 1845, https://www .newspapers.com/image/33032807/.

55. Letter from Ambassador Louis McLane, June 3, 1846, *Correspondence of James K. Polk,* ed. Wayne Cutler (Knoxville: University of Tennessee Press, 2009), 10:193.

56. Chartism was a political reform movement from 1838 to 1857 in Britain, advocating public protests for constitutional changes, including secret ballots, universal male suffrage at age twenty-one, elimination of property requirements for voting, uniform constituencies, and annual elections to reduce corruption. The Radicals were a separate grouping that joined with the Whigs to form the Liberal Party in 1859. Lillibridge, *Beacon of Freedom,* 40.

57. John Clarke, *British Diplomacy and Foreign Policy 1789–1865* (London: Unwin Hyman, 1989), 302.

58. One of the very best parts of Aaron Friedberg's very good book *The Weary Titan* is his insight about "the central role of simplifying, but sometimes misleading, indicators in both public and intergovernmental discussions of the various forms of national power." In the instance of trade, the British government utilized misleading economic indicators because they were the only data available. Aaron Friedberg, *The Weary Titan: Britain and the Experience of Relative Decline, 1895–1905* (Princeton, NJ: Princeton University Press, 1988), 80–81.

59. Merk, "British Party Politics and the Oregon Treaty," 655. The Webster-Ashburton Treaty allowed both countries access to the Great Lakes, established the border between Lake Superior and the Lake of the Woods, extended the agreed border along the forty-ninth parallel to the Rocky Mountains, established grounds

for extradition between the two countries, and pledged to end the maritime slave trade.

60. Henry John Temple, Third Viscount Palmerston to Lord John Russell, quoted in Merk, "British Party Politics and the Oregon Treaty," 668; emphasis in the original. Merk persuasively argues that it was Palmerston's use of public media, rather than the substance of his position, that eventually caused the Liberals' leader, Lord Aberdeen, to force compliance on Palmerston over Oregon.

61. Whether British ambassador Richard Pakenham's rejection of an American offer on July 12, 1845, was part of this stalling strategy or a bungle (Foreign Minister Aberdeen censured the ambassador) is unclear.

62. Pletcher, *The Diplomacy of Annexation*, 322.

63. Henry Nau and Daniel Walker Howe, whose views seldom overlap, both consider Polk too adept a politician to be caught by surprise. But Nau argues that Polk strengthened the American negotiating position by appeal to the Congress and thereby achieved British acceptance of the forty-ninth parallel as the boundary, whereas Howe argues Polk used expected congressional opposition to walk away from a campaign promise to annex all of Oregon. Henry R. Nau, *Conservative Internationalism: Armed Diplomacy under Jefferson, Polk, Truman, and Reagan* (Princeton, NJ: Princeton University Press, 2015); Daniel Walker Howe, *What Hath God Wrought: The Transformation of America, 1815–1848* (Oxford: Oxford University Press, 2009), 722.

64. James K. Polk, "First Annual Message," December 2, 1845, http://www.presidency.ucsb.edu/ws/?pid=29486.

65. Polk, "Inaugural Address," in *Documents of American History*, vol. 1, *To 1898*, ed. Henry Steele Commager (Englewood Cliffs: Prentice-Hall, 1988), 309–310.

66. Perkins, *A History of the Monroe Doctrine*, 79.

67. Polk, "First Annual Message."

68. That Calhoun, who was considered a firebrand during the Monroe administration, was a moderating voice arguing for a narrow interpretation of the doctrine is illustrative of just how much American politics had shifted with Jacksonian populism. I am grateful to Tim Gray for this insight.

69. Perkins, *A History of the Monroe Doctrine*, 82.

70. Michael Turner, *Liberty and Liberticide: The Role of America in Nineteenth Century British Radicalism* (Lanham, MD: Lexington Books, 2014), 104.

71. *New York Tribune*, December 3, 1845.

72. Howard Jones, *Crucible of Power: A History of American Foreign Relations to 1913* (Wilmington: SR Books, 2002), 155.

73. Howe, *What Hath God Wrought*, 719.

74. Jones, *Crucible of Power*, 155.

75. Hunter Miller, *Treaties and Other International Acts of the United States of America* (Washington, DC: U.S. Government Printing Office, 1931–1948), vol. 5, 58; see also Barry Gough, *The Royal Navy and the Northwest Coast of North America, 1810–1914* (Vancouver: University of British Columbia Press, 1971), 70–83.

76. Polk, *Diary*, 241; also quoted in Thomas Leonard, *James K. Polk: A Clear and Unquestionable Destiny*, 117–119. Leonard emphasizes the importance of Britain's fleet deployment in taming Polk's aggressiveness. Polk's claim of surprise is at variance with the descriptions from his ambassador in London and the newspapers sent from that ambassador. It lends support to Howe's view in *What Hath God Wrought*, 717, that in unwinding the crisis Polk "had to play his cards in such a way as to achieve a compromise over Oregon without having to accept responsibility for that compromise."

77. Polk, "Inaugural Address," 309. See also Andrea Kokeny, "British and / or American—The Colonization of the Oregon Country," *Americana* 5, no. 2 (2009), http://americanaejournal.hu/vol5no2/kokeny.

78. "Littell's Living Age," *The Living Age,* May 16, 1846, vol. 9, issue 105, 320.

79. Thomas Hart Benton, quoted in Jones, *Crucible of Power,* 156.

80. Henry John Temple, Third Viscount Palmerston, quoted in "Parliamentary Intelligence," *London Times,* June 30, 1846, 2, https://www.newspapers.com/image/33032682.

81. Merk, "The British Corn Crisis of 1845–46 and the Oregon Treaty," 121. Merk makes a compelling case that British compromise over Oregon was not predominantly influenced by British reliance on wheat imported from the United States (though Britain became a food importer after industrialization), memorably describing that argument as "the serving up of contemporary propaganda as history." See Frederick Merk, "The British Corn Crisis of 1845–46 and the Oregon Treaty," *Agricultural History* 8, no. 3 (1934): 95–123.

82. Lord John Russell, quoted in "Lord John Russell in Glasgow," *The Pembroke Herald and General Advertiser,* January 23, 1846, http://newspapers.library.wales/view/3052123/3052127/42/John%20Smith.

83. The Crimean War of 1854 is more generally considered the point at which public attitudes begin to constrain British foreign policy. And surely putting the Oregon Boundary Dispute in the same category as the Crimean War for its effect within Britain risks a misleading claim of the magnitude of Enver Hoxha that the alliance of China and Albania represented more than a billion people. The Crimean War had a much bigger effect, as it was both a genuine war and an enormously costly one in terms of British casualties, and those visible as journalists reported directly from battlefields as never before. But if domestic antiwar sentiment during and after the Crimean War raised the political cost to Britain for engaging in war, that was not different in type from the pressures on British monarchs in judging their domestic support for foreign campaigns; in the Oregon dispute, British subjects were advocating the opposing state's claim on the same basis—democratic representation—as America was making it.

84. Philip Parrish, reviewing Frederick Merk, "British Party Politics and the Oregon Treaty," *Oregon Historical Quarterly* 33, no. 3 (1932): 281.

85. Crook, "Whiggery and America," 208.

5. DOMESTIC THREAT: AMERICA'S CIVIL WAR

1. The moral cause for which the Civil War is now remembered was still muddied by President Lincoln disavowing emancipation as a war aim and the continuing presence in the Union of several slaveholding states: Delaware, Kentucky, Maryland, and Missouri.

2. John Mearsheimer, *The Tragedy of Great Power Politics* (New York: W. W. Norton and Company, 2001), 248, table 3.3.

3. Henry John Temple, Third Viscount Palmerston, quoted in E. D. Steele, *Palmerston and Liberalism, 1855–1865* (Cambridge: Cambridge University Press, 1991), 295.

4. See Ephraim Douglass Adams, *Great Britain and the American Civil War*, 2 vols. (New York: Longman, Greens, 1925).

5. Peter Thompson, "The Case of the Missing Hegemon: British Nonintervention in the American Civil War," *Security Studies* 16, no. 1 (2007): 98, 107, 116.

6. Adams, *Great Britain and the American Civil War*, 1:2.

7. Stephen R. Rock, "Anglo-U.S. Relations, 1845–1930: Did Shared Liberal Values and Democratic Institutions Keep the Peace?," in *Paths to Peace: Is Democracy the Answer?*, ed. Miriam Fendius Elman (Cambridge, MA: MIT Press, 1997), 117–118.

8. Sheldon Vanauken, *The Glittering Illusion: English Sympathy for the Southern Confederacy* (Regenery Gateway Books, 1989), 10.

9. John Owen, *Liberal Peace, Liberal War: American Politics and International Security* (Ithaca, NY: Cornell University Press, 2000), 129–130.

10. Amanda Foreman, "Disunion: How to Lose Allies and Alienate People," *New York Times,* August 11, 2011, https://opinionator.blogs.nytimes.com/2011/08/11/how-to-lose-allies-and-alienate-people/.

11. Henry John Temple, Third Viscount Palmerston, quoted in H. C. F. Bell, *Lord Palmerston*, vol. 2 (New York: Longmans, Green, 1936), 295.

12. The Clay mission is considered central by Donaldson Jordan and Edwin J. Pratt but Duncan Andrew Campbell believes they overstate its influence. See Donaldson Jordan and Edwin J. Pratt, *Europe and the American Civil War* (Boston: Houghton Mifflin 1931); and Duncan Andrew Campbell, *English Public Opinion and the American Civil War*, vol. 33 (Rochester: Boydell and Brewer, 2003).

13. Kevin Phillips, *The Cousins' Wars: Religion, Politics, and the Triumph of Anglo-America* (New York: Basic Books, 1999), 498.

14. "Our Friends in England A Practical Suggestion" (editorial), *New York Times*, November 8, 1862, http://www.nytimes.com/1862/11/08/news/our-friends-in-england-a-practical-suggestion.html.

15. Phillips, *The Cousins' Wars*, xxiv.

16. Quoted in James McPherson, *Battle Cry of Freedom*, 549.

17. H. C. Allen, *Great Britain and the United States: A History of Anglo-American Relations 1783–1952* (New York: St. Martin's, 1955), 456.

18. Liberal Democrat History Group, "Temple, Henry John (Third Viscount Palmerston)," http://www.liberalhistory.org.uk/resources/temple-henry-john-third-viscount-palmerston/.

19. Henry John Temple, Third Viscount Palmerston, quoted in *Palmerston and Liberalism, 1855–1865* (Cambridge: Cambridge University Press, 1991), 56; also cited in Ben Wilson, *Heyday: The 1850s and the Dawn of the Global Age* (New York: Basic Books, 2016).

20. Allen, *Great Britain and the United States*, 456.

21. Henry John Temple, Third Viscount Palmerston to Queen Victoria, December 5, 1861, quoted in Kenneth Bourne, "British Preparations for War with the North, 1861–1862," *English Historical Review* 76, no. 301 (1961): 630.

22. W. D. Jones, "The British Conservatives and the American Civil War," *American Historical Review* 58 (1953): 529.

23. Joseph Ellis makes this point brilliantly in his evaluation of George Washington's battle plans early in the course of the Revolutionary War. Washington modeled his plans on the textbook thinking of the British Army, which required a more disciplined and better-equipped army than the rebellious colonies could produce. Washington was saved, Ellis persuasively argues, by his willingness to allow subordinate commanders to adapt his concepts. Those subordinate commanders were men like Nathaniel Green and Alexander Hamilton, young men of talent with little invested in the British order and who defined themselves outside it. See Joseph Ellis, *His* Excellency George Washington (New York: Vintage Books, 2005), 23–26.

24. Henry Yates Thomson, quoted in Amanda Foreman, *A World on Fire: Britain's Crucial Role in the American Civil War* (New York: Random House Trade Paperbacks, 2012), 545.

25. William Ewart Gladstone, quoted in Steele, *Palmerston and Liberalism,* 3.

26. William Ewart Gladstone, quoted in E. D. Steele, *Irish Land and British Politics: Tenant-Right and Nationality, 1865–1870* (London: Cambridge University Press, 1974), 45.

27. Carl Schurz, "The Anglo-American Friendship," *Atlantic Monthly,* October 1898, 433–440.

28. Henry John Temple, Third Viscount Palmerston, quoted in Paul Crook, "Whiggery and America: Accommodating the Radical Threat," in *Radicalism and Revolution in Britain, 1775–1848,* ed. Michael T. Davis (London: Palgrave Macmillan UK, 2000), 197.

29. Steele, *Palmerston and Liberalism,* 38.

30. Charles Dickens, *American Notes for General Circulation* (London: Chapman and Hall, 1913), 200.

31. Iain McCalman, "Controlling the Riots: Dickens, Barnaby Rudge and Romantic Revolution," in *History* 84, no. 275 (1999): 461.

32. The 1832 Reform Act expanded the franchise to roughly 20 percent of British males, producing an electorate of 650,000

among a population of fourteen million. See John A. Phillips and Charles Wetherell, "The Great Reform Act of 1832 and the Political Modernization of England," *American Historical Review* 100, 413–414.

33. P. J. Cain, "Economics and Empire: The Metropolitan Context," in *The Oxford History of the British Empire,* vol. 3, *The Nineteenth Century,* ed. Andrew Porter (Oxford: Oxford University Press 2001), 33.

34. Foreman, "How to Lose Allies and Alienate People."

35. Thompson, "The Case of the Missing Hegemon," 122–125, 126.

36. Evelyn Ashley, *The Life and Correspondence of Henry John Temple, Viscount Palmerston,* vol. 2 (London: Bentley, 1879), 218.

37. Paul Kennedy, "The Tradition of Appeasement in British Foreign Policy, 1865–1939," *British Journal of International Studies* 2, no. 3 (1976): 196. Kennedy argues elsewhere that Britain had little strategic interest in intervening in the American Civil War. See Paul Kennedy, *The Rise and Fall of the Great Powers* (New York: Random House, 1987), 178–182.

38. John Clarke, *British Diplomacy and Foreign Policy 1782–1865* (London: Unwin Hyman, 1989), 38.

39. Adams, *Great Britain and the American Civil War,* 1:90.

40. Sir G. C. Lewis to Henry John Temple, Third Viscount Palmerston (regarding the probability of an attack on Canada by America), September 3, 1861, MS PP/GC/LE/144, Palmerston Papers, University of Southampton. Reinforcements were eventually sent during the *Trent* affair, but only as a defensive measure. James Scherer, *Cotton as a World Power* (New York: Stokes, 1916), 275.

41. The British attorney general recommended neutrality on this basis.

42. All the European maritime powers acceded to the Paris Treaty that Britain drafted as part of their effort to abolish the slave trade. When in 1858 the British commenced boarding American ships, the U.S. Senate passed legislation "enabling the President to obtain by force prompt redress for the perpetuation of outrages

upon the flag, soil, or citizens of the United States or their property."
Campbell, *English Public Opinion and the American Civil War,* 20–21.

43. Lincoln later acknowledged the mistake as his own, explaining he
knew little of the law between nations. Bernard Schwartz,
"President Lincoln as a Constitutional Scholar," *American Bar
Association Journal* 67 (1981): 177.

44. Palmerston himself had wanted to reinforce Canada, but could
not muster support for its financing until the *Trent* affair six
months later. Bourne, "British Preparations for War," 631–632.

45. Lincoln said of abolition, "I believe I have no lawful right to do so
and I have no intention to do so." Abraham Lincoln, "First
Inaugural Address of Abraham Lincoln, Monday, March 4, 1861,"
http://avalon.law.yale.edu/19th_century/lincoln1.asp. Lincoln had
also overruled the military governor of Missouri's emancipation
of slaves in that state.

46. Canadians took up arms against their government in 1837
demanding elected political representation. The U.S. government,
hoping the rebellion might result in a sister republic on its
northern border, declared America's neutrality in the conflict,
harboring rebels and even allowed them to openly organize. See
Michael Ducharme, "Closing the Last Chapter of the Atlantic
Revolution: The 1837–38 Rebellions in Upper and Lower Canada,"
Proceedings of the American Antiquarian Society 116, no. 2 (2006):
413–430.

47. Britain's Corn Laws favoring domestic producers (and therefore
higher prices for aristocratic landowners) were repealed in 1846, at
which time it became a net importer of food, principally from
North America. See G. Kitson Clark, "The Repeal of the Corn
Laws and the Politics of the Forties," *Economic History Review* 4,
no. 1 (1951): 1–13.

48. Martin Crawford, *The Anglo-American Crisis of the Mid-Nineteenth
Century* (Athens: University of Georgia Press, 1987), 109. Adams,
Great Britain and the American Civil War (Bibliobazaar, 2006);

Brian Jenkins, *Britain and the War of the Union* (Montreal: McGill-Queen's University Press, 1974); and Donaldson Jordan and Edwin J. Pratt, *Europe and the American Civil War* (New York: Houghton Mifflin, 1931) all credit Seward's threat as engendering caution in British government. Campbell, *English Public Opinion and the American Civil War*, demonstrates the hesitance already existed.

49. Gordon H. Warren, *Fountain of Discontent: The Trent Affair and Freedom of the Seas* (Boston: Northeastern University, 1981), 71, describes the Northern reaction as "a roar of disapproval." See also Howard Jones, *Union in Peril: The Crisis over British Intervention in the Civil War* (Chapel Hill: University of North Carolina Press, 1992), 28.

50. Elizabeth Cobbs Hoffman, "A Dangerous Neutrality," *New York Times,* May 12, 2011, gives a rich feel for the public and government response.

51. D. P. Crook, "Portents of War: English Opinion on Secession," *Journal of American Studies* 33 (1967): 163–179. Clay is elsewhere described as "a brawler and duelist. Whether in the United States or abroad, he typically sported a bowie knife and pair of pistols." David Mayers, *The Ambassadors and America's Soviet Policy* (New York: Oxford University Press, 1995), 39.

52. "Letter from Hon. Cassius M. Clay," reprinted in the *New York Times,* June 5, 1861, http://www.nytimes.com/1861/06/05/news /letter-from-hon-cassius-m-clay.html. That Clay repeated the allegations in Paris, assuring his French hosts they would "sweep England from the map" was likewise resented.

53. Howard Jones attests that Confederate mail was aboard and had the British ship been searched, its seizure would have been uncontested. Jones, *Union in Peril,* 83.

54. Henry John Temple, Third Viscount Palmerston, quoted in Charles Francis Adams, "The Trent Affair," *Proceedings of the Massachusetts Historical Society* 45 (1912): 54.

55. Commenting on the risks unnecessarily run, James Rawley concludes that had the captain "escorted the British ship to a prize court, the episode would have been appealed from public opinion drunk to legal opinion sober." James Rawley, *Turning Points of the American Civil War* (Lincoln: University of Nebraska Press, 1966), 93.

56. Adams, *Great Britain and the American Civil War,* 1:215, 278.

57. Rawley, *Turning Points of the American Civil War,* 86. Scott's services were accepted and diverted to the Civil War.

58. The assessment was Palmerstone's own; throughout the crisis his minister of war remained skeptical of Union intention to risk a two-front war. Robin W. Winks, *The Civil War Years: Canada and the United* States (Montreal: McGill-Queen's University Press, 1998), 53.

59. Russell's hard line is not only evidenced in his correspondence with Prime Minister Palmerston but also in his exchanges with British ambassador Richard Lyons in Washington. See Russell, *Recollections and Suggestions* (London: Longman, Greens, 1875), 275.

60. Rawley, *Turning Points of the American Civil War,* 89; for a draft of Lincoln's dispatch proposing those alternatives, see Roy P. Basler, Marion Dolores Pratt, Lloyd A. Dunlap, eds., *Collected Works of Abraham Lincoln,* vol. 5 (New Brunswick: Rutgers University Press, 1953), 62–64; Jay Monaghan, *Diplomat in Carpet Slippers: Abraham Lincoln Deals with Foreign Affairs* (Lincoln: University of Nebraska Press, 1945), 189–190.

61. Henry John Temple, Third Viscount Palmerston, quoted in Steele, *Palmerston and Liberalism,* 297.

62. Edward Bates, *The Diary of Edward Bates, 1859–1866,* ed. Howard K. Beale (Washington, DC: U.S. Government Printing Office, 1933), 216.

63. Charles Francis Adams to his son, January 10, 1862, in Charles Francis Adams, *A Cycle of Adams' Letters,* vol. 1 (Boston: Houghton Mifflin Company, 1920), 99.

64. Richard Henry Dana, "The Trent Affair," *Proceedings of the Massachusetts Historical Society (1912)*, 45:528.

65. Lord William Russell, quoted in Ephraim Adams, *Great Britain and the American Civil War*, 1:215.

66. The first dispatch demanded release of the envoys, apology, and reparation; subsequent instruction allowed transmission of the text, a week for consideration, latitude to the British envoy to determine if conditions had been met, and "to abstain from menace." Notably, pressure on the government to give the Union some latitude came from the prince consort. Adams, *Great Britain and the American Civil War*, 1:213.

67. Lord William Russell to William Ewart Gladstone, December 13, 1861, cited in Ephraim Douglass Adams, *Great Britain and the American Civil War*, 1:fn447.

68. Russell, not having yet received word from Washington, presciently counseled Palmerston in early January, "I still incline to think Lincoln will submit, but not until the clock is 59 minutes past 11. If it is war, I fear we must summon Parliament forthwith." Lord William Russell to Henry John Temple, Third Viscount Palmerston, quoted in Adams, *Great Britain and the American Civil War*, 1:230.

69. Union attorney general Bates recorded this in his diary as the cabinet consensus. Bates, *The Diary of Edward Bates*, 216.

70. Edward McPherson, *The Political History of the United States of America* (Bedford: Applewood Books, 2009), 338–342.

71. Charles Francis Adams to William Seward, January 10, 1862, quoted in Stephen Tufness, "Expatriate Foreign Relations: Britain's American Community and Transnational Approaches to the U.S. Civil War," *Diplomatic History* 40, no. 4 (2016): 635–663.

72. Confederate agents, quoted in Adams, *Great Britain and the American Civil War*, 1:243.

73. Editorial, "London, Saturday, 1862" *London Times,* January 11, 1862, 6, https://www.newspapers.com/image/32757267/.

74. Adams, *Great Britain and the American Civil War,* 2:34.
75. Charles Francis Adams to his son, April 4, 1862, in Charles Francis Adams, *A Cycle of Adams' Letters,* ed. Worthington Chauncey Ford, vol. 1 (Boston: Houghton Mifflin: 1920), 123.
76. Lord William Russell to Henry John Temple, Third Viscount Palmerston, March 31, 1862, quoted in Howard J. Fuller, *Clad In Iron: The American Civil War and the Challenge of British Naval Power* (Westport: Praeger, 2008), 130.
77. Confederate envoys formally put the question of recognition forward after seeing the extent of Parliamentary support during the July debate.
78. "Correspondence with Mr. Mason respecting Blockade and Recognition," *Parliamentary Papers,* North America, No. 2 (1863), Correspondence with Respecting Blockade, and Recognition of the Confederate States (London: Haerison and Sons, 1863), https://archive.org/stream/correspondencewigrea/correspondence wigrea_djvu.txt, *Lords,* 29. no. 7.
79. Adams, *Great Britain and the American Civil War,* 2:29.
80. Russell, September 17, 1862, quoted in Spencer Walpole, *The Life of John Russell* (London: Longmans, Green, 1889), 349, and in Allen C. Guelzo, *Fateful Lightning: A New History of the Civil War and Reconstruction* (New York: Oxford University Press, 2012), ffn32.
81. Russell's memorandum drew this fabulous rebuttal from Lewis, the minister of war: "A dispassionate bystander might be expected to concur in the historical view of Lord Russell, and to desire that the war should be speedily terminated by a pacific agreement between the contending parties. But, unhappily, the decision upon any proposal of the English Government will be made, not by dispassionate bystanders, but by heated and violent partisans; and we have to consider, not how the proposal indicated in the Memorandum ought to be received, or how it would be received by a conclave of philosophers, but how it is likely to be received by

the persons to whom it would be addressed." George Cornewell Lewis, quoted in Adams, *Great Britain and the American Civil War,* 2:52.

82. Lord William Russell to Henry John Temple, Third Viscount Palmerston, August 24, 1862, quoted in David Herbert Donald, *Why the North Won the Civil War: Six Authoritative Views on the Economic, Military, Diplomatic, Social, and Political Reasons Behind the Confederacy's Defeat* (New York: Touchstone, 1960), 72; Adams, *Great Britain and the American Civil War,* 2:52.

83. Henry John Temple, Third Viscount Palmerston to Russell, quoted in Adams, *Great Britain and the American Civil War,* 2:44.

84. Adams, *Great Britain and the American Civil War,* 2:52. President Lincoln's 1863 Emancipation Proclamation did not emancipate slaves in Union states, only those in states the Union was fighting to subdue.

85. Steele, *Palmerston and Liberalism,* 14.

86. "London, Thursday, November 13th, 1862" (editorial), *London Times,* November 13, 1862, 8.

87. Aaron Friedberg cites the British military as coming to this conclusion in 1896, after the calamity of the Boer War and only as the U.S. Navy moved assertively into the Caribbean. Aaron Friedberg, *The Weary Titan: Britain and the Experience of Relative Decline, 1895–1905* (Princeton, NJ: Princeton University Press, 1988), 99, 135.

88. Kenneth Bourne, "British Preparations for War," 602.

89. Henry John Temple, Third Viscount Palmerston to George Cornewell Lewis, December 31, 1862, MS PP/GC/LE/251, Palmerston Papers, University of Southampton.

90. Francis M. Carroll, "The American Civil War and British Intervention: The Threat of Anglo-American Conflict," *Canadian Journal of History* 47, no. 1 (2012).

91. The courts, rather than Parliament or business interests, had been the motive force in producing legal determinations that

were considerably ahead of either law or public sentiment in most countries—certainly the United States.

92. Phillips, *The Cousins' Wars,* 492.

93. Jones, *Union in Peril,* 225.

94. Thompson, "The Case of the Missing Hegemon," 102–103, argues that Britain had relatively few international concerns, giving it a freer hand.

95. Sir George Cornewell Lewis to Henry John Temple, Third Viscount Palmerston (regarding ordnance matters and the threat of rebellion in Hungary and America), August 23, 1861, MS PP/GC/LE/142, Palmerston Papers, University of Southampton.

96. Frank Lawrence Owsley, *King Cotton Diplomacy: Foreign Relations of the Confederate States of America* (Chicago: University of Chicago Press, 1959), 80.

97. Adams measures as counterfactual the restraint of the British government *despite* the Trent crisis—that is, it ought to have resulted in the Confederate envoys being received, and neutrality reconsidered. Ephraim Adams, *Great Britain and the American Civil War,* 1:235.

98. Palmerston, quoted in E. A. Adamov, "Russia and the United States in the Time of the Civil War," *The Journal of Modern History* 2, no. 4 (1930): 586–602.

99. Sir George Cornewell Lewis to Henry John Temple, Third Viscount Palmerston (regarding gun trials, the threat of rebellion in Hungary, the American Civil War, and arrangements for sending troops to Canada), August 27, 1861, MS PP/GC/LE/143, Palmerston Papers, University of Southampton.

100. R. J. Vincent, *Nonintervention and International Order* (Princeton, NJ: Princeton University Press, 1974), 71, 117.

101. Thompson, "The Case of the Missing Hegemon," 127.

102. Bruce Porter, *War and the Rise of the State: The Military Foundations of Modern Politics* (New York: Free Press, 2002), 264.

103. Phillips, *The Cousins' Wars,* 503.

104. Allen, *Great Britain and the United States,* 503.

105. Anthony Trollope, *North America*, vol. 1 (New York: Harper & Brothers Publishers, 1862), 446.

106. Steele, *Palmerston and Liberalism*, 24.

6. MANIFESTING DESTINY: DEFINING THE NATION

1. In one important element of national power, per capita gross domestic product, the United States surpassed Great Britain in the 1870s; most other elements were apparent only decades later. See Nicholas Crafts, *Britain's Relative Economic Performance* (London: Institute of Economic Affairs, 2002).

2. Henry Adams, *The Education of Henry Adams: An Autobiography* (New York: Modern Library, 1999), 183.

3. Walt Whitman Rostow, *British Economy of the Nineteenth Century: Essays* (Oxford: Clarendon Press, 1948), 68.

4. G. Lowes Dickinson, quoted in Barry Rubin and Judith Colp Rubin, *Hating America: A History* (New York: Oxford University Press, 2004), 46.

5. Benjamin Disraeli, quoted in H. C. Allen, *Great Britain and the United States: A History of Anglo-American Relations, 1783–1952* (New York: St. Martin's, 1955), 523.

6. An estimated eighty thousand African Americans migrated from the former Confederate states by 1870. See Jeanette Greenwood, *First Fruits of Freedom: The Migration of Former Slaves and Their Search for Equality in Worcester, Massachusetts, 1862–1900* (Chapel Hill: University of North Carolina Press, 2010), 2. The 1890 Census shows most blacks remained in the Southern states, with emerging concentrations in the northern urban areas (Chicago, Cleveland, New York City, Philadelphia, Pittsburgh, and Toledo), eastern Kansas, central Missouri, southern Ohio, and scattered areas in the West (Arizona, California, Nevada, New Mexico, and Oklahoma), reflecting migration patterns that began during Reconstruction. U.S. Census Office, *Statistical Atlas of the United States Based on the*

Results of the Eleventh Census (Washington, DC: GPO, 1898), plate 11, https://www.loc.gov/resource/g3701gm.gct00010/?sp=27.

7. Sadly, pervasive racism was not confined to the former Confederate states; it was a California court in 1870 that excluded black children from attending school with whites, establishing the legal basis for racial segregation.

8. Winston Churchill, *A History of the English Speaking Peoples,* vol. 4, *The Great Democracies* (New York: Bantam Books, 1963), 242.

9. Bruce Porter, *War and the Rise of the State: The Military Foundations of Modern Politics* (New York: Free Press, 1994), 262.

10. Walt Whitman, "A Broadway Pageant," in *Drum-Taps,* http:// whitmanarchive.org/published/other/DrumTaps.html.

11. Herman Melville, *Battle Pieces and Aspects of the War* (New York: Harper & Brothers Publishers, 1866), 182.

12. Alfred Thayer Mahan, *The Influence of Sea Power upon History, 1660–1783* (Boston: Little, Brown, 1890); Walter Russell Mead, *God and Gold: Britain, America, and the Making of the Modern World* (New York: Knopf, 2007), 111, takes up Mahan's case.

13. Not even Britain could afford to ignore land wars. Secretary of War Henry Fox told the British House of Commons in 1748 that a solely maritime strategy had been rejected by the government "because our conquests at sea, or in America, would in the end signify nothing if, while we were busied about them, the French should make themselves masters of the continent of Europe." Henry Fox, quoted in Brendan Simms, *Three Victories and a Defeat: The Rise and Fall of the First British Empire, 1714–1783* (New York: Allen Lane, 2007), 353.

14. H. W. Brands, *Andrew Jackson, His Life and Times* (New York: Doubleday, 2005), 536.

15. The 1865 Treaty of Little Arkansas, for example, was concluded by the federal government but required the state of Texas to cede land, which it did not. Ernest Wallace, *Ranald S. Mackenzie on the Texas Frontier* (College Station: Texas A&M University Press, 1993), 22–23.

16. Brands, *Andrew Jackson*, 489-492.

17. W. C. Holden, "Frontier Defense in Texas During the Civil War," *West Texas Historical Association Yearbook* 4 (1928): 27-28.

18. Wallace, *Ranald S. Mackenzie on the Texas Frontier*, 23-24.

19. George A. Forsyth quoted in Patricia Y. Stallard, *Glittering Misery: Dependents of the Indian-Fighting Army* (San Rafael: Presidio Press, 1978), 63.

20. Sucheng Chan, "A People of Exceptional Character: Ethnic Diversity, Nativism, and Racism in the California Gold Rush," in *Rooted in Barbarous Soil: People, Culture, and Community in Gold Rush California*, ed. Kevin Starr and Richard J. Orsi (Berkley: University of California, 2000), 50; and Kevin Starr, "Rooted in Barbarous Soil: An Introduction to Gold Rush Society and Culture," *Rooted in Barbarous Soil*, vii.

21. Carol A. O'Connor, "A Region of Cities" in Clyde A. Milner II, *The Oxford History of the American West*, ed. Clyde A Milner, Carol A. O'Connor, and Martha A. Sandweiss (New York: Oxford University Press, 1994), 543.

22. For many commentators, Conestoga wagons, with their bowed canvas hoods on the vast plains of the West evoked ships on an ocean of grass.

23. R. Ernest Dupuy and Trevor N. Dupuy, *The Encyclopedia of Military History from 3500 B.C. to the Present* (New York: Harper & Row, 1970), 905.

24. Fairfax Downey, *Indian Fighting Army* (New York: C. Scribner's Sons, 1941), 35.

25. R. L. Wilson with Greg Martin, *Buffalo Bill's Wild West: An American Legend* (New York: Random House, 1998), 316.

26. The Rogue River Wars in the Washington Territory of the 1850s illustrate the pattern: provocations of settlers backed by local political power (in this case, Governor Isaac Stevens); calling out militia with the army interposing itself between them and the Native Americans; taking native women and

children into the forts as settlers attacked native villages; attacks spiraling upward in magnitude, and newspapers arguing the native case having their offices attacked. Eventually the army was forced by the federal government to take the settler side.

27. William T. Sherman, quoted in Wilbur S. Nye, *Carbine and Lance: The Story of Old Fort Sill* (Norman: University of Oklahoma Press, 1969), 123. Sherman's criticism gets at another interesting element of life in the vast expanse of the West: for all the emphasis on individualism, many of the problems were best met by communal action. The success of Mormon communities in comparison to others in many instances results from their strong mutual management of resources and sense of communal obligation. The theme is treated by Wallace Stegner in *Beyond the Hundredth Meridian: John Wesley Powell and the Second Opening of the West* (New York: Penguin Books, 1992).

28. Sherman's attitude changed abruptly soon after, when he narrowly escaped an Indian attack.

29. What no Indian tribes mastered were gunsmithing and making ammunition; they all remained reliant on supplies because they could not develop an indigenous production.

30. S. C. Gwynne, *Empire of the Summer Moon: Quanah Parker and the Rise and Fall of the Comanches, the Most Powerful Indian Tribe in American History* (New York: Scribner, 2010), 44.

31. Wallace, *Ranald S. Mackenzie on the Texas Frontier*, 25.

32. Grant was elected president in 1868 and served two four-year terms.

33. Ernest Wallace, *Texas in Turmoil: The Saga of Texas, 1849–1875* (Austin: Steck-Vaughn Company, 1965), 256–257.

34. One of Mackenzie's subordinates during the Civil War, Lieutenant T. F. Vaill, said of him, "By the time we had reached the Shenandoah Valley, he had so far developed as to be a greater terror to both officers and men than [Confederate commander Jubal] Early's grape and canister." T. F. Vaill, quoted in Wallace, *Ranald S. Mackenzie on the Texas Frontier*, 9. But Mackenzie was a

major general at the age of twenty-five due to the Civil War; the challenge of a command so vast at such a young age may account for his severity. Ulysses S. Grant described Mackenzie as "the most promising officer in the army." Ulysses S. Grant, *Memoirs* (New York: Webster, 1894), 659.

35. Philip Sheridan, commander of the Military District of the Missouri, testimony to the Texas Legislature, 1875, quoted in John R. Cook, *The Border and the Buffalo: An Untold Story of the Southwest Plains* (Topeka, KS: Crane and Company, 1907), 113.

36. Wallace, *Ranald S. Mackenzie on the Texas Frontier*, 23.

37. Robert V. Remini, *Andrew Jackson and His Indian Wars* (New York: Viking, 2001), 279.

38. Walter Russell Mead, comment at the meeting of the Hoover Military History Working Group, November 8, 2014; quoted with permission.

39. Dan Elbert Clark, *The West in American History* (New York: Thomas Y. Crowell Company, 1937), 563.

40. Angie Debo, *A History of the Indians of the United States* (Norman: University of Oklahoma Press, 1970), 164–165.

41. Native American tribes widely utilized torture of captives, accounts of which were a centerpiece of American reporting.

42. Frederick Jackson Turner, "The Significance of the Frontier in American History," 1893, http://www.learner.org/workshops /primarysources/corporations/docs/turner.html.

43. John Adams, when challenged by his son Charles whether any thoroughly democratic societies had ever existed in history, answered, "there are many Such Societies in the Forests of America, called Indian Tribes." Joseph J. Ellis, *First Family: Abigail and John Adams* (New York: Knopf, 2010), 162.

44. As in so many other ways, the Comanche are outliers to the general description of Native American cultures, developing neither religion nor governance.

45. One of Andrew Jackson's biographers goes so far as to argue that Jackson rightly believed himself to be preserving the Five Civilized Tribes from complete annihilation by settlers in forcibly removing them. Remini, *Andrew Jackson and His Indian Wars,* 281.

46. Theodore Roosevelt, *The Winning of the West,* vol. 4, *Louisiana and the Northwest* (New York: Putnam's, 1896), 7.

47. Remini, *Andrew Jackson and His Indian Wars,* 278.

48. This section's heading comes from a poem by Alfred, Lord Tennyson, "You Ask Me Why, Tho' Ill at Ease."

    > A land of settled government,
    > A land of just and old renown,
    > Where Freedom slowly broadens down
    > From precedent to precedent . . .

    Alfred, Lord Tennyson, "You Ask Me Why, Tho' Ill at Ease," https://www.poetryfoundation.org/poems-and-poets/poems /detail/45393.

49. Brent E. Kinser, *The American Civil War in the Shaping of British Democracy* (Burlington: Ashgate, 2011), 2, 166; Francis H. Herrick, "The Reform Bill of 1867 and the British Party System," *Pacific Historical Review* 3, no. 2 (1934): 216.

50. Joseph H. Park, "The English Reform Bill of 1867" (PhD diss., University of Columbia, 1920), 133. Herrick disparages the importance of momentum, arguing party politics rather than fear of revolt explains the timing, since Conservative Party members proposed the bill hoping to put a definitive end to voting reform far short of urban representation. He does not satisfactorily explain why the Conservatives would offer any reform rather than maintaining opposition, however. See Herrick, "The Reform Bill of 1867," 222–223n11.

51. Complete enfranchisement of English males would not occur until 1918.

52. Arnold Toynbee, quoted in Martin J. Wiener, *English Culture and the Decline of the Industrial Spirit, 1850–1980* (Cambridge: Cambridge University Press, 1981), 83.

53. John Clarke, *British Diplomacy and Foreign Policy 1782–1865* (London: Unwin Hyman, 1989), 36.

54. Theodore Bromund, "Turnerians before Their Time: Free Land, the Frontier Thesis and the British, 1832–1913," unpublished manuscript, cited with permission of the author.

55. Iain McCalman, "Controlling the Riots: Dickens, Barnaby Rudge and Romantic Revolution," in *Radicalism and Revolution in Britain, 1775–1848,* ed. Michael T. Davis (New York: St. Martin's Press, 2000), 209.

56. Wiener, *English Culture and the Decline of the Industrial Spirit,* 89.

57. James Epstein, "'America' in the Victorian Cultural Imagination," in *Anglo-American Attitudes from Revolution to Partnership,* ed. Fred M. Leventhal and Roland Quinault (Aldershot, England: Ashgate, 2000), 112.

58. E. D. Steele, *Palmerston and Liberalism, 1855–1865* (Cambridge: Cambridge University Press, 1991), 4.

59. Wiener, *English Culture and the Decline of the Industrial Spirit,* 52, 69.

60. Chris Cook, *The Routledge Companion to Britain in the Nineteenth Century, 1815–1914* (Abingdon, England: Routledge, 2005), 68.

61. See Kathleen Burk, *Old World, New World: The Story of Britain and America* (London: Little Brown, 2007), 298–299.

62. H. C. Allen terms 1872–1898 "the quiet years" in Anglo-American relations. Allen, *Great Britain and the United States,* 518.

63. Mark Twain, *Roughing It* (Berkley: University of California Press, 1995), 331.

64. The rate of growth of exports declined, but exports increased in both quantity and value.

65. Primary (e.g., unmanufactured) goods still made up the majority of American exports, however. See S. B. Saul, "Britain and World Trade, 1870-1914," *Economic History Review* 7, no. 1 (1954): 50. American labor productivity levels did not surpass Britain's until 1899; gains centered on more efficient services rather than greater manufacturing productivity. See Stephen Broadberry, "How Did the United States and Germany Overtake Britain? A Sectoral Analysis of Comparative Productivity Levels, 1870-1990," *Journal of Economic History* 58, no. 2 (1998): 378.

66. A. E. Musson, "The Great Depression in Britain, 1873-1896: A Reappraisal," *Journal of Economic History* 19, no. 2 (1959): 199-228.

67. William Cunningham, *The Rise and Decline of the Free Trade Movement* (Cambridge: University Press, 1905), 85-92.

68. Leland H. Jenks, *Migration of British Capital to 1875* (New York: Nelson, 1963), 332. Before 1875, services like shipping compensated for material imports.

69. William Ewart Gladstone, quoted in Steele, *Palmerston and Liberalism, 1855-1865,* 37; see also Iestyn Adams, *Brothers across the Ocean: British Foreign Policy and the Origin of the Anglo-American "Special Relationship" 1900-1905* (New York: St. Martin's Press, 2005), 14.

70. Barry Supple, "National Performance in Personal Perspective," in *Understanding Decline: Perceptions and Realities of British Economic Performance,* ed. Peter Clarke and Clive Trebilcock (New York: Cambridge University Press, 1997), 5.

71. Paul Kennedy, "The Costs and Benefits of British Imperialism 1846-1914," *Past & Present,* no. 125 (November 1989): 187. For a sense of the cultural impact, see Christopher Herbert, *War of No Pity: The Indian Mutiny and Victorian Trauma* (Princeton, NJ: Princeton University Press, 2008), 2.

72. C. K. Harley and D. N. McCloskey, "Foreign Trade and the Expanding International Economy," in *Economic History of Britain*

Since 1700, vol. 2, ed. Roderick Floud and Donald McCloskey (New York: Cambridge University Press, 1981), 50.

73. Avner Offer, "Costs and Benefits, Prosperity, and Security, 1870–1914," in *The Oxford History of the British Empire,* vol. 3, *The Nineteenth Century,* ed. Andrew Porter and William Louis (New York: Oxford University Press, 1998), 702. See also *Understanding Decline: Perceptions and Realities of British Economic Performance,* ed. Peter Clarke and Clive Trebilcock (New York: Cambridge University Press, 1997).

74. T. G. Otte, "Disraeli, the Fifteenth Earl of Derby and the 'War-in-Sight' Crisis," in *Conservatism and British Foreign Policy, 1820–1920: The Derbys and their World,* ed. Geoffrey Hicks (Burlington, VT: Ashgate, 2011), 105–109.

75. Margaret Sprout, "Mahan: Evangelist of Sea Power," in *Makers of Modern Strategy: From Machiavelli to the Nuclear Age,* ed. Peter Paret, Gordon A. Craig, and Felix Gilbert (Princeton, NJ: Princeton University Press, 1986), 424. Aaron Friedberg, *The Weary Titan: Britain and the Experience of Relative Decline, 1895–1905* (Princeton, NJ: Princeton University Press, 1988), 255, also makes this case powerfully for the 1890s.

76. John R. Ferris, *Intelligence and Strategy: Selected Essays* (London: Routledge, 2005), 8.

77. Edward Stanley, Fifteenth Earl of Derby, quoted in *The Parliamentary Debates (Authorized Edition),* vol. 184 (London: Wyman, 1866), 735.

78. Edward Stanley, Fifteenth Earl of Derby, quoted in Otte, "Disraeli, the Fifteenth Earl of Derby and the 'War-in-Sight' Crisis," 114. Otte imparts a priceless characterization of Derby as "stuck, limpet like, to the rock of reassuring notions of British supremacy, even as the rising tide of international politics washed over him" (127).

79. Kinser, *The American Civil War,* 163.

80. Julian Go, *Patterns of Empire: The British and American Empires, 1688 to the Present* (New York: Cambridge University Press, 2011), 25.

81. Clarke, *British Diplomacy and Foreign Policy*, 307.

7. MISSION CREEP: THE VENEZUELAN CRISES

1. Nelson M. Blake, "Background of Cleveland's Venezuelan Policy," *American Historical Review* 47, no. 2 (1942): 259.

2. Robert McElroy, *Grover Cleveland, the Man and the Statesman*, vol. 2 (New York: Harper & Brothers, 1923), 192.

3. Srdjan Vucetic also supports the Venezuelan crises as the seminal moment of constructing a common identity in changing Anglo-American relations, although he attributes it to a newfound sense of racial solidarity. Srdjan Vucetic, *The Anglosphere: A Genealogy of a Racialized Identity in International Relations* (Stanford, CA: Stanford University Press, 2011), 22–53. Vucetic does not provide a justification for why race, a constant element in both countries, would suddenly become so resonant as to dominate policy. He also doesn't account for the countervailing force of Irish nationalism in the relationship, in particular the Anglophobe influence of Irish Americans.

4. "Lord Salisbury and the Nonconformists," *Times* [London, England], February 1, 1896, http://find.galegroup.com/ttda /dispBasicSearch.do?prodId=TTDA&userGroupName =stan90222.

5. A superb survey of primary-source literature from British and Americans illustrative of the Great Rapprochement is provided in Jennie Sloan, "Anglo-American Relations and the Venezuelan Boundary Dispute," *Hispanic American Historical Review* 18, no. 4 (1938): 489–490nn16–19. Sloan also records instances as early as 1895 of British anxiety that the affection it had developed for America was one-sided.

6. Bradford Perkins, *The Great Rapprochement: England and the United States, 1895–1914* (New York: Atheneum, 1968), 156–157.

7. Christopher Layne, "Kant or Cant? Theories of Democratic Peace," in *Theories of War and Peace: An International Security Reader*, ed. Michael Brown (Cambridge, MA: MIT Press, 1998), 198. Layne further argues that Britain permitted America's rise and contested others because "unlike the German, Russian and French challenges, [it] did not seem immediately threatening to vital British interests." This underestimates the value Britain accorded Canada.

8. Theodore Roosevelt to Alfred Mahan, June 8, 1911, cited in Charles Carlisle Taylor, *The Life of Admiral Mahan* (London: John Murray, 1920), 203–204.

9. Henry Adams, *The Education of Henry Adams* (New York: Modern Library, 1931), 363.

10. Robert Arthur Talbot Gascoyne-Cecil, Third Marquess of Salisbury, quoted in George B. Young, "Intervention under the Monroe Doctrine: The Olney Corollary," *Political Science Quarterly* 57, no. 2 (1942): 255.

11. Walter LaFeber, "The Background of Cleveland's Venezuelan Policy: A Reinterpretation," *American Historical Review* 66, no. 4 (1961): 948.

12. Grover Cleveland, "Third Annual Message (First Term)," December 6, 1887, http://www.presidency.ucsb.edu/ws/?pid=29528.

13. The act did have some specific reductions in tariffs, in order that the president might utilize the threat of reversals with foreign countries to attain better market access for American goods. F. W. Taussig, *The Tariff History of the United States (1892)*, 273.

14. Joanne Reitano, *The Tariff Question in the Gilded Age: The Great Debate of 1888* (University Park: Pennsylvania State University Press, 1994), 130.

15. For the tenor of the 1893 testimony, see Associated Press, "Tariff Hearings," *The Herald* [Los Angeles], September 16, 1893, http://chroniclingamerica.loc.gov/lccn/sn85042461/1893-09-16/ed-1/seq-1/.

16. Marc-William Palen, preface to *The Conspiracy of Free Trade: The Anglo-American Struggle Over Empire and Economic Globalization, 1846–1896* (Cambridge, UK: Cambridge University Press, 2016), xi.
17. Ibid.
18. Blake, "Background of Cleveland's Venezuelan Policy," 259.
19. Marc-William Palen, "Protection, Federation and Union: The Global Impact of the McKinley Tariff upon the British Empire, 1890–94," *Journal of Imperial and Commonwealth History* 38, no. 3 (2010): 395–418.
20. R. A. Humphreys, "Anglo-American Rivalries and the Venezuela Crisis of 1895" (presidential address to the Royal Historical Society, December 10, 1966), *Transactions of the Royal Historical Society* 17 (1967): 131–164.
21. George C. Herring, *From Colony to Superpower: U.S. Foreign Relations since 1776* (New York: Oxford University Press, 2008), 307–308.
22. Blake, "Background of Cleveland's Venezuelan Policy," 259.
23. McElroy, *Grover Cleveland, the Man and the Statesman,* 2:192. Cleveland was by no means alone in failing to take up the cause of Monroe's dictum. Dexter Perkins cites an extensive list of European incursions in Latin America in which the United States made no objection or even mention of Monroe between James Polk's grandiloquent 1846 invocation of the dictum and the 1895 Venezuelan crisis. Dexter Perkins, *A History of the Monroe Doctrine* (Boston: Little, Brown, 1955), 170.
24. Arguments that Cleveland was stampeded into action by the press of public opinion are not borne out by his behavior in the crisis; at its height he took a weeklong hunting trip; in instructing Secretary of State Olney, Cleveland declared, "I would not be hurried in the matter even if the Congress should begin grinding again the resolution-of-inquiry mill." Grover Cleveland to Richard Olney, December 3, 1895, in McElroy, *Grover Cleveland, the Man and the Statesman,* 2:183.

25. J. B. McMaster, "Meaning and Application of the Monroe Doctrine," *New York Times,* January 2, 1896.

26. Henry Cabot Lodge, "England, Venezuela, and the Monroe Doctrine," *North American Review* 160 (1895): 657–658.

27. Cleveland's initial restraint demonstrates that the United States wasn't simply looking for an excuse to assert Monroe's doctrine but was instead goaded into it by Britain's diplomacy. Cleveland's policy was communicated to the Venezuelan government on March 25, 1895.

28. Young, "Intervention under the Monroe Doctrine," 255.

29. Thomas Paterson et al., *American Foreign Relations: A History to 1920,* vol. 1 (Boston: Wadworth, 2010), 206.

30. Joseph Chamberlain, quoted in Ernest May, *Imperial Democracy: The Emergence of America as a Great Power* (Chicago: Imprint Publications, 1991), 44–45.

31. John Sumida, *In Defense of Naval Supremacy: Finance, Technology, and British Naval Policy, 1889–1914* (New York: Routledge, 1993), 15.

32. Richard Olney to Joseph Chamberlain, September 28, 1896, Richard Olney Papers, 62, ff. 11084-11088, Library of Congress, Washington, DC. Salisbury held the posts of prime minister and foreign minister concurrently.

33. Young, "Intervention under the Monroe Doctrine," 256, describes the asymmetric advantage as "one of the most persuasive weapons available to American diplomats to coerce foreign chancelleries used to be the threat of relinquishing a matter of foreign policy to Congress."

34. Grover Cleveland, "Address to the Congress," December 17, 1895, in *Presidential Documents: The Speeches, Proclamations and Policies,* ed. Fred L. Israel and Jim F. Watts (New York: Routledge, 2000), 184.

35. Ibid., 182–183.

36. Sir Michael Hicks Beach, quoted in McElroy, *Grover Cleveland, the Man and the Statesman,* 2:196.

37. Richard F. Hamilton, *America's New Empire: The 1890s and Beyond* (New Brunswick, NJ: Transaction, 2010), 131.

38. Edward P. Kohn, *This Kindred People: Canadian-American Relations and the Anglo-Saxon Idea* (Kingston, ON: McGill-Queens University Press), 22.

39. Grover Cleveland, quoted in McElroy, *Grover Cleveland, the Man and the Statesman,* 2:193; emphasis in the original.

40. McElroy, *Grover Cleveland, the Man and the Statesman,* 2:195.

41. I am grateful to Andrew Lambert for his emphasis on this element of the strategic calculation. Andrew Lambert, "The Transfer of Power Between the UK and United States," paper presented at conference "Grand Strategy and the Anglo-American Worldview," King's College London, November 13, 2014. Cited with permission of the author.

42. Paul Kennedy, *The Realities behind Diplomacy: Background Influences on British External Policy, 1865–1980* (London: Allen and Unwin, 1981), 254–257; A. E. Campbell, *Britain and the United States,* 29–40.

43. Aaron Friedberg, *The Weary Titan: Britain and the Experience of Relative Decline, 1895–1905* (Princeton, NJ: Princeton University Press, 1988), 197.

44. Ibid., 162.

45. Sloan, "Anglo-American Relations," 495; Blake, "Background of Cleveland's Venezuelan Policy," 259, describes Cleveland's policy as "among the most crudely assertive ever issued by responsible American statesmen."

46. Arthur Balfour, quoted in Sloan, "Anglo-American Relations," 494.

47. McElroy, *Grover Cleveland, the Man and the Statesman,* 2:197.

48. "Chronicle of the Week," *The Tablet* 85, no. 2852 (London: January 5, 1895); see also *Congressional Record: The Proceedings and Debates, Fifty Third Congress, Third Session, XXVII* (Washington, DC: Government Printing Office, 1895), 1833.

49. Perkins, *The Great Rapprochement*, 19. See also Sloan, "Anglo-American Relations," 496; Blake, "Background of Cleveland's Venezuelan Policy," 261; and Bertha Ann Reuter, *Anglo-American Relations in the Spanish-American War* (New York: The MacMillan Company, 1924), 42.

50. J. A. S. Grenville, *Lord Salisbury and Foreign Policy at the Close of the Nineteenth Century* (London: Athlone, 1964), 55; Lloyd C. Gardner, Walter F. LaFeber, and Thomas J. McCormick, *Creation of the American Empire: U.S. Diplomatic History* (Chicago: Rand McNally, 1973), 241.

51. Kenneth Bourne, *Britain and the Balance of Power in North America, 1815–1908* (Berkeley: University of California Press, 1967), 340. Salisbury had the support of newspapers and "jingoes" (this term for militant imperialists had already perked from Britain to America, and was in general use in both countries' political debates), but they were forces he railed against in British politics.

52. "Lord Salisbury's Reference at the Guildhall," *London Times*, November 11, 1896, 6.

53. McElroy, *Grover Cleveland, the Man and the Statesman*, 2:200.

54. Otto Schoenrich, "The Venezuela-British Guiana Boundary Dispute," *American Journal of International Law* 43, no. 3 (1949): 526.

55. Cleveland reported in his annual message to Congress that "the provisions of the treaty are so eminently just and fair that the assent of Venezuela thereto may confidently be anticipated." Grover Cleveland, "Fourth Annual Message (Second Term)," December 7, 1896, http://www.presidency.ucsb.edu/ws/?pid=29537.

56. E. David Steele, *Lord Salisbury* (London: UCL, 1999), 332.

57. Congressional opposition had scattered motives: concern that arbitration would erode Congress's constitutional prerogatives, hostility from Irish Americans, personal animosity toward the secretary of state and, most important, monetary policy. Nearly all of the twenty-six votes against the treaty had been cast by "silver men." "To Work on for Arbitration," *New York Times*, May 7,

1897. The British government ascribed blame for the treaty's failure entirely to the influence of Irish Americans, who had mobilized to affect political processes and gained power in urban centers like New York and Boston that were crucial to national political campaigns, including the one that brought Cleveland to power. Salisbury opposed home rule for Ireland, further embittering Anglophobe sentiment. Noel Ignatiev, *How the Irish Became White* (New York: Routledge, 1995), 19–20.

58. Friedberg, *The Weary Titan*, 173–174.

59. Ibid., 134–148.

60. Admiral Jackie Fisher, quoted in Friedberg, *The Weary Titan*, 197.

61. Serge Ricard, "The Roosevelt Corollary," *Presidential Studies Quarterly* 36, no. 1 (2006): 17–26.

62. Only Chile and Costa Rica escaped, and only because of oligarchs tightly controlling the political process.

63. Theodore Roosevelt, "First Annual Message," December 3, 1901, http://www.presidency.ucsb.edu/ws/?pid=29542.

64. Joseph B. Bishop, *Theodore Roosevelt and His Time Shown in His Letters*, vol. 1 (New York: Charles Scribner's Sons, 1920), 222.

65. As Seward W. Livermore conclusively shows, the General Board had been siting Caribbean port locations and drawing up plans for naval forces needed were the Monroe Doctrine to be enforced. Both the fleet maneuvers and Dewey's appointment, while doubtless useful, significantly predated tensions over Venezuela. Dewey's appointment was not made for the pointed foreign policy message to Britain and Germany during the crisis, but because he was the foremost admiral in service. Seward W. Livermore, "Theodore Roosevelt, the American Navy, and the Venezuelan Crisis of 1902–1903," *American Historical Review* 51, no. 3 (1946): 462.

66. The German government had a year earlier communicated its plans in writing to Secretary of State Hay, consulted with both Hay and Roosevelt, and received no objections. Perkins, *A History of the Monroe Doctrine*, 218.

67. Roosevelt's story is hotly contested among historians. Biographer Edmund Morris recounts Roosevelt recollecting long after the fact, having said, "I should be obliged to interfere, by force if necessary, if Germany took any action that looked like the acquisition of territory in Venezuela or elsewhere in the Caribbean," and gave Germany ten days to clarify its position or he would send Dewey with his fleet along the Venezuelan coast. Roosevelt's retroactive account does not accord with the American, British, or German documentary evidence, as Dexter Perkins demonstrates, and the German ambassador was not even in Washington when Roosevelt claims to have delivered the ultimatum. Perkins also notes that Roosevelt's account came in the run-up to World War I, when prejudice against Germany ran high. Perkins, *A History of the Monroe Doctrine*, 217–219.

68. Matthias Maass, "Catalyst for the Roosevelt Corollary: Arbitrating the 1902–1903 Venezuela Crisis and Its Impact on the Development of the Roosevelt Corollary to the Monroe Doctrine," *Diplomacy and Statecraft* 20, no. 3 (2009): 383–402.

69. Livermore, "Theodore Roosevelt, the American Navy, and the Venezuelan Crisis," 464.

70. It would actually make the most sense for Roosevelt's threat to have occurred in this context, demanding Germany act with greater restraint.

71. Edmund Morris, "A Matter of Extreme Urgency: Theodore Roosevelt, Wilhelm II, and the Venezuela Crisis of 1902," *Naval War College Review* 55, no. 2 (2002): 74.

72. Perkins recounts the Anglo-German negotiations in detail. Oswald von Richthofen, the German foreign minister, explicitly cited concern about American reaction when arguing against the British proposal. Germany was also conscious of the likelihood Britain would be credited by America with forcing Germany to arbitration. Perkins, *A History of the Monroe Doctrine*, 218–219.

73. Theodore Roosevelt, quoted in Perkins, *A History of the Monroe Doctrine*, 221.

74. United Kingdom, *The Hansard Parliamentary Debates*, 4 ser., vol. 116 (London: Wyman and Sons, 1902), 1263.

75. "Mr. Balfour in Liverpool," *Times* [London, England], February 14, 1903.

76. Perkins makes a spirited factual defense of German ameliorations during the crisis. Perkins, *A History of the Monroe Doctrine*, 220–224.

77. Notably, even though that July 1902 German diplomatic note came six months after President Roosevelt's stern public injunction against any creditor holding territory in the western hemisphere, Secretary of State Hay's reply to the German government did not explicitly reiterate the president's red line.

78. Admiral George Dewey, "Journal of the Commander-in-Chief, December 1902-January 1903," entry for January 13, 1903, cited in Seward W. Livermore, "Theodore Roosevelt, the American Navy, and the Venezuelan Crisis of 1902–1903," 462. It is, of course, germane that being a navy man he would naturally consider the flotilla to have had a significant effect.

79. The Court of Arbitration had been established in 1899, an outcome of the first Hague peace conference. The United States and Great Britain were architects of its creation and founding members.

80. Theodore Roosevelt, quoted in Mark T. Gilderhus, "The Monroe Doctrine: Meanings and Implications," *Presidential Studies Quarterly* 36, no. 1 (2006): 11. See also Maass, "Catalyst for the Roosevelt Corollary."

81. H. W. Brands, "The Rooseveltian Roots of the Bush Doctrine," in *La montée en puissance des Etats-Unis: de la Guerre hispano-américaine a la guerre de Corée (1898–1953)*, ed. Pierre Melandri and Serge Ricard (Paris: Harmattan, 2004), 74.

82. Theodore Roosevelt, "Transcript of Theodore Roosevelt's Corollary to the Monroe Doctrine (1905)," http://www.ourdocuments .gov/doc.php?doc=56&page=transcript. Serge Ricard considers the corollary a useful means Roosevelt was seeking to repair the "glaring inadequacy" of American doctrine; his account ignores not only the arbitration decision but also the tentative and humanitarian sales pitch Roosevelt made to the nation for support of the policy. Ricard, "The Roosevelt Corollary," 19.

83. Walter LaFeber argues that "it is the Roosevelt Doctrine, not Monroe's, that Dulles, Acheson, Johnson, Reagan and Weinberger had in mind when they justified unilateral U.S. intervention in the affairs of Latin American states." Walter LeFeber, "The Evolution of the Monroe Doctrine from Monroe to Reagan," in *Redefining the Past: Essays in Diplomatic History in Honor of William Appleman Williams,* ed. Lloyd C. Gardner (Corvallis, OR: Oregon State University Press, 1986), 139–140.

84. Alan Brinkley, *The Unfinished Nation: A Concise History of the American People* (New York: McGraw-Hill, 2008), 596.

85. That Roosevelt himself had long believed in assertive application of American power is evident from his writings. See Theodore Roosevelt, "The Monroe Doctrine," in *Presidential Addresses and State Papers,* vol. 3 (New York: The Review of Reviews, 1910), 231–234; and Theodore Roosevelt, "The Monroe Doctrine," in *The Works of Theodore Roosevelt,* vol. 13 (New York: Charles Scribner's Sons, 1906), 49–65.

86. Roosevelt, "First Annual Message."

87. Roosevelt, "Transcript of Theodore Roosevelt's Corollary."

88. *Selections from the Correspondence of Theodore Roosevelt & Henry Cabot Lodge, 1884–1918,* ed. Charles F. Redmond (Cambridge: Da Capo Press, 1971), I, 200.

89. Livermore, "Theodore Roosevelt, the American Navy, and the Venezuelan Crisis," 463.

90. Young, "Intervention under the Monroe Doctrine," 278.

91. It may be compared in the private realm to the boom in Anglo-American marriages that occurred as American wealth was married to British stature around the same time.

92. Theodore Roosevelt to William Roscoe Thayer, quoted in Joseph Bucklin Bishop, *Theodore Roosevelt and His Time* (New York: Charles Scribner's Sons, 1920), 14.

93. H. C. Allen, *Great Britain and the United States* (New York: St. Martin's Press 1955), 563.

94. Otto von Bismarck, quoted in Wolf von Schierbrand, *Germany: The Welding of a World Power* (New York: Doubleday, Page & Company, 1902), 352.

95. John Hay to Henry Cabot Lodge, quoted in Forrest Davis, *The Atlantic System* (New York: Reynal & Hitchcock, 1941), 97.

96. Otto von Bismarck, quoted in Kathleen Burk, *Old World, New World: The Story of Britain and America* (London: Little, Brown, 2007), 380.

97. Richard Olney, "International Isolation of the United States," *Atlantic Monthly* 81 (1898): 582.

8. US VERSUS THEM: THE SPANISH-AMERICAN WAR

1. *New York Times,* late September 1898, quoted in Bertha Ann Reuter, *Anglo-American Relations in the Spanish-American War* (New York: The MacMillan Company, 1924), 113.

2. James A. Field Jr., "American Imperialism: The Worst Chapter in Almost Any Book," *American Historical Review* 83 (1978): 644.

3. This description of Roosevelt and his circle can be found in Evan Thomas, *The War Lovers: Roosevelt, Lodge, Hearst and the Rush to Empire, 1898* (New York: Little, Brown, 2010), 5–12.

4. Lloyd C. Gardner, Walter F. LaFeber, and Thomas J. McCormick (although writing earlier than Thomas) refute the "rush to empire" impetus, arguing that "the large-policy imperialists were the most colorful and fascinating opinion leaders of their day. In fact, however, their numbers were few and the influence was

slight. Yet historians have lavished attention on them almost in inverse proportion to their importance, perhaps because they make such good copy." Lloyd C. Gardner, Walter F. LaFeber, and Thomas J. McCormick, *Creation of the American Empire: U.S. Diplomatic History* (Chicago: Rand McNally, 1973), 229.

5. Hugh DeSantis, "The Imperialist Impulse and American Innocence, 1865–1900," in *American Foreign Relations: A Historiographical Review*, ed. Gerald K. Haines and J. Samuel Walker (Westport, CT: Greenwood Press, 1981), 65–90; Edward P. Crapol, "Coming to Terms with Empire: The Historiography of Late-Nineteenth-Century American Foreign Relations," *Diplomatic History* 16 (1992): 573–597; Field, "American Imperialism," 644–68.

6. Ted Curtis Smythe, *The Gilded Age Press, 1865–1900* (Westport, CT: Praeger, 2003), 192; G. Wayne King, "Conservative Attitudes in the United States toward Cuba (1895–1898)," in *The Proceedings of the South Carolina Historical Association 1973*, ed. Hewitt D. Adams (Spartanburg, North Carolina: South Carolina State Library, 1973), 94–104, http://dc.statelibrary.sc.gov/bitstream/handle/10827/23804/SCHA_Proceedings_1973.pdf?sequence=1&isAllowed=y.

7. In 1870, President Grant attempted to annex Santo Domingo and was rebuffed by Congress. President Harrison's 1892 proposal to annex Hawaii was not acted on by Congress before it was retracted by President Cleveland upon his election. McKinley submitted Hawaii legislation early in the course of his presidency; Congress debated inconclusively for more than nine months.

8. While not so termed, insurgency and successful tactics for countering insurgencies were reasonably well understood, even at the time of the Spanish-American War. British parliamentarian Edmund Burke had concluded during the American rebellion a hundred years earlier that "the use of force alone is but temporary; it may subdue for a moment but it does not remove the necessity of subduing again. And a country is not to be governed

that is perpetually to be conquered." That militaries understood the complex politico-military orchestration necessary to success is evidenced in the U.S. Marine Corps' Small Wars manuals. See, for example, Major Samuel. M. Harrington, "The Strategy and Tactics of Small Wars," *Marine Corps Gazette,* December 1921, 474–491; Harrington, "The Strategy and Tactics of Small Wars," *Marine Corps Gazette,* December 1922, 84–93.

9. John L. Offner, "McKinley and the Spanish-American War," *Presidential Studies Quarterly* 34, no. 1 (2004): 51.

10. William McKinley, "First Annual Message," December 6, 1897, http://www.presidency.ucsb.edu/ws/?pid=29538.

11. David S. Trask, *The War with Spain in 1898* (Lincoln: University of Nebraska Press, 1996), 2–3; Offner, "McKinley and the Spanish-American War," 54.

12. The American ambassador in Madrid advocated to the Spanish Britain's model of unity with Ireland.

13. Trade figures are from United States Tariff Commission, Stanley Kuhl Hornbeck, Jacob Viner, Clive Day, and Walter B. Palmer, *Reciprocity and Commercial Treaties* (Washington, DC: Government Printing Office, 1919), 324–325, https://babel.hathitrust.org/cgi/pt?id=nyp.33433024590782;view=1up;seq=7.

14. Offner, "McKinley and the Spanish-American War," 54–55.

15. S. C. Gwynne, *Empire of the Summer Moon* (New York: Scribner, 2010), 62. Gwynne is also incredibly insightful in pointing out that Spain's style of colonization worked best against societies with strong centralized control, such as the Aztec and Inca.

16. Trask, *The War With Spain in 1898,* 24.

17. McKinley making such worldwide preparations demonstrates the sinking of the *Maine* was not the sole cause of conflict, nor was the president pushed into action by the Congress. Those who would use McKinley's order as evidence of an imperialist predilection need recognize that it occurred in the context of collapsing confidence in reform of Spanish policy in Cuba.

18. Benjamin R. Beede, *The War of 1898, and U.S. Interventions, 1898–1934: An Encyclopedia* (New York: Rutledge, 1994), 148.

19. Offner, "McKinley and the Spanish-American War," 56.

20. Admiral Hyman Rickover, father of the American nuclear submarine force and abrasively independent thinker, studied the sinking and also determined it to have been caused by explosion of the ship's own ordnance.

21. Graham A. Cosmas, "The Shaping of Military Policy," and "Mobilization Begins: Strategy Changes," in *An Army for Empire: The United States Army and the Spanish-American War* (College Station, TX: Texas A&M University Press), chaps. 3–4.

22. The argument that McKinley was stampeded by the Congress needs to account for the president's orchestration of activity: he commissioned the navy report, timed its release, provided military and diplomatic support to Senator Redfield Proctor in Cuba and met with him prior to the speech. Offner, "McKinley and the Spanish-American War," 56–57.

23. William McKinley, "War Message," April 11, 1898, https://www.mtholyoke.edu/acad/intrel/mkinly2.htm.

24. A contrary view, much more in line with Latin American attitudes about American imperialism, is Louis A. Pérez, "The Meaning of the Maine: Causation and the Historiography of the Spanish-American War," *Pacific Historical Review* 58, no. 3 (1989): 293–322.

25. McKinley, "War Message."

26. Offner, "McKinley and the Spanish-American War," 57–61, describes McKinley as delaying the deadline several days and himself prodding the Europeans into offering a deal he could then reject, but it isn't obvious what that would have gained McKinley, and Offner provides no explanation. The rejection irritated European governments, wasn't needed for congregating Americans around war, and drove up the costs to Britain for their support. Bertha Ann Reuter's description of British ambassador

Julian Pauncefote reluctantly agreeing to European pressure and privately assuring McKinley Britain did not support the effort rings truer, especially in light of subsequent outrage exhibited by the British Parliament and newspapers—if McKinley had generated the effort, the British government most likely would have dampened down domestic criticism of their role in it as responsive to American encouragement. Bertha Ann Reuter, *Anglo-American Relations in the Spanish-American War.*

27. William McKinley, "Message to Congress Requesting a Declaration of War with Spain," April 11, 1898, http://www.presidency.ucsb.edu/ws/?pid=103901.

28. Ibid.

29. Ibid.

30. Ibid.

31. Ibid.

32. Congressional Record, 55th Congress, 2nd Session (1898) 31:3988.

33. Harry Thurston Peck, *Twenty Years of the Republic, 1885–1905,* 553.

34. Dexter Perkins, *A History of the Monroe Doctrine,* 198.

35. Reuter, *Anglo-American Relations in the Spanish-American War,* 109.

36. Editorial, *London Times,* December 12, 1898, 11.

37. "An Anglo-American Alliance," in *The Advocate of Peace (1894–1920)* 60, no. 6 (1898): 128–129.

38. James Bryce, "The Essential Unity of Britain and America," *Atlantic Monthly* 82 (1898): 22–29.

39. Charles A. Kupchan, *How Enemies Become Friends: The Sources of Stable Peace* (Princeton, NJ: Princeton University Press, 2010), 83.

40. "The Terrible Disaster to the United States," *Times* [London, England], February 17, 1898, http://find.galegroup.com.stanford.idm.oclc.org/ttda/infomark.do?&source=gale&prodId=TTDA&userGroupName=stan90222&tabID=T003&docPage=article&searchType=AdvancedSearchForm&docId=CS151577169&type=multipage&contentSet=LTO&version=1.0.

41. "The United States National Defence Bill," *Times* [London, England], March 10, 1898; "Europe Not To Interfere," *New York Times,* March 11, 1898.

42. United Kingdom, *The Hansard Parliamentary Debates,* 4 ser., vol. 54 (London: Wyman and Sons, 1902), 1526.

43. Ibid., 418–419.

44. "The United States and Spain," *Spectator,* April 9, 1898, 8:501.

45. Reuter, *Anglo-American Relations in the Spanish-American War,* 71–72.

46. Editorial, *Ottawa Citizen,* July 1, 1898, cited in Reuter, *Anglo-American Relations in the Spanish-American War,* 105.

47. Reuter, *Anglo-American Relations in the Spanish-American War,* 71; William Archibald Dunning, *The British Empire and the United States* (New York: Charles Scribner's Sons, 1914), 321–322.

48. George C. Herring, *From Colony to Superpower: U.S. Foreign Relations since 1776* (New York: Oxford University Press, 2008), chap. 8.

49. Cosmas, *An Army for Empire,* 110.

50. The American consul at Manila, William R. Day, reported, "Our crews are all hoarse from cheering, and while we suffer for cough drops and throat doctors, we have no use for liniment or surgeons." William R. Day, "Naval Battle of Manila Bay, May 1, 1898," June 17, 1898, http://www.history.navy.mil/research /library/online-reading-room/title-list-alphabetically/s/selected -documents-of-the-spanish-american-war/u-s-consul-at-manila .html.

51. Kaiser Wilhelm II, quoted in "The German Emperor on the American Peril," *Spectator,* June 26, 1898, 78:907.

52. Walter F. Bell, "Great Britain: Policies and Reactions to the Spanish-American War," in *The Encyclopedia of the Spanish- American and Philippine-American Wars: A Political, Social, and Military History,* vol. 1, *A–L,* ed. Spencer Tucker (Santa Barbara, CA: ABC CLIO, 2009), 258. It should be noted that Bell believes Dewey and others overstate the importance of British assistance at Manila Bay.

53. Reuter believes that if the United States had stated its intention to occupy the Philippines, confrontation with the Germans could have been avoided; she ascribes the American silence to a discomfort in accepting that notion of empire. Reuter, *Anglo-American Relations in the Spanish-American War*, 137.

54. Ibid., 147.

55. Donald M. Seekins, "Historical Setting—Outbreak of War, 1898," in *Philippines: A Country Study*, ed. Ronald E. Dolan (Washington, DC: Library of Congress, 1991), 22–27.

56. Dino Buenviaje, "Great Britain," in *The Encyclopedia of the Spanish-American and Philippine-American Wars: A Political, Social, and Military History*, vol. 1, A–L, ed. Spencer Tucker (Santa Barbara, CA: ABC CLIO, 2009), 255–256.

57. *Annual Report of the Navy Department* (Washington, DC: GPO 1898), 66; George Dewey, *The Autobiography of George Dewey, Admiral of the Navy* (New York: Charles Scribner's Sons, 1913), 188.

58. Dewey, *The Autobiography of George Dewey*, 266.

59. Ibid., 266.

60. Reuter, *Anglo-American Relations in the Spanish-American War*, 147.

61. "Cuba and the Far East" (editorial), *New York Times*, March 6, 1898.

62. *The Bookman: Twenty Years of the Republic*, vol. 22 (New York: Dodd, Mead and Company, 1906), 487.

63. McKinley, "War Message."

64. Ibid.

65. Cosmas, *An Army for Empire*, 110. Gardner, LaFeber and McCormick believe the McKinley Administration having drawn up contingency plans for dispatch of twenty thousand troops to Manila in advance of the war constitutes an intention to have occupied the Philippines. Gardner, LaFeber, and Thomas J. McCormick, *Creation of the American Empire*, 256.

66. H. Wayne Morgan, *America's Road to Empire: The War with Spain and Overseas Expansion* (New York: John Wiley & Sons, 1965), 225.

67. Lewis Gould, *The Presidency of William McKinley* (Lawrence: Regents Press of Kansas, 1980), 117.

68. Bradford Perkins, *The Great Rapprochement: England and the United States, 1895–1914* (New York: Atheneum, 1968), 241.

69. Reuter, *Anglo-American Relations in the Spanish-American War,* 176.

70. Gould, *The Presidency of William McKinley,* 98–99.

71. "The First Philippine Commission," in Dean Conant, *The Philippines: Past and Present* (London: Mills & Boon, 1914).

72. Frank H. Golay, *Face of Empire: United States–Philippine Relations, 1898–1946* (Madison: University of Wisconsin-Madison, 1998), 50.

73. Britain's argument faltered in Congress on Britain having taken over the unfortified Suez Canal from France. David McCullough, *The Path between the Seas: The Creation of the Panama Canal 1870–1914* (New York: Simon and Schuster, 1977), 256.

74. Arthur Balfour, quoted in Iestyn Adams, *Brothers across the Ocean: British Foreign Policy and the Origin of the Anglo-American "Special Relationship" 1900–1905* (New York: Tauris Academic Studies, 2005), 79.

75. Walter L. Arnstein, "Queen Victoria and the United States," in *Anglo-American Attitudes from Revolution to Partnership,* ed. Fred M. Leventhal and Roland Quinault (Aldershot, England: Ashgate, 2000), 101.

76. Theodore Roosevelt, quoted in Adams, *Brothers across the Ocean,* 225.

77. William Howard Taft, quoted in Adams, *Brothers across the Ocean,* 226.

78. James K. Hosmer, "The American Evolution: Dependence, Independence, and Interdependence," *Atlantic Monthly* 81 (1898): 29–36.

79. Joseph Chamberlain, speech in Birmingham, printed in *Sacramento Daily Union,* May 14, 1898.

80. L. M. Gelber, *The Rise of Anglo-American Friendship* (London: Oxford University Press, 1938), 89–92.

81. Earl of Selborne, quoted in Eric Edelman, "A Special Relationship in Jeopardy," *American Interest*, July 1, 2010, http://www.the-american -interest.com/2010/07/01/a-special-relationship-in-jeopardy/.

82. Count Paul Metternich, Memorandum, printed in Prince von Bulow, *Memoirs, 1897–1903* (London: Chiswick Press, 1932), 422; also cited in Kenneth Bourne, *Britain and the Balance of Power in North America, 1815–1908* (Berkeley: University of California Press, 1967), 342.

83. Gelber, *The Rise of Anglo-American Friendship*, 27.

84. James Kendall Hosmer, *The American Evolution, Dependence, Independence, Interdependence* (New York: Houghton, Mifflin, 1898).

85. John Hay, *Addresses, of John Hay* (New York: The Century Co., 1906), 77–80.

86. "How the American Press View the South African Situation," *The Literary Digest* 10, no. 26, January 1900–June 1900 (New York: Funk and Wagnals, 1900), 777.

87. "An Anglo-American Alliance," in *The Advocate of Peace (1894–1920)* 60, no. 6 (1898): 128.

88. "Mr. Chamberlain's Speech," *New York Times*, May 15, 1898.

89. "The Possible Anglo-American Alliance," *The Economist*, May 28, 1898.

9. EUROPEAN POWER: WORLD WAR I

1. Adam J. Tooze, *The Deluge: The Great War, America and the Remaking of the Global Order, 1916–1931* (New York: Penguin, 2015), 29.

2. Brock Millman, "A Counsel of Despair: British Strategy and War Aims, 1917-18," *Journal of Contemporary History* 36, no. 2 (2001): 249.

3. Patrick Devlin, *Too Proud to Fight: Woodrow Wilson's Neutrality* (New York: Oxford University Press, 1975), 143–44.

4. Arthur S. Link, *The Struggle for Neutrality, 1914–1915* in *Vol. 3 of Wilson* (Princeton, NJ: Princeton University Press, 1947–1965), 105.

5. Woodrow Wilson, *Foreign Relations of the United States* (Washington, DC: U.S. Government Printing Office, 1915), supplement, 393. Wilson had always been suspected by neutralists of having Anglophone sympathies; see Edwin Borchard and William Lage, *Neutrality for the United States* (New Haven: Yale University Press, 1937), 34–37, 57.

6. Robert Hannigan, *The New World Power: American Foreign Policy, 1898–1917* (Philadelphia: University of Pennsylvania Press, 2002), 241–243.

7. Benjamin O. Fordham, "Revisionism Reconsidered: Exports and American Intervention in World War I," *International Organization* 61, no. 2 (2007): 289.

8. Viscount Grey of Fallodon, *Twenty-Five Years, 1892–1916* (New York: Frederick A. Stokes Company, 1925), 2:126–128.

9. Woodrow Wilson, "Address Delivered at the First Annual Assemblage of the League to Enforce Peace: 'American Principles,'" May 27, 1916, http://www.presidency.ucsb.edu/ws/index.php?pid=65391.

10. For a sense of just how exasperated the British were with Wilson, see the comments of Charles Hardinge in Sterling Kernek, "The British Government's Reactions to President Wilson's 'Peace' Note of December 1916," *Historical Journal* 13, no. 4 (1970): 747n78. For the text of Wilson's note, see "President Wilson's Peace Note, December 18, 1916," https://wwi.lib.byu.edu/index.php/President _Wilson%27s_Peace_Note,_December_18,_1916.

11. David Lloyd George, Prime Minister's Personal Correspondence, E/2/13/6, Lloyd George Papers, Parliamentary Archives, London, UK.

12. Sir Cecil Spring-Rice, December 24, 1916, cited in Kernek, "The British Government's Reactions to President Wilson's 'Peace' Note of December 1916," 740.

13. Woodrow Wilson, quoted in David Trask, *The AEF and Coalition Warmaking, 1917–1918* (Lawrence: University of Kansas Press, 1993), 3; Wilson to Colonel Edward M. House, July 21, 1917, quoted in Ray

Stannard Baker, *Woodrow Wilson: Life and Letters* (Garden City, NY: Doubleday, 1927–1939), 7:180.

14. The British government had assessed the issue once previously, in October 1916.

15. Kernek, "The British Government's Reactions to President Wilson's 'Peace' Note of December 1916," 727.

16. Ibid., 736.

17. Ernest May, *The World War and American Isolation, 1914–1919* (Cambridge, MA: Harvard University Press, 1959), 416.

18. Ibid., 422–423. Wilson described the opponents as "[a] little group of willful men, representing no opinion but their own, [who] have rendered the great government of the United States helpless and contempt." Link, *The Struggle for Neutrality, 1914–1915* in *Vol. 3 of Wilson*, 362. In fact, national origin (German and Irish American voters in congressional districts) and reliance on exports were the major influences in congressional voting. Fordham, "Revisionism Reconsidered," 302.

19. Kernek, "The British Government's Reaction to President Wilson's 'Peace' Note of December, 1916," 742.

20. And of those 236 American deaths, 128 were in a single instance, the 1915 sinking of the *Lusitania*. Clinton Grattan, *Why We Fought* (New York: The Vanguard Press, 1929), 163.

21. Link, *The Struggle for Neutrality, 1914–1915* in *Vol. 3 of Wilson*, 291–97, 391.

22. Kernek, "The British Government's Reaction to President Wilson's 'Peace' Note of December, 1916," 741.

23. Woodrow Wilson, "Address of President Woodrow Wilson to the U.S. Senate, 22 January 1917," http://www.firstworldwar.com /source/peacewithoutvictory.htm.

24. Charles Austin Beard, *The Devil Theory of War: An Inquiry into the Nature of History and the Possibility of Keeping out of War* (New York: Greenwood Press, 1936), 22–23.

25. Fordham, "Revisionism Reconsidered," 286.

26. Ibid., 305.
27. Porfirio Diaz, Mexican President from 1896 to 1911, is reputed to have said, "¡Pobre México! ¡Tan lejos de Dios y tan cerca de los Estados Unidos!" (Poor Mexico! So far from God and so close to the United States!).
28. Even then, anti-British sentiment was so strong that British manipulation was suspected until Zimmerman admitted to having sent the telegram. Michael Meyer, "The Mexican-German Conspiracy of 1915," *Americas* 23, no. 1 (1966): 76.
29. Catherine O. Peare, *The Woodrow Wilson Story: An Idealist in Politics* (New York: Thomas Y. Crowell, 1963), 235.
30. Rothwell, *British War Aims and Peace Diplomacy 1914–1918* (Oxford: Clarendon Press, 1973), 162–163; Millman, "A Counsel of Despair," 245.
31. Interesting as Lloyd-George's activist policies were, neither William Philpott, Priscilla Roberts, nor Brock Millman consider them to have contributed much to winning the war. Millman emphasizes the postwar complications of the foreign policy moves requiring greater autonomy for colonies and creating "strategic orphans" when Britain turned its attention back to the western front. William J. Philpott, *Anglo-French Relations and Strategy on the Western Front* (New York: St. Martin's Press, 1996), 164; Priscilla Roberts, "Tasker H. Bliss and the Evolution of Allied Unified Command, 1918: A Note on Old Battles Revisited," *Journal of Military History* 65, no. 3 (2001): 672; Millman, "A Counsel of Despair," 270.
32. Peare, *The Woodrow Wilson Story*, 235.
33. Kathleen Burk, "Great Britain in the United States, 1917-1918: The Turning Point," *International History Review* 1, no. 2 (1979): 233.
34. Devlin, *Too Proud to Fight: Woodrow Wilson's Neutrality*, 619–635.
35. Burk, "Great Britain in the United States," 229.
36. Trask, *The AEF and Coalition Warmaking*, 4.
37. Burk, "Great Britain in the United States," 234.
38. Ibid., 236–240.

39. Lord Northcliffe to Geoffrey Robinson, July 1, 1917, File 1917, Northcliffe Papers, Times Archives, London.

40. Trask, *The AEF and Coalition Warmaking*, 5.

41. Spencer Tucker, Laura Matysek Wood, and Justin D. Murphy, eds., *The European Powers in the First World War: An Encyclopedia* (New York: Garland, 1996), 1.

42. David R. Woodward, *World War I Almanac* (Lexington: University Press of Kentucky, 1998), 191–192.

43. Jehuda Lothar Wallach, *Uneasy Coalition: The Entente Experience in World War I* (Westport, CT: Greenwood Press, 1993), 114. The French, interestingly enough, were more indulgent, with Marshall Joffre saying in sympathy, "No great nation having a proper consciousness of its own dignity—and America perhaps less than any other—would allow its citizens to be incorporated like poor relations in the ranks of some other army and fight under a foreign flag." Marshall Joffre, quoted in Trask, *The AEF and Coalition Warmaking*, 6.

44. Trask, *The AEF and Coalition Warmaking*, 142; Spencer C. Tucker, *World War I: The Definitive Encyclopedia and Document Collection* (Santa Barbara, CA: ABC-CLIO, 2014), 2.

45. Tasker Bliss, quoted in Trask, *The AEF and Coalition Warmaking*, 5.

46. B. J. C. McKercher, "Reckoning with the Myth of the American Expeditionary Force: The United States and the Allied War Coalition, 1917–1918," *Reviews in American History* 23, no. 2 (1995): 285.

47. Millman, "A Counsel of Despair," 253.

48. Trask, *The AEF and Coalition Warmaking*, 1.

49. David Stevenson, *Cataclysm: The First World War as Political Tragedy* (New York: Basic Books, 2004), 383.

50. Whittle Johnston, "Reflections on Wilson, and Problems of World Peace," in *Woodrow Wilson and a Revolutionary World, 1913–1921*, ed. Arthur S. Link (Chapel Hill: University of North Carolina Press, 1982), 193; see also Allen Lynch, "Woodrow

Wilson and the Principle of 'National Self-Determination': A Reconsideration," *Review of International Studies* 28, no. 2 (2002): 429.

51. Bullitt Lowry, "Pershing and the Armistice," *Journal of American History* 55, no. 2 (1968): 281. Pershing's edict would result in 3,500 more American casualties.

52. Fordham, "Revisionism Reconsidered," 278.

53. Allen Lynch, "Woodrow Wilson and the Principle of 'National Self-Determination,'" 428.

54. B. J. C. McKercher, review of *Trial by Friendship: Anglo-American Relations 1917–1918* by David R. Woodward, *Albion: A Quarterly Journal concerned with British Studies* 26, no. 1 (1994): 199.

55. Aaron Friedberg details Britain's increasingly desperate hopes that in return for Royal Navy support Japan would provide the land forces to Britain could not to counter Russia on the Indian subcontinent. Aaron Friedberg, *The Weary Titan: Britain and the Experience of Relative Decline, 1895–1905* (Princeton, NJ: Princeton University Press, 1988), 268.

56. Robert O'Neill, "Churchill, Japan, and British Security in the Pacific 1904–1942," in *Churchill*, ed. Robert Blake and William Louis (Oxford: Clarendon Press, 1996), 276.

57. David Stevenson, "French War Aims and the American Challenge, 1914–1918," *Historical Journal* 22, no. 4 (1979): 877.

58. Norman Gordon Levin, *Woodrow Wilson and World Politics: America's Response to War and Revolution* (New York: Oxford University Press, 1968), vii.

59. Woodrow Wilson, "President Woodrow Wilson's Fourteen Points," January 8, 1918, http://avalon.law.yale.edu/20th_century/wilson14.asp.

60. Victor Mamatey, *The United States and East-Central Europe* (Princeton, NJ: Princeton University Press, 1957), 41–42.

61. Marc Trachtenberg, "Versailles after Sixty Years," *Journal of Contemporary History* 17, no. 3 (1982): 490–491.

62. Bernard M. Baruch, "American Delegation to Negotiate Peace: Memoranda, Comments and Notes in Diary Form," entry for June 2, 1919, p. 60, Baruch Papers, Firestone Library, Princeton University.

63. David Lloyd George to Imperial War Cabinet, quoted in Marc Trachtenberg, "The Question of Realism," *Security Studies* 13, no. 1 (London: Taylor & Francis, 2003), 156–194.

64. "Clemenceau Will Support Britain on Freedom of the Sea," *The Brooklyn Daily Eagle,* December 30, 1918, 1.

65. This superb analysis is from Sally Marks, "Mistakes and Myths: The Allies, Germany, and the Versailles Treaty, 1918–1921," *Journal of Modern History* 85, no. 3 (2013): 638–640. See also Kenneth R. Rossman, "The Legend of Versailles," *Social Science* 20, no. 3 (1945): 168–172.

66. David Lloyd George, *Memoirs of the Peace Conference,* vol. 1 (New Haven: Yale University Press, 1939), 266–73.

67. Seth Tillman, *Anglo-American Relations at the Paris Peace Conference of 1919* (Princeton, NJ: Princeton University Press, 1961), 112, 12. See also Trachtenberg, "Versailles after Sixty Years," 499.

68. Marks, "Mistakes and Myths," 658.

69. Anthony Lentin, "Lloyd George, Clemenceau and the Elusive Anglo-French Guarantee Treaty, 1919: 'A Disastrous Episode'?," in *Anglo-French Relations in the Twentieth Century,* ed. Alan Sharp and Glyn Stone (New York: Routledge, 2000), 104–120.

70. Woodrow Wilson, "Address to Congress on International Order," February 11, 1918, http://www.presidency.ucsb.edu/ws/index.php?pid=110448; *The Public Papers of Woodrow Wilson: War and Peace; Presidential Messages, Addresses, and Public Papers (1917–1924),* ed. Howard Savoy Leach, vol. 1 (New York: Harper, 1927), 182.

71. I. M. Destler, "Treaty Troubles: Versailles in Reverse," *Foreign Policy* 33 (1978–1979): 45.

72. D. E. Ellwood, *The Shock of America: Europe and the Challenge of the Century* (Oxford: Oxford University Press, 2012), 1.

73. The Wilson administration's rationale was that German submarine warfare took American lives, while the British blockade only interrupted American goods en route to market. Lloyd C. Gardner, Walter F. LaFeber, and Thomas J. McCormick, *Creation of the American Empire: U.S. Diplomatic History* (Chicago: Rand-McNally, 1973), 319–326.

74. For a sense of just how impoverishing the war had been, see the accounts of Tasker Bliss, an American envoy to Britain and France, in Papers Relating to the Foreign Relations of the United States, the Lansing Papers, 1914–1920, Volume II, 763.72 Su/99, https://history.state.gov/historicaldocuments/frus1914-20v02/d147.

75. B. C. J. McKercher, *Anglo-American Relations in the 1920s: The Struggle for Supremacy* (Hampshire, UK: Macmillan Press, 1991), 2.

76. Ernest May, "Foreword," in *The Washington Conference, 1921–22: Naval Rivalry, East Asian Stability and the Road to Pearl Harbor,* ed. Erik Goldstein and John Maurer (Portland: Frank Cass Publishers, 1994), front matter.

77. Wilson famously enthused, "At last the world now knows America as the savior of the world!" Woodrow Wilson speaking on the League of Nations to a luncheon audience in Portland OR. 66th Cong., 1st sess. Senate Documents: Addresses of President Wilson (May–November 1919), vol. II, no. 120, 206.

78. McKercher, *Anglo-American Relations in the 1920s,* 4.

79. Narratives of an America greedy for global power have difficulty explaining the hearty public opposition to international involvement that Americans exhibited even at the dawn of American hegemony.

80. Woodrow Wilson, "Final Address in Support of the League of Nations," September 25, 1919, http://www.americanrhetoric.com/speeches/wilsonleagueofnations.htm.

81. Tod Lindberg, *The Heroic Heart: Greatness Ancient and Modern* (New York: Encounter Books, 2015), traces the evolution of British attitudes in poetry from the war.

82. Akira Iriye, *The Cambridge History of American Foreign Relations,* vol. 3, *The Globalizing of America, 1913–1945,* 32.

83. Adam Tooze, *The Deluge: The Great War, America and the Remaking of the Global Order, 1916–1931* (New York: Penguin, 2015), 8.

IO. IMPOSING POWER: THE WASHINGTON NAVAL TREATIES

1. Kathleen Burk, *Old World, New World: Great Britain and America from the Beginning* (New York: Atlantic Monthly Press, 2008), 387, describes the attitude as one in which "they believed that the US was self-evidently more liberal, democratic and peaceful, and should stay apart from too close links with European powers, which might serve to pull it into conflict."

2. An excellent timeline of the cultivation of racial solidarity in the Anglo-American relationship in the 1890s can be found in Bradford Perkins, *The Great Rapprochement: England and the United States, 1895–1914* (New York: Atheneum, 1968), chap. 9.

3. Adam Tooze, *The Deluge: The Great War, America and the Remaking of the Global Order, 1916–1931* (New York: Penguin, 2015), 6.

4. Warren F. Kimball, "Franklin D. Roosevelt and World War II," *Presidential Studies Quarterly* 34, no. 1 (2004): 85, quotations marks in the original.

5. Tooze, *The Deluge,* 11.

6. These were the five main naval powers in East Asia; Germany, having been constrained by the Versailles Treaty and Russia—after its drubbing by Japan in the 1902 war, Great War losses, and undergoing the Bolshevik Revolution—were no longer serious concerns.

7. Cecelia Lynch, *Beyond Appeasement: Interpreting Interwar Peace Movements in World Politics* (Ithaca, NY: Cornell University Press, 1999), 131.

8. Quincy Wright, "The Washington Conference," *American Political Science Review* 16, no. 2 (1922): 287.

9. Burk, *Old World, New World,* 382.

10. The British even had hopes that the Japanese could provide ground troops for the defense of India, implicit in the 1905 renegotiation of the alliance. As Arthur Balfour described the 1905 treaty, "Japan can depend upon *our* Fleet for defending Korea, etc., and we can depend upon *her* Army to aid us on the North-West Frontier if India is imperiled in that quarter." Arthur Balfour, quoted in Ian H. Nish, *The Anglo-Japanese Alliance: The Diplomacy of Two Island Empires 1984–1907* (London: The Athlone Press, 1972), 354–358; emphasis in the original.

11. John H. Maurer, "Arms Control and the Washington Conference," in *The Washington Conference, 1921–22: Naval Rivalry, East Asian Stability and the Road to Pearl Harbor,* ed. Erik Goldstein and John Maurer (Portland: Frank Cass Publishers, 1994), 287.

12. Eric Goldstein, "The Evolution of British Diplomatic Strategy for the Washington Conference," in *The Washington Conference, 1921–22: Naval Rivalry, East Asian Stability and the Road to Pearl Harbor,* ed. Erik Goldstein and John Maurer (Portland: Frank Cass Publishers, 1994), 14.

13. Winston Churchill, quoted in Goldstein, "The Evolution of British Diplomatic Strategy," 15.

14. Maurer, "Arms Control and the Washington Conference," 269.

15. Iestyn Adams, *Brothers Across the Ocean: British Foreign Policy and the Origin of the Anglo-American "Special Relationship" 1900–1905* (New York: St. Martin's Press, 1999), 216.

16. B. J. C. McKercher, "The Politics of Naval Arms Limitation in Britain in the 1920s," in *The Washington Conference, 1921–22: Naval Rivalry, East Asian Stability and the Road to Pearl Harbor,* ed. Erik Goldstein and John Maurer (Portland: Frank Cass Publishers, 1994), 43.

17. Maurer, "Arms Control and the Washington Conference," 274–275.

18. Lynch, *Beyond Appeasement,* 131.

19. Warren G. Harding, quoted in Roger Dingman, *Power in the Pacific: The Origins of Naval Arms Limitation, 1914–1922* (Chicago: University of Chicago Press, 1977), 157.

20. Thomas H. Buckley, *The United States and the Washington Conference, 1921–1922* (Knoxville: University of Tennessee, 1970), 11–19.

21. William R. Braisted, "The Evolution of the United States Navy's Strategic Assessments in the Pacific, 1919–1931," in *The Washington Conference, 1921–22: Naval Rivalry, East Asian Stability and the Road to Pearl Harbor,* ed. Erik Goldstein and John Maurer (Portland: Frank Cass Publishers, 1994), 104.

22. Ibid., 106.

23. Tooze, *The Deluge,* 6, comments, "If there was a European victor it was Britain."

24. Goldstein, "The Evolution of British Diplomatic Strategy," 4.

25. Gregory C. Kennedy, "Britain's Policy-Making Elite, the Naval Disarmament Puzzle, and Public Opinion, 1927–1932," *Albion: A Quarterly Journal Concerned with British Studies* 26, no. 4 (1994): 623–624.

26. Sir Auckland Geddes, quoted in Goldstein, "The Evolution of British Diplomatic Strategy," 10. Curzon, too, worried that the United States would use debt to force a cessation of Britain's shipbuilding program.

27. British Foreign Office, "Anglo-Japanese Alliance," March 10, 1921, cited in Goldstein, "The Evolution of British Diplomatic Strategy," 10.

28. George Nathaniel Curzon, First Marquess Curzon of Kedleston, cited in Goldstein, "The Evolution of British Diplomatic Strategy," 12.

29. Winston Churchill, cited in Goldstein, "The Evolution of British Diplomatic Strategy," 13.

30. McKercher, "The Politics of Naval Arms Limitation," 43.

31. Goldstein, "The Evolution of British Diplomatic Strategy," 7.

32. DBFP 404, Wellesley, "General Survey of Political Situation in Pacific and Far East with reference to the Forthcoming Washington Conference," October 20, 1921, quoted in Goldstein, "The Evolution of British Diplomatic Strategy," 20.

33. Michael Graham Fry, "The Pacific Dominions and the Washington Conference, 1921–1922," in *The Washington Conference, 1921–22: Naval Rivalry, East Asian Stability and the Road to Pearl Harbor,* ed. Erik Goldstein and John Maurer (Portland: Frank Cass Publishers, 1994), 64–65.

34. Ibid., 72.

35. CAB 23/39, Conference of Ministers, July 25, 1921, quoted in Goldstein, "The Evolution of British Diplomatic Strategy," 17–18.

36. Victor Wellesley, quoted in Goldstein, "The Evolution of British Diplomatic Strategy," 20.

37. Goldstein, "The Evolution of British Diplomatic Strategy," 16.

38. Alexandre Bracke, quoted in Joel Blatt, "The Parity That Meant Superiority: French Naval Policy towards Italy at the Washington Conference, 1921–22, and Interwar French Foreign Policy," *French Historical Studies* 12, no. 2 (Autumn 1981): 244.

39. Blatt, "France and the Washington Conference," in *The Washington Conference, 1921–22: Naval Rivalry, East Asian Stability and the Road to Pearl Harbor,* ed. Erik Goldstein and John Maurer (Portland: Frank Cass Publishers, 1994), 210.

40. Ibid., 228–232.

41. Ibid., 240.

42. Buckley, *The United States and the Washington Conference,* 112. It is on this basis that the conference is sometimes considered a failure for France. See Blatt, "The Parity That Meant Superiority," 243.

43. Ernest Andrade, "The Cruiser Controversy in Naval Limitations Negotiations, 1922–1936," in *Military Affairs* 48, no. 3 (1984): 113–120.

44. Michael Barnhart, "Domestic Politics, Interservice Impasse, and Japan's Decisions for War," in *History and Neorealism,* ed. Ernest R. May, Richard Rosecrance, and Zara Steine (New York: Cambridge University Press, 2010), 185–189. The Japanese government managed to outrage both its navy, which argued for absolute parity with Britain and the United States, and its army, which had used

commitment to the Anglo-Japanese defense treaty to justify taking German possessions in China during World War I.

45. The treaties consisted of the arms limitation treaty, the Four-Power Treaty ending the Anglo-Japanese alliance, the Nine-Power Treaty opening trade with China, the Shantung Treaty returning Japanese-held territory, and treaties allocating transoceanic telegraph cable routes.

46. Wright, "The Washington Conference," 291.

47. Lodge permitted no hearings before the Senate Foreign Relations Committee nor the House Committee on Naval Affairs, giving navalists no venue to express concern. Buckley, *The United States and the Washington Conference,* 133.

48. Wright, "The Washington Conference," 291.

49. Goldstein, "The Evolution of British Diplomatic Strategy," 9.

50. Stephen Roskill, *Admiral of the Fleet Earl Beatty, The Last Naval Hero: An Intimate Biography* (New York: Athenaeum, 1981), 302–303.

51. Allen W. Dulles, "The Threat of Anglo-American Naval Rivalry," *Foreign Affairs* 7, no. 2 (1929): 174.

52. Correlli Barnett, *The Collapse of British Power* (London: Faber and Faber, 2011), 272.

53. Tooze, *The Deluge,* 12, summarizes, "America did not even build its full quota of ships. It was enough that everyone knew that it could. Economics was the pre-eminent medium of American power, military force was a by-product."

54. John Ferris, "The Symbol and the Substance of Seapower: Great Britain, the United States and the One-Power Standard, 1919–1921," in B. C. J. McKercher, *Anglo-American Relations in the 1920s: The Struggle for Supremacy* (London: Palgrave Macmillan, 1991), 79–80.

55. Maurer, "Arms Control and the Washington Conference," 279.

56. B. C. J. McKercher, *Transition of Power: Britain's Loss of Pre-eminence to the United States, 1930–1945* (Cambridge: Cambridge University Press, 1999), 44.

57. Robert O'Connell, *Sacred Vessels: The Cult of the Battleship and the Rise of the U.S. Navy* (Oxford: Oxford University Press, 1991), 1–8.

58. Allen W. Dulles, "The Threat of Anglo-American Naval Rivalry," *Foreign Affairs* 7 (January 1929): 173–182; David Carlton, "Great Britain and the Coolidge Naval Disarmament Conference of 1927," *Political Science Quarterly* 83, no. 4 (1968): 573; Stephen Roskill, *Naval Policy between the Wars*, vol. 1, *The Period of Anglo-American Antagonism, 1919–1929* (Annapolis: Naval Institute Press, 2016).

59. Robert Vansittart, quoted in McKercher, *Transitions of Power*, 49.

11. SHARP RELIEF: WORLD WAR II

1. Mark M. Lowenthal, "INTREPID and the History of World War II," *Military Affairs* 41, no. 2 (1977): 88–90.

2. David Reynolds, "Rethinking Anglo-American Relations," *International Affairs* 65, no. 1 (1988): 90.

3. Henry B. Ryan, "Different Ends of the Telescope: Great Britain's Problems with American Opinion during World War II," *Australasian Journal of American Studies* 3, no. 2 (1984): 18.

4. George P. Auld, "The British War Debt: Retrospect and Prospect," *Foreign Affairs* 16, no. 4 (1938): 640–650.

5. The 1941 Lend-Lease Act permitted the United States government, although neutral, to provide without payment assistance to "the government of any country whose defense the President deems vital to the defense of the United States." It was widely used to skirt the restrictions of the 1939 Neutrality Act. U.S. Department of State, Office of the Historian, Lend-Lease and Military Aid to the Allies in the Early Years of World War II, https://history.state.gov/milestones/1937-1945/lend-lease.

6. Warren F. Kimball, "Lend-Lease and the Open Door: The Temptation of British Opulence, 1937–1942," *Political Science Quarterly* 86 (1971): 232–259.

7. Warren F. Kimball, "Going to War," *Presidential Studies Quarterly* 34, no. 1 (2004): 84–85.

8. Reynolds, "Rethinking Anglo-American Relations," 105.

9. Neville Chamberlain, quoted in Richard A. Harrison, "A Neutralization Plan for the Pacific: Roosevelt and Anglo-American Cooperation, 1934–1937," *Pacific Historical Review* 57, no. 1 (988): 56.

10. Raymond E. Burnett, *Gentlemanly Capitalism and British Imperialism: The New Debate on Empire* (Routledge: New York, 2014), 153.

11. Harrison, "A Neutralization Plan for the Pacific," 57.

12. Ibid., 52.

13. David Reynolds, *The Creation of the Anglo-American Alliance, 1937–1941: A Study in Competitive Co-operation* (Chapel Hill: University of North Carolina Press, 1982), 18.

14. Warren F. Kimball, ed., *Churchill and Roosevelt: The Complete Correspondence* (Princeton, NJ: Princeton University Press, 1984), 1:37.

15. By September 1940, Churchill had to inform Roosevelt that Britain could no longer pay for supplies. Kimball, *Churchill and Roosevelt*, 1:87–111.

16. Robert Shogan, *Hard Bargain* (Boulder: Westview Press, 1999), 207; Fred Pollack, "Roosevelt, the Ogdensburg Agreement, and the British Fleet," *Diplomatic History* 5, no. 3 (1981): 203–219.

17. Justus Doenecke, *Storm on the Horizon: The Challenge to American Intervention, 1939–1941* (Lanham: Rowman and Littlefield Publishers, Inc., 2000), 126. See also U.S. Department of State, Office of the Historian, "Lend-Lease and Military Aid to the Allies in the Early Years of World War II," https://history.state.gov/milestones/1937-1945/lend-lease.

18. "Texts of Roosevelt's Addresses at Boston Garden and Hartford," *New York Times*, October 31, 1940, 12A; see also James MacGregor Burns, *Roosevelt: The Lion and the Fox* (New York: Harvest, 1984), 449.

19. Harry Hopkins, quoted in Michael Fullilove, *Rendezvous with Destiny: How Franklin D. Roosevelt and Five Extraordinary Men Took America into the War and into the World* (New York: Penguin, 2014), 126.

20. Warren Kimball, *The Most Unsordid Act* (Baltimore: Johns Hopkins Press, 1969), 90.

21. Reynolds, "Rethinking Anglo-American Relations," 93.

22. Advocates of the special relationship often glide over the direct parallels between the London and Moscow missions. Both were to assess the political leadership and judge societal capacity for sustained resistance to Hitler, ask what assistance the leadership wanted the United States to provide. And Hopkins returned nearly identical reports in both cases, personalizing the nation in both Stalin and Churchill.

23. Fullilove, *Rendezvous with Destiny,* 329

24. Ibid., 327

25. Reynolds, "Rethinking Anglo-American Relations," 94.

26. Donald G. Stevens, "World War II Economic Warfare: The United States, Britain, and Portuguese Wolfram," *Historian* 61, no. 3 (1999): 542.

27. Martin Gilbert, *The Churchill War Papers: An Ever-Widening War* (New York: W. W. Norton, 2000), 3:235.

28. The Cabinet Papers, British National Archives, CAB 65/19, WM 84/41, August 19, 1941; Warren F. Kimball, "Franklin D. Roosevelt and World War II," *Presidential Studies Quarterly* 34, no. 1 (2004): 83.

29. Robert E. Sherwood, *Roosevelt and Hopkins, An Intimate History* (New York: Harper and Brothers, 1948), 365.

30. The terrific phrase is Mark Stoler's: "The 'Pacific-First' Alternative in American World War II Strategy," *International History Review* 2, no. 3 (1980): 445.

31. David Reynolds, *The Creation of the Anglo-American Alliance,* 213–219.

32. John D. Millett, "World War II: The Post-Mortem Begins," *Political Science Quarterly* 61, no. 3 (1946): 325.

33. Mark Harrison, "Resource Mobilization for World War II: The U.S.A., U.K., U.S.S.R., and Germany, 1938–1945," *Economic History Review* 41, no. 2 (1988): 177.

34. Lowenthal, "INTREPID and the History of World War II," 88.
35. Kimball, "Franklin D. Roosevelt and World War II," 96.
36. James R. Leutze, *Bargaining for Supremacy: Anglo American Naval Collaboration, 1937–1941* (Chapel Hill: University of North Carolina Press, 1977), 219.
37. Mark A. Stoler, "The 'Pacific-First' Alternative in American World War II Strategy," *International History Review* 2, no. 3 (1980): 449.
38. Dwight D. Eisenhower, *The Papers of Dwight David Eisenhower: The War Years, 1941–1945*, vol. 1, ed. Alfred D. Chandler Jr. (Baltimore: Johns Hopkins University Press, 1970), 145-148, 205-208.
39. Mark A. Stoler, *Allies and Adversaries: The Joint Chiefs of Staff, the Grand Alliance, and U.S. Strategy in World War II* (Chapel Hill: University of North Carolina Press, 2000), 79. Both Stimson and Marshall would subsequently claim the threat had merely been a negotiating tactic to pressure Britain into a cross-channel invasion date, not a serious reconsideration of American strategy. Henry L. Stimson, *On Active Services in Peace and War* (New York: Harper & Brothers, 1947), 425; Forrest C. Pogue, *George C. Marshall,* vol. 2, *Ordeal and Hope, 1939–1942* (New York: Viking, 1966), 34.
40. George Marshall, "Memorandum, Chief of Staff to President: Latest British Proposals Relative to Bolero and Gymnast," July 10, 1942, Record Group 165, WDCSA BOLERO, National Archives, College Park, MD.
41. Louis Morton, "Germany First: The Basic Concept of Allied Strategy in World War," in *Command Decisions,* ed. Kent R. Greenfield (Washington, DC: Methuen & Co. Ltd., 1960), 11.
42. George C. Marshall to Ernest King, memorandum, July 15, 1942, WDCA 38 1 War Plans, folder 1, National Archives, College Park, MD; Stoler, "The 'Pacific-First' Alternative," 438-439.
43. Stoler, *Allies and Adversaries,* 117.
44. General Thomas Handy to chief of staff, "American-British Strategy," memorandum, November 8, 1942, WDCSA 381, National Archives, College Park, MD.

45. U.S. Marine Corps general Jim Mattis believes the British were justified in their hesitation on the basis that American forces were not hardened enough to prevail against the Wehrmacht in battle, and fearing losses would cause the United States to shift its effort to the Pacific. James N. Mattis, interview with the author, Stanford, CA, October 29, 2016.

46. Millett, "World War II," 330.

47. Ibid., 326.

48. Ibid., 326.

49. Ryan, "Different Ends of the Telescope," 18.

50. Henry B. Ryan, "Different Ends of the Telescope," *Australasian Journal of American Studies* 3, no. 2 (December 1984): 18.

51. Anthony Eden, quoted in ibid., 19.

52. John Balfour, quoted in B. J. C. McKercher, *Transition of Power: Britain's Loss of Global Preeminence to the United States, 1930–1945* (Cambridge: Cambridge University Press, 2004), 308.

53. Ryan, "Different Ends of the Telescope," 21.

54. Ibid., 27.

55. Reynolds, "Rethinking Anglo-American Relations," 107; U.S. Department of State, *Foreign Relations of the United States Diplomatic Papers: The Conferences at Cairo and Tehran* (Washington, DC: U.S. Government Printing Office, 1943), 486.

56. Francis O. Wilcox, "The Monroe Doctrine and World War II," *American Political Science Review* 36, no. 3 (1942): 435.

57. Arnold Wolfers even considered the U.S.-hemispheric compacts a suitable basis for British-American relations after the war. Arnold Wolfers, "Anglo-American Post-War Coöperation and the Interests of Europe," *American Political Science Review* 36, no. 4 (1942): 656.

58. Stevens, "World War II Economic Warfare," 541.

59. Reynolds, *The Creation of the Anglo-American Alliance*, 13–16, 77–78, 269–82; Alan P. Dobson, *Anglo-American Relations in the Twentieth Century* (New York: Routledge, 1955), 81–90.

60. Ryan, "Different Ends of the Telescope," 27.
61. Reynolds, "Rethinking Anglo-American Relations," 103.
62. Dwight D. Eisenhower, "1945 Proclamation no. 1 to the People of Germany," quoted in Michael R. Bechloss, *The Conquerors: Roosevelt, Truman and the Destruction of Hitler's Germany* (New York: Simon and Schuster, 2002), 159.
63. Millett, "World War II," 326.

12. LESSONS FROM A PEACEFUL TRANSITION

1. Paul Kennedy, "The Tradition of Appeasement in British Foreign Policy, 1865–1939," *Review of International Studies* 2, no. 3 (October 1976): 196.
2. Ernest May, *Imperial Democracy: The Emergence of America as a Great Power* (New York: Harcourt, Brace & World, 1961), 267.
3. *Anagnorisis* is Aristotle's term for the moment of character realization in drama. Aristotle, *Poetics,* line 1452a.
4. Martin Crawford, *The Anglo-American Crisis of the Mid-Nineteenth Century* (Athens: University of Georgia Press, 1987), 107.
5. National Bureau of Statistics of China, *China Statistical Yearbook 2006,* 734, 1025, http://www.stats.gov.cn/tjsj/ndsj/2006/indexeh .htm.
6. Paul Franco, "Hegel and Liberalism," *The Review of Politics* 59, no. 4 (Autumn 1997): 831.
7. G. John Ikenberry, *After Victory: Institutions, Strategic Restraint, and the Rebuilding of Order after Major Wars* (Princeton, NJ: Princeton University Press, 2000).
8. Charles Kupchan, *No One's World: The West, the Rising Rest, and the Coming Global Turn* (New York: Oxford University Press, 2000).
9. Azar Gat, "The Return of Authoritarian Great Powers," *Foreign Affairs* 86, no. 4 (2007): 59–69.

Acknowledgments

Condi Rice once again helped me chart my course by setting me on the path of writing this book. Steve Krasner encouraged me to think the shared sovereignty over Oregon illustrated something unique about the interaction between the United States and Britain. The indefatigable Lawry Freedman thought I was on to something, which helped me persevere. Walter Russell Mead cheerily urged me on.

Tod Lindberg did me the great favor of gently telling me the first draft was awful and helped me to identify the proper standard of performance. I'm so appreciative of my colleagues who read this manuscript with a critical eye to improvement: Stephen Randolph, the historian of the U.S. Department of State; Elizabeth Cobbs of Texas A&M University; and Tom Donnelly of the American Enterprise Institute. The joint University of Texas–King's College London conference "Grand Strategy and the Anglo-American Worldview" gave me an invaluable opportunity to present an outline and a version of Chapter 8 as I was writing and get feedback from some of the best historians of the subject.

My magnificent nephews, Barrett Eller Schake and Connor Lafitte Schake, contributed early archival research and listened to the plotline of this book more times than anyone should have to. Stalwart

Sean O'Grady, my research assistant, showed the equipoise of his classicist's training in checking my work at the end. Three of my favorite students, Nick Drake, Kevin Mott, and Libby Johnson, also put shoulder to the wheel when I needed help, for which I'm very grateful.

Ryan Evans, the founder of War on the Rocks, helped me get my foundering ship off the rocks, for which I am deeply in his debt. Martyn Frampton did a complete stranger a great professional courtesy; he will never have to buy a drink or a meal in my proximity. And finally, I'm grateful to my editor at Harvard University Press, Ian Malcolm, who believed in this book and in me.

Index